REVISE FOR

SCIENCE GCSE

SUFFOLK

GILL ALDERTON
DAVID BERRINGTON
MICHAEL BRIMICOMBE

Heinemann

HIGHER

Heinemann Educational Publishers
Halley Court, Jordan Hill, Oxford, OX2 8EJ
a division of Reed Educational & Professional Publishing Ltd

Heinemann is a registered trademark of Reed Educational &
Professional Publishing Ltd.

OXFORD   MELBOURNE   AUCKLAND
JOHANNESBURG   BLANTYRE   GABORONE
IBADAN   PORTSMOUTH NH (USA)   CHICAGO

First published 1998

ISBN 0 435 57864 2

02 01
10 9 8 7 6

Edited by June Thompson

Designed and typeset by Ken Vail Graphic Design

Illustrated by Graham-Cameron Illustration (Virginia Gray),
Graeme Morris, Sam Vail (Ken Vail Graphic Design)

Cover artwork by Stephen May

Printed and bound in the UK by Bath Press

Contents

How to use this book

This book is divided into two parts:
- the first part will help you revise for the exam at the end of year 10
- the second part helps you revise for the exam at the end of year 11.

You will also have to revise certain topics of the year 10 material for the exam at the end of year 11. These topics are clearly marked in the book by a vertical black line in the margin of the text, as shown here.

Each part is divided into chapters on AT2 (biology), AT3 (chemistry) and AT4 (physics).

Helping you revise

1 At the end of each chapter is a *Concept map*. This will help you check that you remember everything you need to know and will help you see the connections between topics more clearly.

   The best plan is to make your own personal map of the subject which makes your own connections between topics.

   The concept maps show all the year 11 material in heavy bold type and with dark arrows. They also have the year 10 topics in fainter type and with white arrows so that you can see how the whole subject fits together. The concept maps for year 10 show only what you cover in year 10.

2 The words in **bold** are all key words you need to know. A useful revision idea would be to build up your own glossary of these as you work through the book. For quick reference to a word or topic use the *Index* at the back of the book.

3 There are lots of questions in the book and they are an important part of your revision. There are:
   - simple questions to help you stop and think about the subject as you read.
   - questions at the end of each chapter to help you practise for the exam.

The answers to all these are at the back of the book so you will never get stuck.

Good luck with your exams!

Year 10

The basics of life

The seven signs of life

All living things carry out the following seven activities. This makes them different from non-living things.

1 **M**ovement – animals move their whole bodies, plants move as they grow.
2 **R**eproduction – they make new individuals like themselves.
3 **S**ensitivity – they are aware of, and can respond to, changes in their surroundings.
4 **G**rowth – they all get bigger.
5 **R**espiration – they release energy from their food.
6 **E**xcretion – they get rid of waste products they have made.
7 **N**utrition – animals eat, plants make their own food by photosynthesis in their leaves.

Cells – the building blocks of life

All living things are made of cells. The cells are so tiny that you can only see them using a microscope.

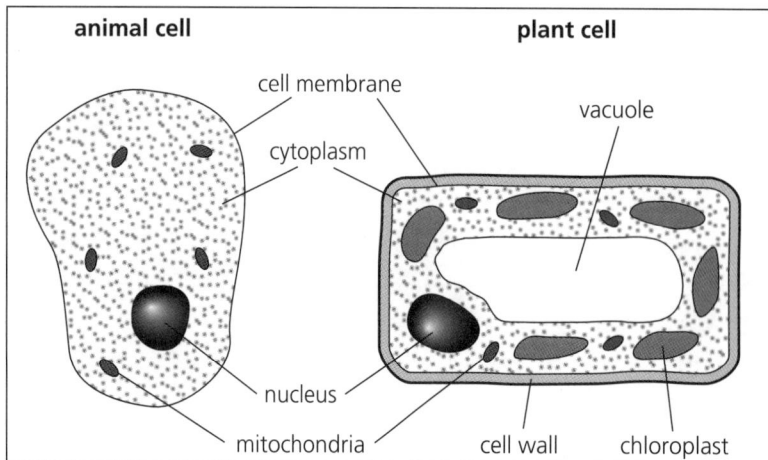

Cells contain:
- a **nucleus** to control everything a cell does
- **cytoplasm** – a watery jelly in which most of the cell's reactions occur
- a **cell membrane**, which controls what goes in and out of the cell
- **mitochondria**, which release energy from food (respiration).

Plant cells also have a few extras:
- a **cellulose cell wall** to help support the plant – think of the size of tall trees, and remember they don't have any bones to hold them up
- **chloroplasts** to contain the chlorophyll needed for photosynthesis
- large **cell vacuole**, a space filled with a fluid called cell sap.

The main chemical in cells is water.

Now do this

1 The first letters of each activity make the words 'Mrs Gren'. Cover up the list and use 'Mrs Gren' to help you write down all of the activities.

2 Which of the following are living things: coal, wood, plastic, maggots, grass, feathers, an oak tree and a sausage?

The right cell for the job

Cells contain the same basic parts, but they also have important differences. They are specialised to do different jobs. These are examples:

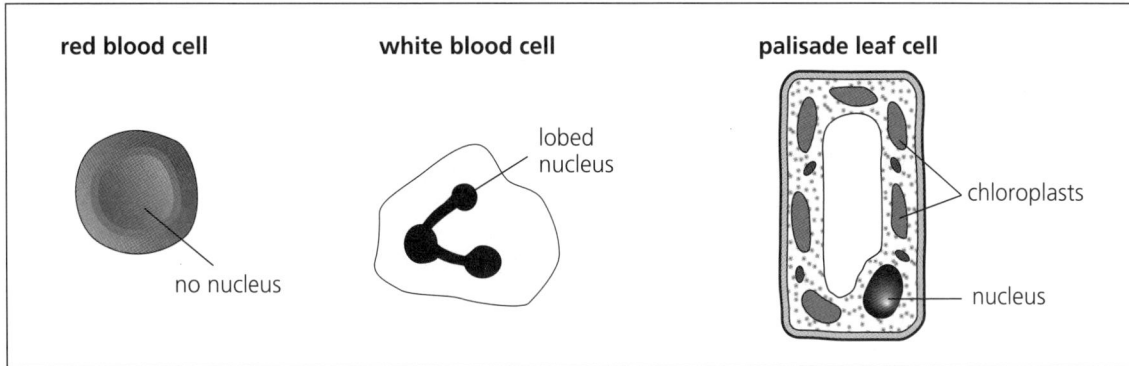

red blood cell

no nucleus

white blood cell

lobed nucleus

palisade leaf cell

chloroplasts

nucleus

Red blood cells carry oxygen. They have no nucleus, to make more space for oxygen. White blood cells fight infection, and they can change their shape to engulf microbes. Palisade leaf cells near the surface of leaves are long and thin with lots of chloroplasts to trap light for photosynthesis.

Cells, tissues and organs

Tissues are groups of cells which do the same job, e.g. muscle cells make up muscle tissue.

Organs are different types of tissues grouped together to do one job, e.g. muscle and gland tissues make up the stomach.

Organs working together form an **organ system**, e.g. the stomach and several other organs are part of the digestive system.

Now do this

3 Which part of a plant cell
   a is needed for photosynthesis
   b controls what moves in and out of the cell
   c supports the plant?
4 A red blood cell is peculiar because it does not have a nucleus. Why?

Digestion

The food you eat has to reach all your cells to release the energy needed to keep you alive. Food also provides the raw materials for growth and maintenance.

So that it reaches the cells, food has to be broken down into small enough pieces to be carried in the blood to the cells. This breaking down is called **digestion**, and it occurs in the **digestive system**.

Digesting what you eat

This is what happens:
- **digestion** is the breakdown of large, insoluble pieces of food into small, soluble pieces
- digestion is helped by the production of **digestive juices** by parts of the digestive system
- digestive juices contain special chemicals, called **enzymes**, which speed up digestion
- there are many different enzymes. Each one has its own type of food to break down
- **bile** is produced in the liver and stored in the **gall bladder**. It is *not* an enzyme. It helps to break down lipids (fats) by **emulsifying** them. This means breaking large droplets of fat into much smaller droplets, thereby increasing the surface area for the enzyme, lipase, to attack
- bile is alkaline, and therefore helps to neutralise the acids coming out of the stomach.

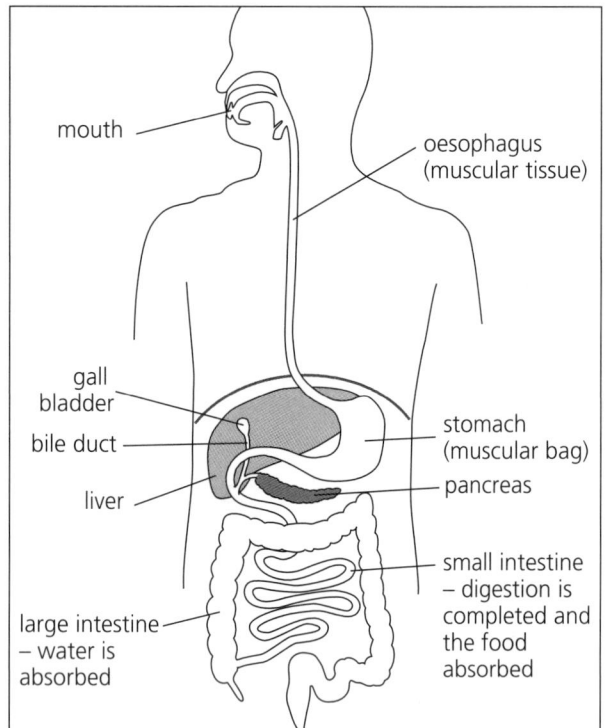

mouth
oesophagus (muscular tissue)
gall bladder
bile duct
liver
stomach (muscular bag)
pancreas
small intestine – digestion is completed and the food absorbed
large intestine – water is absorbed

Now do this

1   Explain what digestion is.

2   Where in the body is bile produced, and what does it do in the digestive system?

3   Explain how enzymes help with digestion.

Digestive juices

The stomach makes an enzyme to digest certain foods. This enzyme needs acid conditions for it to work well. Therefore the stomach also makes an acid to provide the enzyme with the right conditions to work well. An added bonus is that the acid kills any germs on the food!

The pancreas makes other enzymes which digest food. These enzymes are released into the small intestine together with juices from the liver. These juices neutralise the acid from the stomach so that the enzymes from the pancreas can work.

Enzymes are proteins which speed up (catalyse) reactions in living things. They will only work at the correct pH, and are also affected by temperature:
- too cold, movement is slow – the enzyme and food do not collide often enough for a fast reaction
- too hot – enzymes are destroyed.

Absorption and the small intestine

The small intestine has lots of finger-like projections called **villi**, which increase the surface area for the absorption of digested food.

The small intestine is adapted for food absorption:
- it is very long
- the villi give a huge surface area
- the walls are very thin and permeable
- it has a good blood supply to transport digested food.

Now do this

4 Give **two** uses of stomach acid.

5 Name **two** parts of the digestive system that produce enzymes.

6 Explain how all enzymes are affected by temperature.

One villus, lots of villi

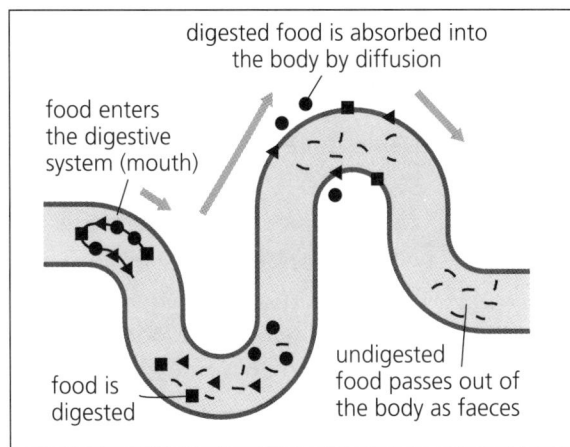

digested food is absorbed into the body by diffusion

food enters the digestive system (mouth)

food is digested

undigested food passes out of the body as faeces

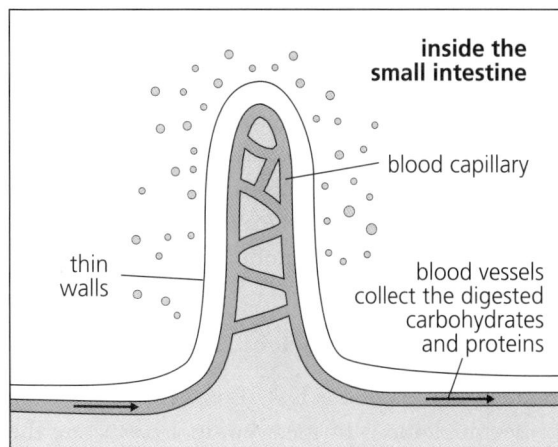

inside the small intestine

blood capillary

thin walls

blood vessels collect the digested carbohydrates and proteins

Peristalsis

Food is squeezed through the digestive system by the muscles in the walls of the oesophagus, stomach and intestines. This squeezing action is called **peristalsis**.

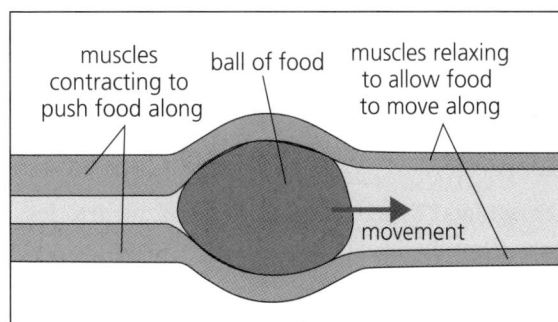

muscles contracting to push food along

ball of food

muscles relaxing to allow food to move along

movement

Now do this

7 Explain how the small intestine is adapted for the absorption of food.

8 What is peristalsis, and why is it so important?

Circulation and transport

Your body needs a transport system to carry materials such as oxygen and food to all the body cells. The transport system has three main parts: **blood** to carry the materials; a network of tubes called **blood vessels** for the blood to pass through; and a pump called the **heart**.

Blood

Blood is made up of the following components:

- **plasma** is a watery fluid, which transports digested foods, water, hormones, and waste products such as urea and carbon dioxide
- **white blood cells** defend the body against disease

- **platelets** help with blood clotting

- **red blood cells** transport oxygen around the body. They are adapted to do this because:
  1 they do *not* contain a nucleus and therefore there is more room inside them
  2 they have a large surface area
  3 they contain haemoglobin, which combines reversibly with oxygen

> **oxygen + haemoglobin ⇌ oxyhaemoglobin**

In areas where there is lots of oxygen, e.g. the lungs, oxyhaemoglobin is formed, but in areas where there is little oxygen, e.g. actively respiring cells, oxyhaemoglobin breaks down to release the oxygen.

Now do this

1 Name **three** materials transported by plasma.

2 Explain how red blood cells are adapted to transport oxygen.

3 Where do the following materials enter and leave the blood: oxygen, carbon dioxide, food?

4 The formation of oxyhaemoglobin is reversible. Why is this important?

Blood vessels

Blood is carried throughout the body in blood vessels. There are three different types of blood vessel.

Arteries

Carry blood at high pressure away from the heart..

small lumen

Thick elastic muscular wall to withstand high blood pressure.

Capillaries

Link arteries and veins, allowing materials to be exchanged with surrounding tissues.

Walls only one cell thick to allow materials to diffuse in and out. Materials moving out form tissue fluid.

Veins

Carry blood at a lower pressure back to the heart.

wide lumen

Thin muscular walls because the blood is no longer at high pressure. Contain valves to prevent blood flowing backwards.

Double circulatory system

A double circulatory system means that one blood cell passes through the heart twice on each complete trip around the body.

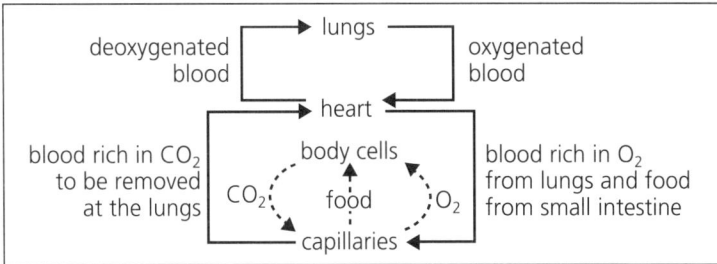

Now do this

5 Give **two** differences between an artery and a vein.

6 What is the advantage of a double circulatory system?

The advantage is that oxygenated blood returns to the heart so it can be sent out around the body at higher pressure. This means that more blood flows around the body to all tissues.

Heart

Blood has to be pumped around the body, and this is the job of the heart. The heart is made of muscle. It has four chambers and four valves.

The four chambers are the right and left atria, which collect incoming blood from the veins, and the very muscular right and left ventricles, which contract to squirt blood out into the arteries at high pressure. It needs the pressure because some of the blood has a long way to go!

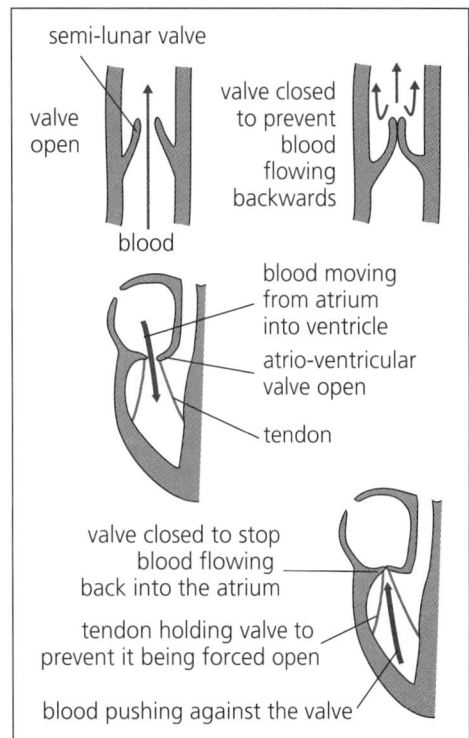

Now do this

7 Name the thick muscular chambers of the heart.

8 Why is it necessary to have valves between the chambers of the heart?

9 Name **one** other part of the body where there are valves, and explain their function.

Look at the arrows in the heart. They show the direction the blood flows. The valves stop the blood flowing backwards. The valves that stop blood flowing back into the atria from the ventricles are named after their position between the atria and ventricles. They are called the **atrio-ventricular valves**. The other valves are called the **semi-lunar valves**. These are named after their shape. They guard the entrance to the arteries leaving the heart and they are the shape of a half moon.

Breathing

You breathe in air to take oxygen into your body to be used in respiration (to release energy from your food). Releasing energy from food produces carbon dioxide, which needs to be removed from the body. Therefore **breathing** is **gas exchange**. Gas exchange occurs in the **lungs**, which are in the chest, protected by the **ribs**.

Gas	Air in	Air out
O_2	21%	16%
CO_2	0.04%	4%
N_2	78%	78%
H_2O vapour	variable	saturated

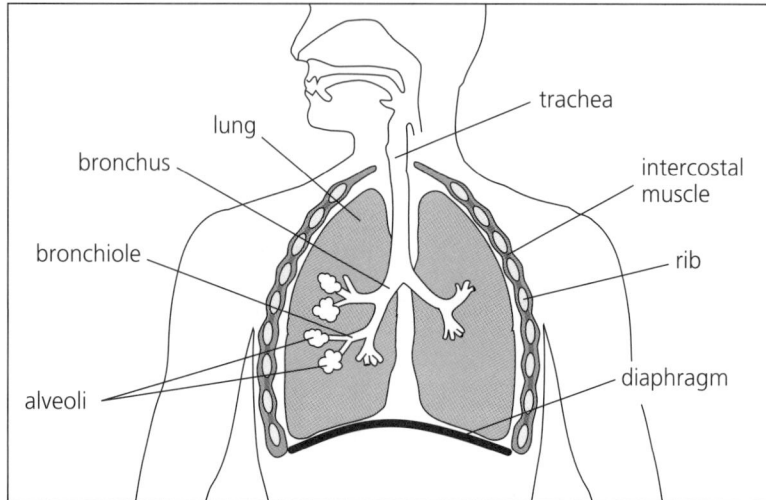

Gas exchange

The **bronchus** and **bronchioles** carry air into the lungs. At the end of the bronchioles are lots of little air sacs called **alveoli**. The alveoli are where gas exchange occurs.

One alveolus, lots of alveoli

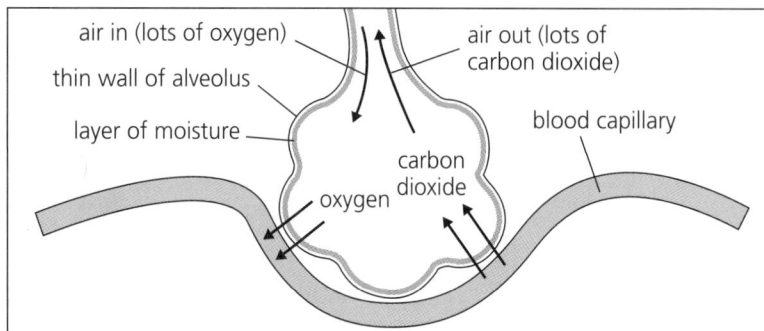

The alveoli are good at gas exchange because they have:
- a large surface area (there are thousands of alveoli)
- moist surfaces which make diffusion faster
- thin walls, which make diffusion faster
- lots of blood capillaries to carry the gases.

In the alveolus oxygen moves from a high concentration (lots of oxygen) through the thin wall into the blood capillary where there is a low concentration of oxygen (very little oxygen). Movement from a high to a low concentration like this is called **diffusion**. There is a high concentration of carbon dioxide in the blood, so carbon dioxide diffuses out of the blood into the alveolus.

Now do this

1 Why do we need oxygen?

2 Explain why oxygen diffuses from the alveoli into the blood.

3 Give **three** ways in which alveoli are adapted for gas exchange.

Breathing in and breathing out

When we breathe in (inhale), the lung volume increases and therefore the air pressure decreases. When we breathe out (exhale) the lung volume decreases and the air pressure increases. Therefore the air pressure in the lungs is continuously changing. The bronchi and larger bronchioles have pieces of cartilage in their walls to support them and prevent them from collapsing as the air pressure changes.

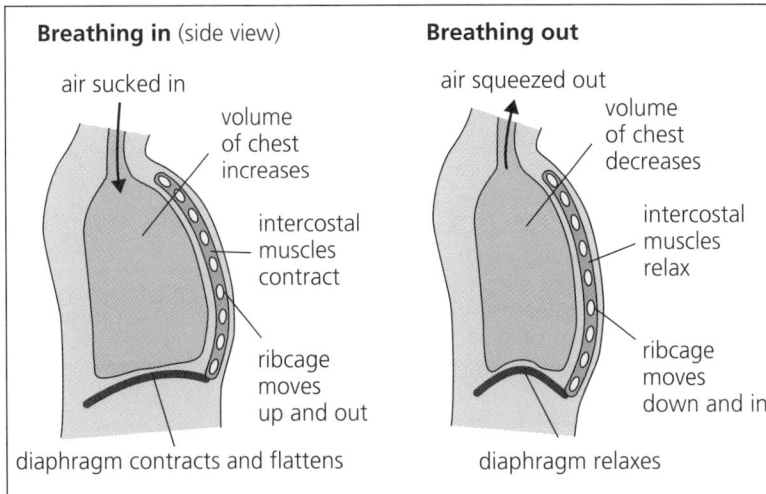

Breathing in (side view)

air sucked in

volume
of chest
increases

intercostal
muscles
contract

ribcage
moves
up and out

diaphragm contracts and flattens

Breathing out

air squeezed out

volume
of chest
decreases

intercostal
muscles
relax

ribcage
moves
down and in

diaphragm relaxes

Now do this

4　Describe the changes in the position of the ribs and diaphragm that cause inhalation and exhalation.

5　Explain why the bronchi and larger bronchioles contain pieces of cartilage.

Keeping the lungs clean

Air often contains germs and dust. To help keep the lungs clean the trachea produces a sticky **mucus** to trap invaders. It also has small hairs called **cilia** which beat together to move the mucus away from the lungs.

air down
to lungs

mucus
moving
up

a mucus-
producing
cell

cells
lining
trachea

cillia beating

Smoking stops the cilia beating. This allows germs and mucus into the lungs. The germs increase the risk of infection, e.g. bronchitis. The mucus irritates the lungs causing coughing, e.g. smokers' cough. Chemicals in the smoke destroy alveoli. This makes gas exchange more difficult and may cause the disease emphysema. Some of the chemicals cause lung cancer.

Now do this

6　Explain the link between irritating chemicals in cigarette smoke and lung damage.

Nervous system

Sense organs

We are aware of and can respond to changes in our surroundings. These changes are called **stimuli** and they are detected by parts of the body called **receptors**. Receptors often form part of a **sense organ**.

- The eye is a sense organ and responds to the stimulus light.
- The ear detects sound and balance.
- The nose detects chemicals (smell and taste).
- The tongue detects chemicals (taste).
- The skin detects touch, pressure and temperature change.

The eye

lens – changes shape to bend the light

cornea – starts to bend the light

pupil – allows light into the eye

iris – controls the amount of light entering the eye

retina – contains light-sensitive cells (receptors) to detect light stimulus

optic nerve – carries nervous message to the brain

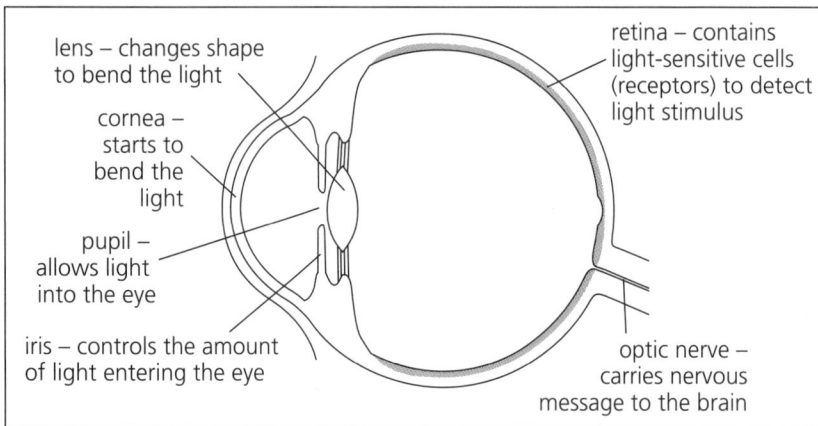

The iris is the coloured bit of your eye.

pupil

circular muscles relaxed

radial muscles contracted

pupil

circular muscles contracted

radial muscles relaxed

In dim light the pupil is large and the iris becomes smaller. This allows more light in.

In bright light the pupil is small and the iris becomes larger. This prevents too much light damaging the retina.

Now do this

1 Which of the body's receptors gather information about the following: touch, smell, light, sound and balance?

2 What are the functions of the following parts of the eye: retina, iris, optic nerve and lens?

3 Describe how the muscles in the iris change to prevent too much light damaging the retina.

The nervous system

To enable us to respond to stimuli quickly, the receptors and sense organs need to be able to communicate with other parts of the body. This is the job of the **nervous system**. The nervous system is made up of two parts:

1 the **central nervous system**, which is the spinal cord and brain
2 the **peripheral nervous system**, which is the network of nerve cells (**neurones**) connecting all parts of the body to the central nervous system.

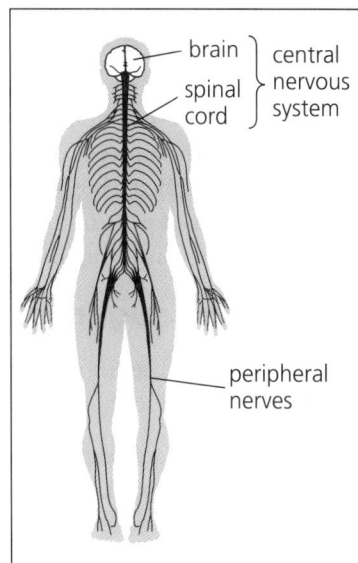

Sending a message

There are two types of neurones and they are named after the messages they carry. Messages come into the central nervous system from receptors via neurones called **sensory nerve cells** or **sensory neurones**. Neurones carrying messages away from the central nervous system are called **motor neurones**.

The diagram shows the structure of a motor neurone.

The end of one neurone is not connected to the next one. There is a little gap between them. This is called the **synapse**. Messages passing along a neurone are electrical but when they reach the synapse they release a chemical which diffuses across the synapse and spreads the message to the next neurone. Only one side of the synapse can make the chemical messenger. So nervous messages only go in one direction.

A motor neurone

Reflex actions

What happens when you touch something hot?

1 Temperature receptors detect the hot stimulus.
2 The receptors send the message along a sensory neurone to the central nervous system.
3 The central nervous system sends the message along a motor neurone to a muscle (an **effector**).
4 The muscle contracts moving your hand away from the hot object.

> **stimulus** → **receptor** → **sensory neurone** → **central nervous system** →
> **motor neurone** → **effector(muscle)** → **response (hand moves)**

This is called a **reflex action**.

Reflex actions are:
• fast
• automatic (without thinking)
• protective.

Examples include blinking, swallowing and sneezing.

Now do this

4 Give **three** ways in which motor neurones are adapted to do their job.
5 What is a synapse? Suggest one advantage of synapses.
6 Describe the paths taken by a nervous message in the reflex action resulting from a dog biting your hand.

Hormones

Alongside the nervous control in your body, some activities are also controlled by **hormones**. These are chemical messengers produced by groups of cells called **glands**. Hormones travel in the blood plasma and work on groups of cells in the body. Each hormone acts in a particular way, on a particular group of **target cells**.

Controlling sugar (glucose) levels

All cells need glucose for energy. But you need to have the right amount of glucose available in your blood. Too much or too little can be fatal.

The hormone that controls the amount of glucose is called **insulin**. This is produced by the pancreas. When there is too much glucose in the blood, the pancreas releases insulin. Insulin lowers the level of glucose by:
- making cells take up more glucose
- making **liver** cells change glucose to **glycogen**. This is then stored in the liver.

Some people do not make any insulin, or do not make enough. This means they suffer from **diabetes**. In these cases the level of glucose in the blood can go up and down wildly. Many diabetics control their blood glucose level by injecting themselves with insulin. The amount of insulin a diabetic needs depends on their diet and activity.

Controlling sexual development

The changes which take place during adolescence (the stage of children growing into adults) are controlled by hormones.

As girls grow older their ovaries start to produce the hormone **oestrogen**. Oestrogen causes a number of changes in girls. They:
- start their menstrual cycle (have periods)
- develop breasts
- grow pubic and underarm hair
- grow taller.

These are called **secondary sexual characteristics**.

In boys, the development of secondary sexual characteristics is controlled by the hormone **testosterone**, which is produced by the testes. The effect is that boys:
- grow taller
- develop a longer penis
- grow pubic, underarm and facial hair
- develop a deeper voice.

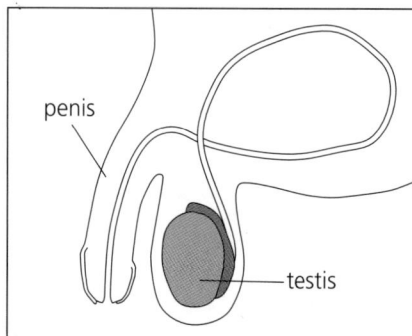

Now do this

1 Give **three** female secondary sexual characteristics.

2 Explain why hormones (chemical messages) are likely to take longer to affect the body than nervous messages.

Controlling the menstrual cycle

Two hormones control a woman's menstrual cycle, **oestrogen** and **progesterone**.

What these hormones do:
- oestrogen repairs the uterus wall
- progesterone keeps the uterus wall thick and in position
- oestrogen and progesterone together control **ovulation** (ovaries releasing eggs).

progesterone keeps
the uterus lining thick

yellow body
produces
progesterone

ovary

lining of uterus

days

menstruation

ovary – yellow body
stops producing
progesterone because
the woman is not pregnant

lining of uterus
leaves the
body because
progesterone
is not produced

egg starting
to develop

ovary starts to
produce oestrogen

ovulation (egg
leaves the ovary)

forms
yellow
body

ovary

oestrogen causes
uterus wall to thicken

Preventing pregnancy ...

Hormones can be used in **contraceptive pills** to prevent ovulation and make the body think it is pregnant. This means that a woman will not release eggs and therefore cannot get pregnant.

... and helping pregnancy

Some women have difficulty in getting pregnant. Hormones can be used to help them produce more eggs, which will increase their chances of getting pregnant.

Controlling growth

Growth is controlled by **growth hormone**. This is produced by the **pituitary gland** in the brain. Too little growth hormone causes **dwarfism**. This is when a person does not grow enough. Too much growth hormone produces a giant. This is when a person grows too much.

Fight or flight

The hormone **adrenaline** prepares the body for action. It is produced by the two **adrenal glands**. It makes the heart beat faster. This forces blood around the body more rapidly, delivering more oxygen and glucose to the muscles to release more energy.

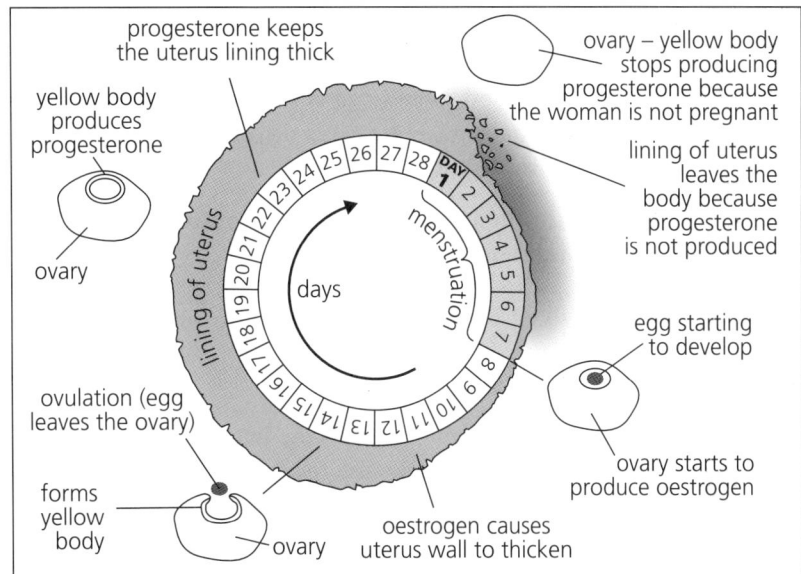

Now do this

3   Explain why a pregnant woman will not menstruate.

4   How do contraceptive pills work?

5   What part does oestrogen play in the menstrual cycle?

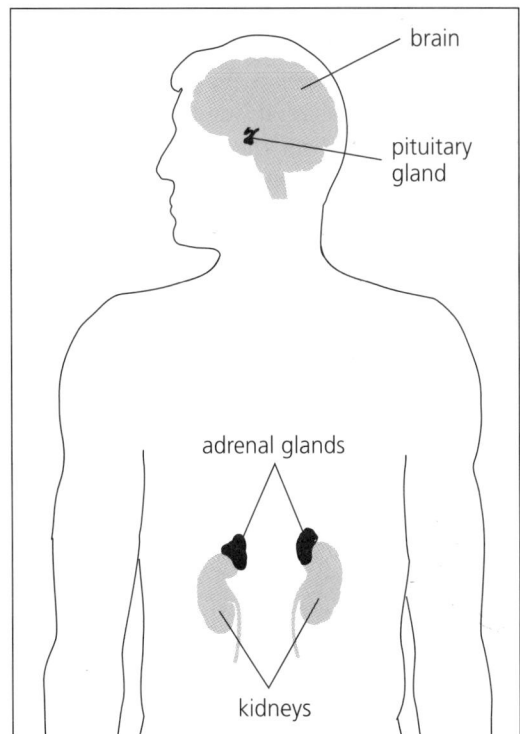

brain

pituitary
gland

adrenal glands

kidneys

Control in plants

Plants do not have a nervous system and so usually cannot respond as quickly as animals. They react to stimuli more slowly. Their reactions are controlled by hormones called **auxins**, which are produced in shoot and root tips. The auxins dissolve in water and are then transported through the plant.

Auxins regulate cell growth and development to control:
• growth of shoots and roots
• flowering
• ripening of fruit.

How do plants grow?

The shoots of a plant always grow towards the light. They do this because leaves need the light to make the food needed for plants to grow. They make their food by photosynthesis (see page 74).

Growing towards the light is called **phototropism**. 'Photo' means light and 'tropism' means growth.

Plant roots always grow downwards in the direction of gravity. They need to do this to find the water the plant needs, and to anchor the plant in the ground.

??? Now do this

1   Give **two** uses of auxins in plants.
2   Explain how auxins travel around a plant.

I don't understand... I turn it round every week!

Auxins control the direction plants grow by making different parts grow at different speeds. To make a shoot grow towards the light, auxins make its shaded side grow faster, resulting in the tip bending over towards the light. To make a root grow downwards, auxins make the top side of the root grow faster, resulting in the tip curving downwards.

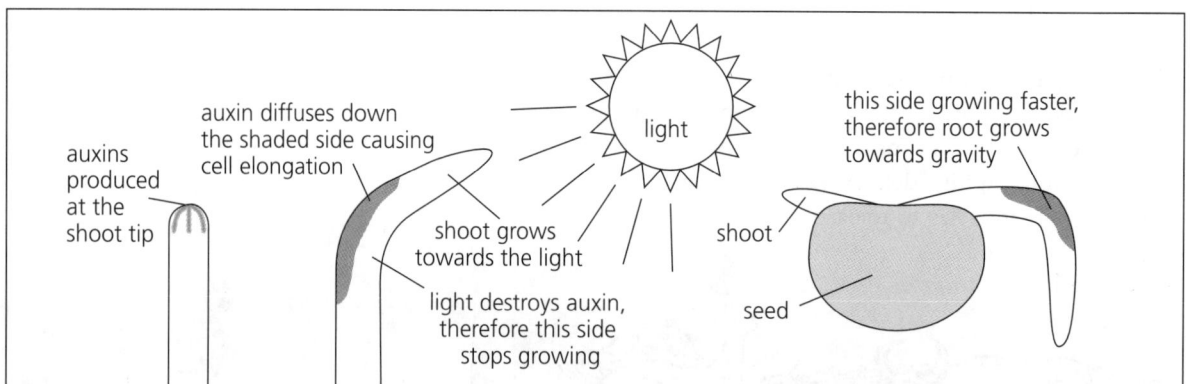

auxins produced at the shoot tip

auxin diffuses down the shaded side causing cell elongation

light

shoot grows towards the light

light destroys auxin, therefore this side stops growing

this side growing faster, therefore root grows towards gravity

shoot

seed

Using plant hormones

We use synthetic auxins to trick plants and make them behave in ways which are more convenient for us.

Making more plants

It can take some time for plants to produce young new plants naturally. Cutting shoots off plants and dipping them in auxins makes them grow roots. Gardeners use auxins, known as rooting powder, to make new plants.

Ripening fruit

Auxins can also be used to slow down fruit ripening. This is useful for farmers who have a long way to take their fruit to the shops. If they treat it in this way it stops the fruit getting overripe before it gets to the customers.

Selective weedkillers

Selective weedkillers contain auxins which speed up the growth of selected plants. This makes them grow too fast and die. For example, if there are weeds with broad leaves growing in a lawn, a weedkiller can be used which will kill only those weeds and not the grass.

broad-leaved weeds growing faster than the grass will die

grass

Now do this

3   Name **two** stimuli plants respond to. Explain why it is important that plants can respond to these stimuli.

4   Describe **two** commercial uses of auxins in agriculture.

5   Explain what is meant by a 'selective' weedkiller.

6   Explain how a bulb planted upside down manages to grow.

Ecosystems

Ecology is the study of living things and the way they react with each other and with their surroundings (**environment**). To make it easier to study, the environment is divided into lots of smaller areas called **ecosystems**.

For example, a rock pool is an ecosystem.

Every ecosystem is made up of **two** parts:

- the **habitat**, which is the non-living part, e.g. the water and rocks in the rock pool
- the **populations** of plants and animals, which are the living part. A population includes all members of the same species. In the rock pool there would be a population of crabs, a population of sea lettuce, a population of sea anemone, and many more. All the populations make up the **community**.

rocks and water (habitat)

sea anemone

shrimp

sea lettuce

seaweed

Blenny

crab

Finding out about populations

There are a number of ways to find out what populations live in a habitat and how many members each has.

1 You can count the plants on a piece of land by using a metal or wooden frame called a **quadrat**. For example, if you wanted to know the number of daisies in a field, you put the quadrat on the ground and count the number of daisies inside it. You multiply this number by how many quadrats would cover the whole field. This gives you a rough estimate of the size of the daisy population on the field.

2 You can collect insects and other very small creatures by sweeping a **net** through the undergrowth and then sucking them into a special jar called a **pooter**. This gives you some idea of the animals living in the habitat and a rough idea of their numbers. ▶

3 You can collect small nocturnal animals by ▶ digging small **pitfall traps** and covering them over. The animals which fall in can be identified and released the next day.

Now do this

1 Describe the two parts of an ecosystem.

2 What populations would you sample using:
a a pooter
b a quadrat
c a pitfall trap?

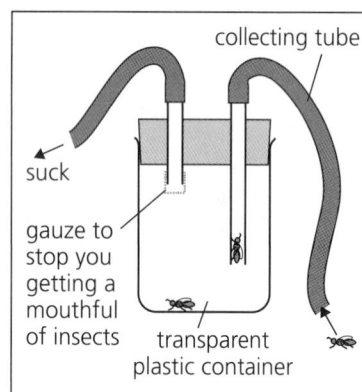

collecting tube

suck

gauze to stop you getting a mouthful of insects

transparent plastic container

Using a pooter

bits of leaf-litter to disguise the trap

pieces of stick supporting a stone lid

hole dug in soil

yoghurt pot

bait

drainage holes

A pitfall trap

Surviving in the environment

Living things need water, space, light, minerals, food and shelter. The size of each population in a habitat depends on how much of all these resources is available. When a population becomes too large for the resources in its habitat, it stops growing.

Living things also **compete** against each other for these resources. The size of a population of one species often depends on how well it competes against other populations for what it needs. Sometimes a newly introduced species thrives, e.g. grey squirrels have out-competed the native British red squirrel because they are bigger and more aggressive. In Australia, rabbits have become a real nuisance because they have no natural predator and are therefore breeding unchecked.

If wheat is planted closely, the farmer can increase the yield because more wheat can be fitted into the field. But if the plants are too close together they compete for space, water and light, and do not grow as well. This results in a reduced yield.

Adapting to survive

Each population is **adapted** to survive in its particular habitat. For example:

polar bear – very cold habitat	camel – an arid habitat	fish – water
• thick coat of fur to keep body heat in • large body means it loses less heat to the air.	• long thin legs • does not sweat very much • no layer of fat under the skin • hump of stored fats can be broken down to provide water.	• streamlined to move easily through the water • waterproof scales • fins for swimming • gills for 'breathing'.

Plants are also adapted to survive. For example, small plants on woodland floors flower very early before the leaves grow on trees and block the light from the Sun. Many plants also have to protect themselves against animals to survive. They use spines, stings or poisons to avoid being eaten.

Predator and prey relationships

Predators are animals which eat other animals (their **prey**). Predators are more likely to catch their prey if they:
• are **camouflaged** and difficult to see, like a polar bear in the snow
• have large teeth, claws, sting or poison to kill their 'food'
• have good senses – sight, hearing or smell – to find the 'food'.

Prey try to escape being caught by:
• camouflage that makes them hard to see, e.g. a stick insect
• colours which warn that they are unpleasant to eat, e.g. yellow and black wasps
• tasting horrible – predators soon learn which caterpillars are tasty.

Predators depend upon prey, so if the numbers of prey in a habitat go down, then some predators will starve and the number of predators will also go down.

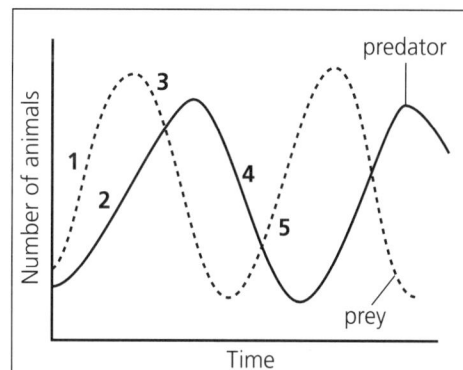

1 Prey has plenty of food, so breeds and increases in number.
2 More prey means more food for predators, so predators breed and their numbers increase.
3 More predators eating more prey means prey numbers decrease.
4 Fewer prey, therefore some predators starve.
5 Fewer predators, therefore not so many prey eaten and prey numbers start to increase again.

Food chains

Feeding relationships

Green plants make their own food (glucose and starches) using energy from the Sun. They are called **producers** because they convert the light energy from the Sun into chemical energy (food), which is stored in organic compounds such as glucose and starch. Other living things are called **consumers** because they have to get their food by eating (consuming) green plants or other animals.

All animals rely on plants, even if they do not eat them directly. Animals may eat other animals but there is always an animal which eats only plants (a **herbivore**) at the start of the line. Animals which eat only meat are called **carnivores**. Animals which eat plants and meat are called **omnivores**.

Feeding relationships can be drawn as a **food chain**. Some of the energy captured from light by plants is passed down the food chain as plants and animals are eaten. The Sun is the source of energy for *all* food chains.

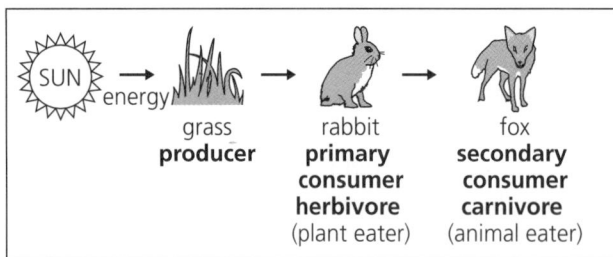

Hint

The arrow *must* point towards the animal that is eating, because it shows the direction the energy is moving in.

grass → rabbit   means the rabbit eats the grass

grass ← rabbit   would mean that the grass eats the rabbit!

	grass	rabbit	fox
	producer	**primary consumer herbivore** (plant eater)	**secondary consumer carnivore** (animal eater)

Each feeding level is called a **trophic level**. The first trophic level contains the producers, the second trophic level the herbivores or primary consumers, and subsequent trophic levels contain all the carnivores. Because most living things eat more than one type of food, a food chain is usually changed into a **food web** in which all the feeding relationships are shown.

Pyramid of numbers

Another way of showing feeding relationships is as a **pyramid of numbers**. Here, each trophic level is represented by a block. The size of the block represents the number of individuals.

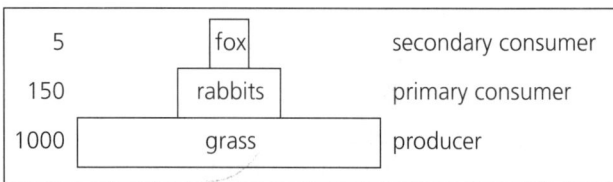

5	fox	secondary consumer
150	rabbits	primary consumer
1000	grass	producer

Now do this

1   On a moorland the main plant is heather, which is the food for lots of animals, including rabbits, grouse, bees and deer. There are also several fox families and a pair of eagles, which survive by hunting the grouse and rabbits.

  a Name **one** moorland producer, **one** primary consumer and **one** predator.

  b Draw **two** food chains using some of the living things mentioned in the passage.

  c Draw pyramids of numbers based on your food chains.

But it does not always work, for example:

		tertiary consumer	fleas	1000
10	blue tits	secondary consumer	cat	1
200	caterpillars	primary consumer	mice	100
1	oak tree	producer	wheat	1000

Don't be put off – always put the producer at the bottom and arrange the other feeding levels above it, keeping to the order in which they appear in a food chain.

Pyramid of biomass

A more accurate way of representing feeding relationships is to produce a **pyramid of biomass**. Here the size of the block represents the mass of the animals and plants feeding at that level, rather than the number. Samples of the

1 kg	blue tits	secondary consumer
200 kg	caterpillars	primary consumer
10 000 kg	oak tree	producer

plants and animals are heated in an oven to remove their water content and then their dry mass is recorded. The dry mass is used to construct the pyramid. A pyramid of biomass for the oak tree example is shown.

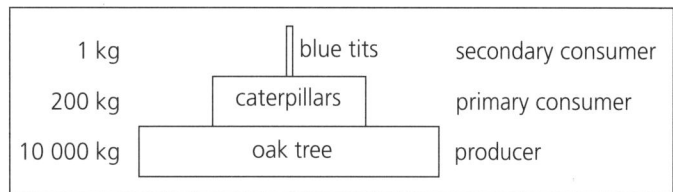

As you move along a food chain, energy is lost from each trophic level. Some is lost as heat energy, some as waste materials (excretion), and some through death. This can be shown pictorially:

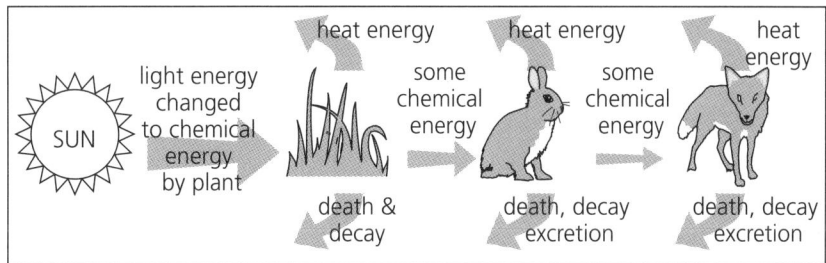

SUN — light energy changed to chemical energy by plant → heat energy → some chemical energy → heat energy → some chemical energy → heat energy

death & decay   death, decay excretion   death, decay excretion

Therefore there is less energy available at each step of the food chain. This is why a pyramid of biomass gets progressively smaller as it moves along the food chain.

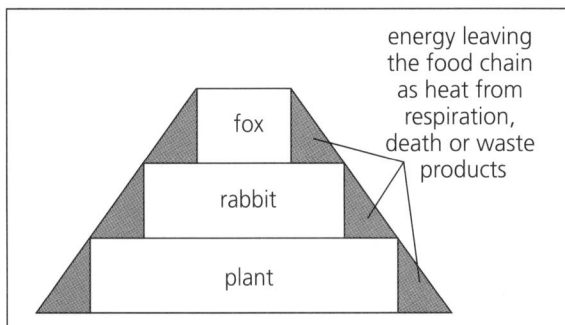

fox
rabbit
plant

energy leaving the food chain as heat from respiration, death or waste products

An area of land can produce more plant food, and therefore feed more people, than if the same area is used to produce meat.

Now do this

2   In what form does energy enter the environment?

3   What is the difference between a food chain and a food web?

4   Explain why a pyramid of biomass is a more accurate representation of an ecosystem than a pyramid of numbers.

5   Explain why most food chains are restricted to only four trophic levels.

Cycling and decay

What happens to all the dead bodies and waste produced by organisms in a food chain? In every ecosystem there are living things called **decomposers** which feed on dead plants and animals and their waste materials.

Some **bacteria** and **fungi** are decomposers. They make dead things **decay** so that the useful substances these things contain can be used again by other living things. One of these useful substances is carbon, which is part of all living things because it is present in all proteins, carbohydrates and fats. Decomposers return carbon to the atmosphere as carbon dioxide, and plants remove it from the atmosphere to convert it into carbohydrates during photosynthesis. Therefore a cycle is produced.

Decomposers are living things and therefore have the same needs as other living things. They need:
- food – the material they are going to decompose
- moisture
- oxygen
- warm temperatures.

The carbon cycle

In the carbon cycle:
- soil bacteria and fungi release carbon dioxide into the air as they respire; they also return minerals to the soil
- plants and animals release carbon dioxide into the air as they respire
- carbon dioxide is used by plants for photosynthesis
- energy in some decomposing materials becomes trapped as fossil fuels, e.g. coal, oil
- burning fossil fuels releases carbon dioxide
- burning all organic materials, including wood, paper and animal tissues, releases carbon dioxide.

Now do this

1 Name **two** groups of living organisms which can act as decomposers.

2 Explain why decomposers are so important within an ecosystem.

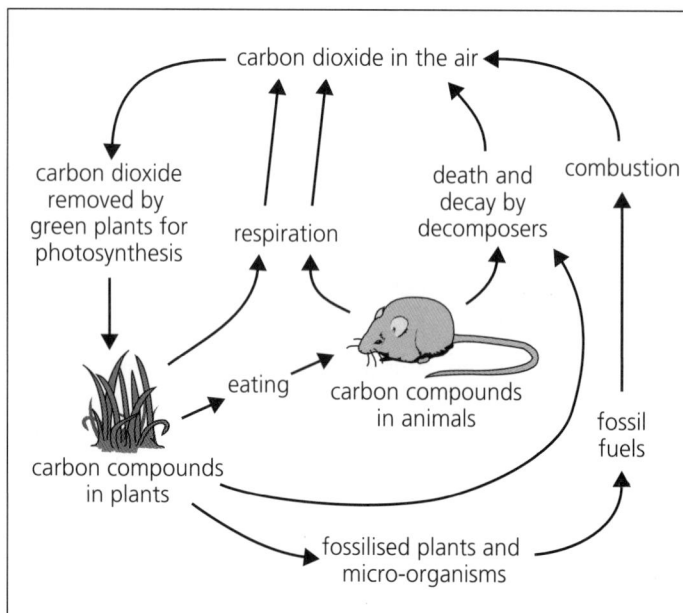

carbon dioxide in the air

carbon dioxide removed by green plants for photosynthesis

respiration

death and decay by decomposers

combustion

eating

carbon compounds in animals

carbon compounds in plants

fossil fuels

fossilised plants and micro-organisms

Now do this

3 Describe **three** ways in which human activities are in danger of upsetting the carbon cycle.

4 State the main way in which carbon dioxide is removed from the atmosphere.

The nitrogen cycle

In addition to carbon, nitrogen is vital to living things. It is needed to make proteins, which animals and plants need to grow. Although the atmosphere contains a large amount of nitrogen, atmospheric nitrogen must be changed into soluble nitrates and nitrites before it can be used by most living things.

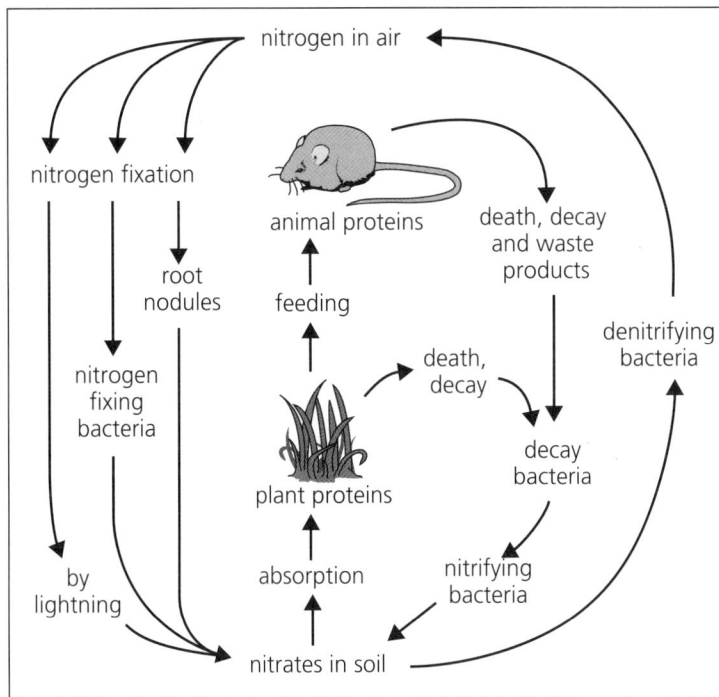

The nitrogen cycle at work

- Nitrogen-fixing bacteria convert atmospheric nitrogen into amino acids and proteins. Some of these bacteria are free living in the soil and others live in the root nodules of leguminous plants, e.g. clover, beans, peas.
- Lightning converts atmospheric nitrogen into nitrates.
- Plant roots absorb nitrates from the soil and convert them into amino acids and proteins.
- Decay bacteria convert proteins and urea into ammonia.
- Nitrifying bacteria add nitrates to the soil by converting ammonia into nitrates.
- Farmers artificially boost the nitrate content of soil by adding fertilisers.
- Farmers can also boost the nitrate content of soil by ploughing plant remains, especially leguminous plant remains, back into the soil so they can decay.

Now do this

5   The nitrogen cycle involves nitrogen-fixing bacteria, denitrifying bacteria and nitrifying bacteria. Explain the **three** different roles they have in the cycle.

6   Explain why traditional farming techniques include crop rotation, in which every five years a field is planted with beans and, instead of cropping the beans, the farmer ploughs them back into the soil.

The human influence on the environment

The human population is growing rapidly, all the time producing more mouths to feed. More land is required for food production. Some areas of land which are not suitable for plant crops are used to graze sheep or deer, but the rest is increasingly being used for intensive food production.

Intensive food production ensures that the chemical energy produced remains in the food, plant or animal, for us to eat, rather than being lost as energy to:
- competing plants (weeds)
- pests
- heat – farm animals kept indoors do no use up as much energy in keeping warm. Therefore intensive food production improves the efficiency of energy transfer.

Farmers can produce more food if they use:
- **herbicides** to kill weeds which otherwise compete with their crop
- **pesticides** to kill pests which otherwise might eat their crop
- **fertilisers** to provide extra nitrates and minerals for the crop to grow
- **intensive practices**, e.g. hedge removal to make larger fields
- **biological control** – non-chemical methods of pest control, e.g. using ladybirds to eat the aphids in greenhouses.

Intensive farming practices cause practical problems and ethical problems.

Damaging the food chain

Herbicides may kill plants which are an important part of a food chain. Animals which normally feed on them either die or find something else to eat, possibly the crop itself.

Pesticides may kill non-pest organisms either directly or through the food chain. The following is an example of this:

wheat ⟶ greenfly ⟶ ladybird ⟶ blue tit

If the pesticide kills the ladybirds, then the blue tits may well starve, and the greenfly population will become enormous because there will be no ladybirds left to eat them.

Pollution

Fertilisers provide plants with the extra nitrates and minerals they need to enable them to grow big and strong. The fertilisers have to be soluble so that the plant can take them up through the roots. But this means that if too many are added to the crop, or if it rains hard after they have been added, there is a good chance they will be washed (**leached**) out of the soil and into nearby waterways.

rain

nitrate fertiliser

nitrates dissolve in rain water

nitrate-rich water flows into stream

Fertilisers leaching into waterways cause **nitrate pollution**. This results in a waterway of dead and decomposing plants and animals beneath a layer of surface-growing plants (often algae). Lack of oxygen and/or light kills the rest of the living things in the waterway. This process is called **eutrophication**.

Destruction of habitats

Removing hedges destroys habitats. Many insects and birds which live in hedges act as predators of pest species. Without a home their numbers will decline. The farmer will then have more pests to control.

Treatment of animals

Intensive farming of animals raises an ethical problem. Many animals are reared indoors where they can be fed and checked for disease regularly. However, a growing number of people do not like this form of farming. They claim that it is the wrong way to treat animals and are calling on farmers to go in for more **free-range farming** where animals are free to live outside in fields and outdoor pens.

Other problems

The human population continues to grow rapidly and threatens the planet with the following forms of pollution.
- Nitrate-rich sewage enters the waterways.
- More people means more household waste.
- Sulphur dioxide dissolves in rainwater to form **acid rain,** which kills plants and attacks some buildings.
- Carbon dioxide is a **greenhouse gas** and causes heat to be trapped in the atmosphere, leading to **global warming** and its possible consequences of:
  - ice caps melting
  - increased sea levels
  - loss of low-lying habitats.

It is the developed countries, including the UK, which have the smallest populations but the greatest impact on global pollution, because of their access to global resources – for example, fossil fuels.

Now do this

1. Describe **three** ways in which farmers can improve the yield of their crops.
2. Give **one** advantage and **one** disadvantage of using a pesticide.
3. Explain the process of eutrophication and its effects on waterways.

Remember that, although the animals are kept inside, the food they eat still has to be grown outside, and therefore a reasonably large area of land is still needed to support them.

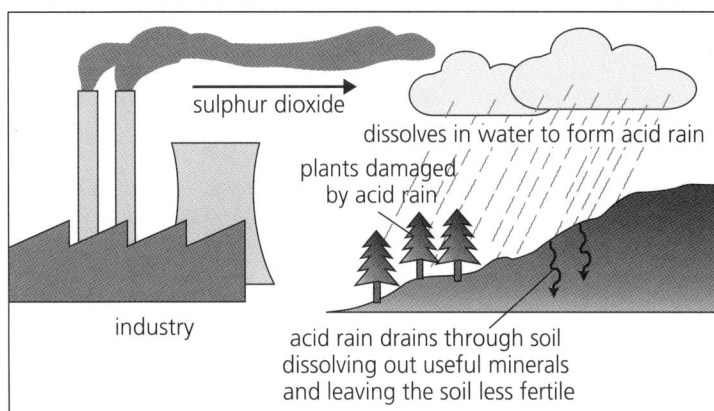

Formation of acid rain

Now do this

4. State **two** environmental problems associated with the increases in the human population, and suggest ways of overcoming them.

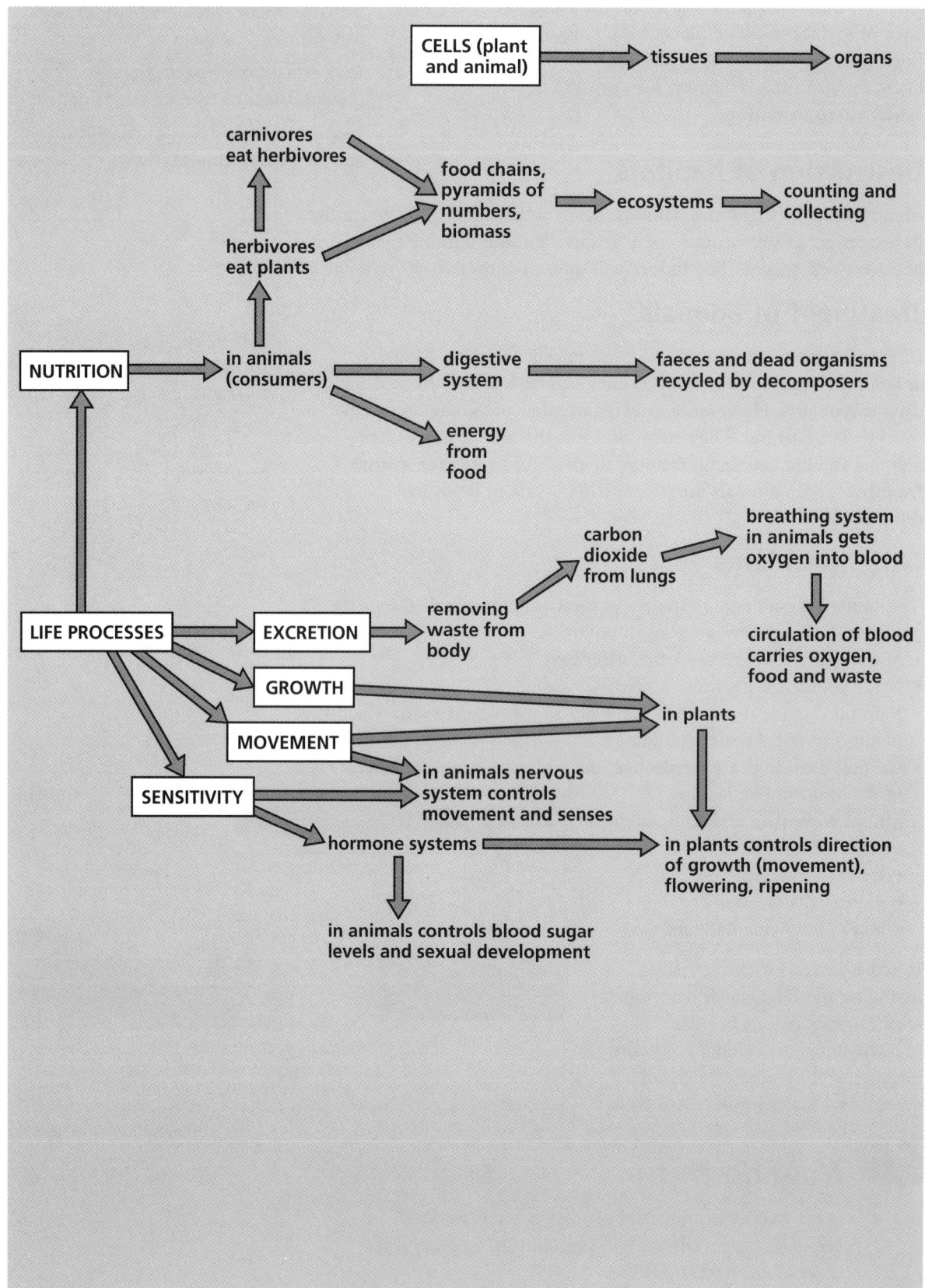

Concept map

CELLS (plant and animal) → tissues → organs

carnivores eat herbivores → food chains, pyramids of numbers, biomass → ecosystems → counting and collecting

herbivores eat plants → food chains, pyramids of numbers, biomass

NUTRITION → in animals (consumers) → digestive system → faeces and dead organisms recycled by decomposers

in animals (consumers) → energy from food

LIFE PROCESSES → EXCRETION → removing waste from body → carbon dioxide from lungs → breathing system in animals gets oxygen into blood → circulation of blood carries oxygen, food and waste

GROWTH → in plants

MOVEMENT → in plants

in animals nervous system controls movement and senses

SENSITIVITY → hormone systems → in plants controls direction of growth (movement), flowering, ripening

hormone systems → in animals controls blood sugar levels and sexual development

Exam questions

1 This question is about digestion. Enzymes in the mouth, stomach and small intestine help to digest food.

a What do enzymes do to food during digestion? [1]

b Bile also helps to digest food. Which food type does bile help to digest? [1]

c How does bile help to digest this food type? Explain as fully as you can. [2]

d When food has been digested it is then absorbed. This occurs in the small intestine. Write down **two** ways the small intestine is adapted to absorb digested food. [2]

[6 marks]

2 Look at the drawing. It shows a section through an alveolus.

a An alveolus is adapted for efficient gaseous exchange. Explain **three** ways in which the alveolus is adapted for oxygen uptake. [3]

b The alveoli are connected to the trachea by a system of tubes called the bronchioles and bronchi. Like the trachea, many of these contain pieces of cartilage in their linings. Write down what these pieces of cartilage are used for. [2]

[5 marks]

3 This question is about blood.

a Red blood cells contain a chemical substance that carries oxygen.

i Write down the name of this chemical substance. [1]

ii Write down a word equation for the reaction between this substance and oxygen. [1]

iii This reaction is reversible. Write down where in the body this reaction works in reverse. [2]

b Blood is carried in arteries, veins and capillaries. Complete the following table. [5]

Blood vessel	Function	Adaptation
	to carry blood at high pressure	
capillary		walls only one cell thick
	to carry blood at low pressure back to the heart	

[9 marks]

4 Look at the drawing. It shows a person frightened by a charging bull.

Adrenaline is released in the body of the person. It travels round the body in the bloodstream, preparing the body for action.

a Write down the name given to chemical messengers like adrenaline. [1]

b How does adrenaline prepare the body for action? Explain as fully as you can. [4]

[5 marks]

5 This question is about the plant hormone auxin. Auxin is produced in the tip of the shoot. Auxin causes shoots to grow towards the light.

a Write down the name of this response to light. [1]

b Suggest why this response is beneficial for plants. [2]

c Explain as fully as you can how auxin causes shoots to bend towards the light. [3]

[6 marks]

6 By accident, Martin trod on a drawing pin. He moved his foot away very quickly. This is called a reflex action.

a Describe the nerve pathway which allows this reflex action to happen. [3]

b Write down **two** other examples of reflex actions. [2]

c Nerve cells, or neurones, are well adapted for carrying messages. Write down **two** of these adaptations. [2]

[7 marks]

7 In America some farmers keep their pigs in indoor pens. The floors of these pens are metal slats which allow urine and waste to drop through into a reservoir. In some areas, nitrate-rich material from these reservoirs has seeped out into local waterways, causing widespread nitrate pollution. Explain fully what effect nitrate pollution can have on a waterway. [4]

[4 marks]

8 The diagram shows some different types of cells.

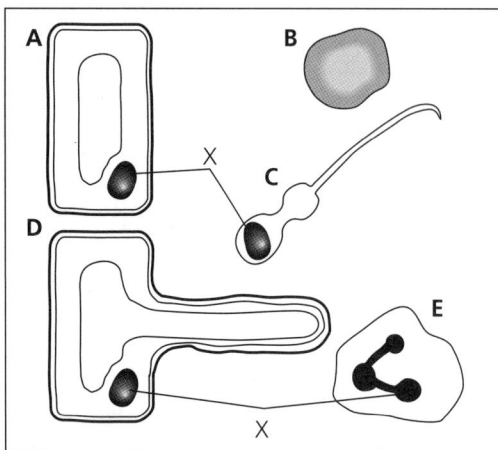

a Write down the name of structure X and its function? [2]

b Cell B does not contain structure X. Suggest a reason for this. [1]

c Cell C contains lots of mitochondria.

i What is the function of mitochandria? [1]

ii Why is it an advantage for this cell to contain lots of mitochondria? [1]

d Name one chemical which is made in cell A and is found in a high concentration in cell B. [1]

e Name one chemical which is taken up by cell D and transported to cell A. [1]

f Write down **two** of the cells which are plant cells, and give a reason for your choice. [3]

[10 marks]

9 Look at the diagram. It shows a model gut.

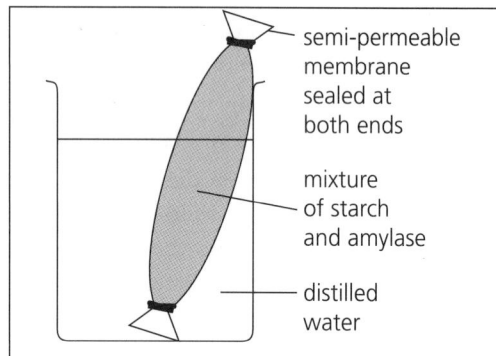

semi-permeable membrane sealed at both ends

mixture of starch and amylase

distilled water

a Inside the model gut are enzymes. What do enzymes do in your digestive system? [2]

At the start of the experiment the model gut was filled with starch and enzyme. After 30 min the distilled water was tested and found to contain glucose.

b Explain where the glucose has come from. [2]

c What does the distilled water represent in the model gut? [1]

d The distilled water does not contain any starch. Suggest a reason for this. [1]

A second model gut was set up with starch and enzyme, but this time the enzyme was boiled for 5 min before the experiment.

e What would you expect to find in the distilled water after 30 min and why? [3]

[9 marks]

10 Here is a section through an eye.

a On the diagram label the cornea, retina and lens. [3]

b What is the function of these parts of the eye? [3]

c Briefly describe how the muscles in the iris controls how much light enters the eye. [4]

d What is the name given to this type of reaction? [1]

e Suggest one advantage of it to the body. [1]

[12 marks]

11 This question is about the menstrual cycle.

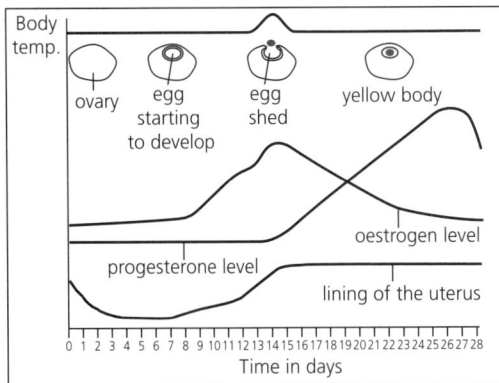

The figure shows the changes which occur during the menstrual cycle.

a What happens during days 1–7 of the cycle? [1]

b What is the main function of the hormone oestrogen? [1]

c On which day does ovulation occur? [1]

d If fertilisation occurs, explain what you would expect to happen to the progesterone level. [2]

e Some women use their body temperature as a form of birth control. Suggest one reason why this might not be very reliable. [1]

[6 marks]

12 Kim wanted to find out which species lived in a small wood near to his home. He wanted to sample the plants and the animals living in the wood. Explain how he could use each piece of apparatus to sample the wood.

a A quadrat. [3]

b A sweep net and pooter. [3]

c A pitfall trap. [3]

[9 marks]

13 Look at the food web of a pond.

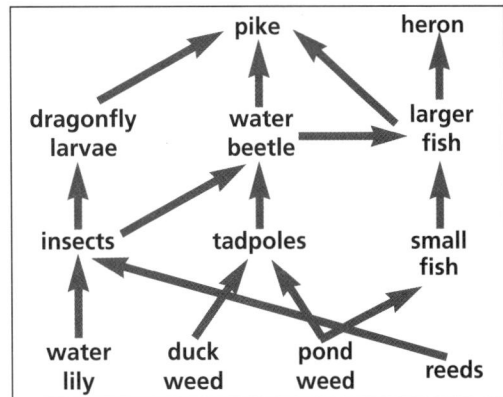

a Draw two different food chains from the food web. [3]

b What do the arrows in the food chain represent? [1]

c Explain why most food chains are limited to only four trophic levels. [2]

d Write down a possible food chain which would result in organisms moving from the pond food chain to a terrestrial food chain. [3]

[9 marks]

14 The figure shows a simplified nitrogen cycle.

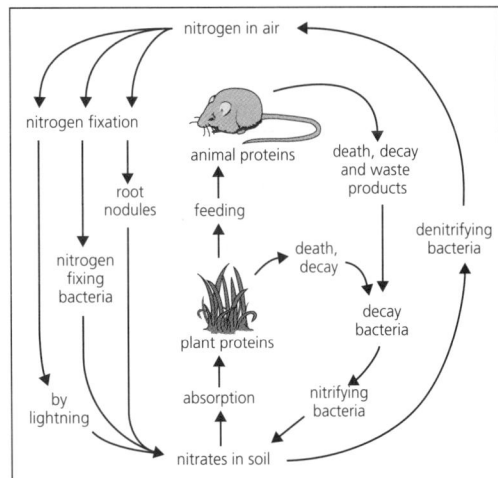

a Why do living things need nitrogen? [1]

b Explain why most living things cannot use the nitrogen in the air. [2]

c What does nitrogen fixation mean? [1]

d Give two ways in which farmers can increase the nitrogen content of their fields. [2]

[6 marks]

Atoms, elements, compounds and mixtures

Atoms, molecules and elements

The particles inside all chemicals are made from **atoms**. There are 104 different types of atom known. Each different type of atom is a different **element**. Some common elements are hydrogen, carbon, oxygen, sulphur, iron.

The particles inside a chemical might be single atoms on their own, or they might be made from groups of atoms. A small group of atoms combined together is called a **molecule**. Molecules can be made from atoms of one element, or from atoms of several different elements.

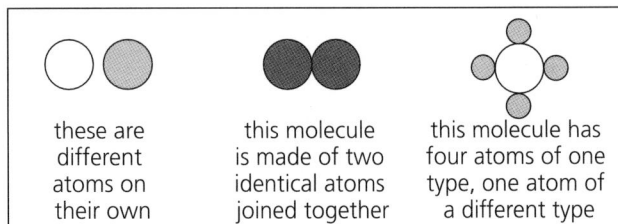

these are different atoms on their own

this molecule is made of two identical atoms joined together

this molecule has four atoms of one type, one atom of a different type

Enormous groups of atoms are called **giant structures** – you will come across these later.

Compounds and chemical bonds

Atoms of different elements can join together to make **compounds**. Compounds are always made from more than one element.

The atoms inside a compound are held to each other by **chemical bonds**.

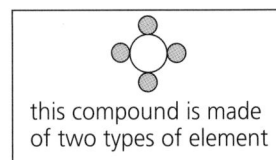

this compound is made of two types of element

Mixtures

Substances can be mixed together without them joining. They do not form compounds, they stay as mixtures. For example, air is a mixture of gases such as oxygen and nitrogen. Sea water is a mixture of water and salt – the salt is dissolved in the water, but it does not form a compound with the water. Substances in a mixture do not join, so they are easy to separate out.

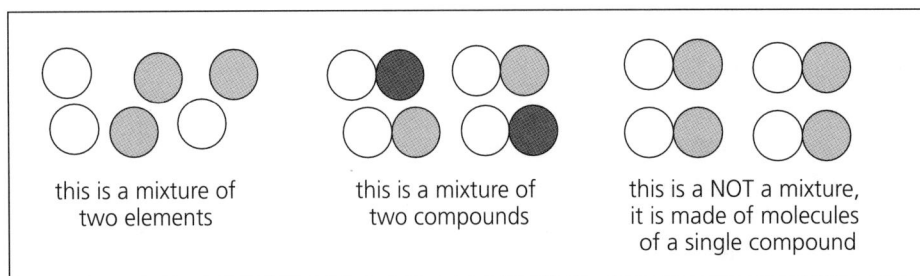

this is a mixture of two elements

this is a mixture of two compounds

this is a NOT a mixture, it is made of molecules of a single compound

Now do this

1 Which are compounds in the following list:
   hydrogen, hydrogen sulphide, oxygen, sugar, nitric acid, carbon?

2 Which are mixtures in the following list:
   salt and sand, sodium chloride, sugar, water, salty water?

Separation techniques

Substances in a mixture are not joined together, so you can separate them out again using one of these methods.

Filtration

Use filtration to separate undissolved solid from a liquid. You could use this to get sand from a mixture of sand and salty water.

Evaporation/crystallisation

You can use this techique to get a solid from a solution. Gently heat the mixture so that the liquid evaporates into the air and the solid stays behind as crystals. You could you use this to get salt out of salty water.

Distillation

You can use distillation to get a pure liquid back out of a solution of a solid in a liquid. You heat the solution in a flask. The liquid boils and turns into a gas. The gas goes through a condenser, and the cold surfaces inside the condenser turn the gas back into a liquid – it **condenses**.

Fractional distillation

Solutions made of two liquids cannot be separated by normal distillation – both liquids will evaporate when you heat the solution. You will have to use a **fractionating column** instead. Crude oil is a mixture of liquids which is separated by fractional distillation.

Chromatography

You can use chromatography to see how many chemicals there are in a solution.

Put a drop of solution on a strip of filter paper and dip the end in water. As the water goes up the paper the chemicals separate and each moves a different distance up the paper.

You could use chromatography to see how many coloured dyes there are in black ink.

mixture splits into two spots as the water rises

mixture put on to a line on the filter paper

??? Now do this

3 Here are some separation problems. Some separations can be done by using just one of the techniques in the table. Others will need more than one method. Copy the table and tick the techniques that you need for each separation.

Separation problem	Technique		
	Dissolve	Filter	Evaporate
To get solid salt out of salty water (like the sea)			
To get sand from sand mixed with salty water			
To get solid salt from sand mixed with salty water			
To get solid salt from sand mixed with salt crystals			

Solids, liquids and gases

Everything is made of very small particles that are too small to
see. The particles are always moving; the hotter they are the more
they move. Particles are arranged in different ways in solids,
liquids and gases.

Solids

The particles are close together. The particles stay in the same
places, so solids keep their shape – even though the vibrations
increase as the solid gets hotter. You can't move the particles any
closer, so solids can't be compressed into a smaller space. The
forces between the particles are strong.

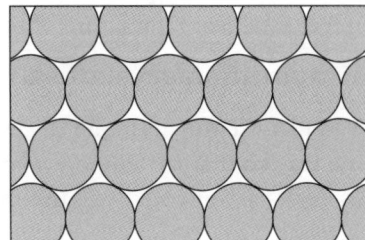

Liquids

Usually the particles are *slightly* further apart than in a solid.
They can now move about, so liquids do not have a fixed shape.
You still can't move the particles any closer so liquids can't be
compressed into a smaller space. When a liquid gets hotter, the
particles move faster.

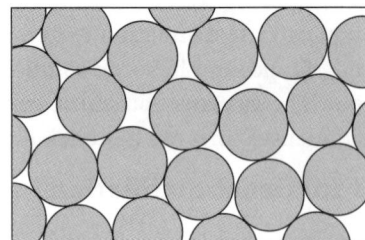

Gases

The particles are *very* far apart. This means that gases have no
shape and it is easy to compress them into a small space. In gases
the forces between the particles are very weak, so they don't stick
together.

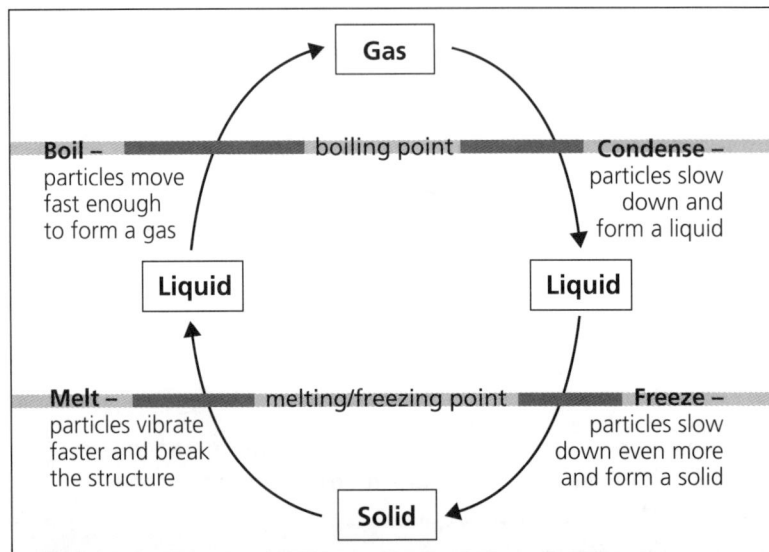

Gas

Boil – | boiling point | **Condense –**
particles move | particles slow
fast enough | down and
to form a gas | form a liquid

Liquid   **Liquid**

Melt – | melting/freezing point | **Freeze –**
particles vibrate | particles slow
faster and break | down even more
the structure | and form a solid

Solid

Now do this

1   Give **two** ways in which liquid particles are similar to
    gas particles.

2   Why are solids hard?

Linking particles together

Physical changes

water ⟵⟶ steam

When water boils it changes from a liquid into steam. It is easy to change steam back into liquid water. The molecules inside the water move further apart when it boils but the molecules do not change: no new substance has been made. This is called a **physical change**. Dissolving is another physical change.

Dissolving things

Dissolving a solid in a liquid is a physical change; it is easy to get the solid and the liquid back apart. Sugar dissolves in water because the forces between the water and the sugar molecules are stronger than the weak forces that hold one sugar molecule to the next. Substances such as calcium carbonate will *not* dissolve because the forces holding the calcium carbonate particles together are stronger than the forces between the water and the calcium carbonate.

A substance that will dissolve is **soluble**. A substance that won't dissolve is **insoluble**. The liquid that it dissolves in is a **solvent**. The solvent with the substance dissolved in it is a **solution**. Water is a very useful solvent; lots of chemicals will dissolve in it.

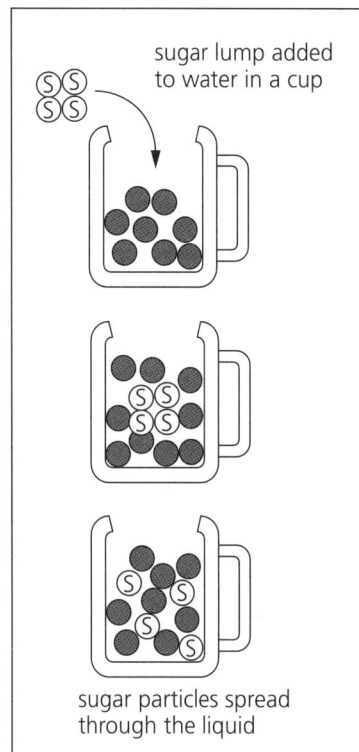

sugar lump added to water in a cup

sugar particles spread through the liquid

Chemical reactions

When sodium combines with chlorine, the two substances turn into sodium chloride – something totally new. This is a **chemical reaction**.

For changes like this to happen the bonds inside the chemicals must break up and new ones form. This isn't easy, so chemical reactions are very dificult to undo.

Most chemical reactions either need heating to make them start or give out heat as they happen – this is one sign that a chemical reaction is taking place.

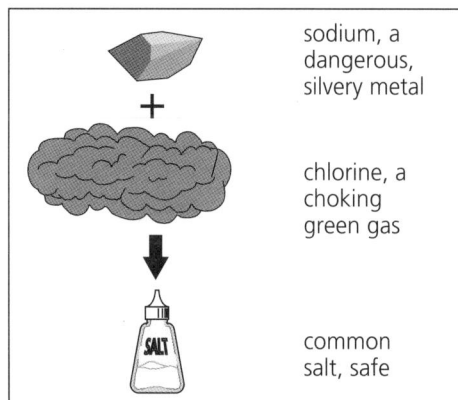

sodium, a dangerous, silvery metal

+

chlorine, a choking green gas

common salt, safe

Now do this

3 When you put iron filings into copper sulphate solution, the solution gets warm, it changes colour, and it is difficult to get the iron filings and copper sulphate back again. What are the **two** clues that tell you that this is a chemical change?

4 Copy and complete the following sentences:

When steam is cooled it turns back into liquid water; we say that it has _____. If you put sugar into water the sugar will _____. Water behaves as a _____. The water and sugar make a _____.

Symbols, formulae and chemical equations

Symbols for the elements

- Elements have symbols of either one or two letters.
- If the symbol has one letter, that letter must be a capital.
- If the symbol has two letters, the first letter is a capital
  the second letter is a little letter, e.g. Fe.

Formulae for compounds

The formula for a compound tells us which elements are inside the compound. It also tells us how many atoms of each element are in the compound.

The formula of a hydrogen molecule is H_2.
It is made of two hydrogen atoms bonded together.

molecule diagram	formula
H—H	H_2

The formula of hydrogen chloride is HCl.
It is made of one atom of hydrogen and one atom of chlorine bonded together.

molecule diagram	formula
H—Cl	HCl

If the molecule of a compound contains different numbers of atoms inside it, write the numbers of each element in small letters after each symbol in the formula.

The formula of water is H_2O.
It has two atoms of hydrogen and one atom of oxygen bonded together. See how the '2' comes after the 'H' in H_2O.

molecule diagram	formula
H—O—H	H_2O

The formula $(NH_4)_2SO_4$ looks more complicated. It is made of two atoms of N, eight atoms of H, one atom of S and four atoms of O.

??? Now do this

1 Copy and complete this table for the following compounds:
   HCl, H_2O, CH_4, $AlCl_3$, H_2SO_4, $C_6H_{12}O_6$.

Formula	Number of atoms in the formula	Number of different elements

2 Write down the formula of the hydrogen sulphide molecule shown in this diagram: H—S—H

3 Write down the formula of ammonia shown in this diagram:
$$\begin{matrix} H \\ \\ H \end{matrix} \Big\rangle N{-}H$$

4 Write down the formulae for the following metal compounds:
   magnesium chloride (Mg Cl Cl), iron oxide (Fe Fe O O O).
   (the chemical bonds are not shown)

What is a chemical equation?

A chemical equation tells us what happens in a chemical reaction. The chemicals at the start are the **reactants**, and they change into the **products**.

Nothing is left over at the end.

sodium	+	chlorine	→	sodium chloride
reactant	+	reactant	→	product

In this reaction two chemicals have turned into one product chemical. All the atoms inside the two reactants are now inside the product chemical.

Balancing equations

All the atoms inside the reactant molecules end up inside the product molecules, so equations always have the same number of atoms on each side of the equation sign.

For example, hydrogen gas and chlorine gas will react with each other.

hydrogen + chlorine → hydrogen chloride

Warning
You can only change the numbers *in front of* a formula. Never change any other numbers in the equation!

The symbol equation *might* look like this

$$H_2 + Cl_2 \rightarrow HCl$$ ✗

This means that there are two atoms of hydrogen and two of chlorine on the left, but only one of each on the right.

To balance this up we make sure that all the atoms of hydrogen and chlorine are used.

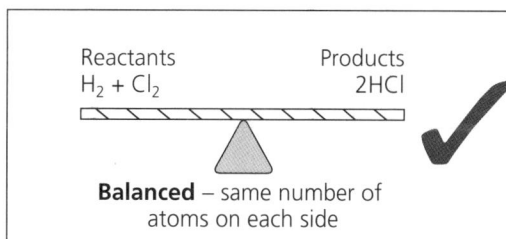

$$H_2 + Cl_2 \rightarrow 2HCl$$ ✓

Products
HCl
Reactants
$H_2 + Cl_2$
✗
Not balanced – not enough atoms on the right

Reactants
$H_2 + Cl_2$
Products
2HCl
✓
Balanced – same number of atoms on each side

Now do this

5 Copy each equation, then write down all the atoms of each element on **a** the reactant side **b** the product side. State whether the equation balances.

$Mg + O_2 \rightarrow 2MgO$

$CH_4 + 2O_2 \rightarrow CO_2 + 2H_2O$

6 Copy and complete these equations – there is a line for each missing number.

$H_2 + Cl_2 \rightarrow \underline{}HCl$

$Mg + \underline{}HCl \rightarrow MgCl_2 + H_2$

$C_3H_8 + 5O_2 \rightarrow \underline{}CO_2 + \underline{}H_2O$

$C_2H_4 + \underline{}O_2 \rightarrow 2CO_2 + 2H_2O$

Rates of reactions

Chemical reactions happen at different speeds. You can see some of them around you. Rusting is a slow chemical reaction. Burning is a fast chemical reaction. Explosions are even faster! The speed of a reaction is called its **rate**.

Speeding up reactions

Reactions happen when reactant particles collide and turn into products. Most ways of speeding up reactions make the particles collide more often – there are more collisions per second; the frequency of the collisions increases. There are several ways of making a reaction go faster.

- Increase the **temperature**. Reactant particles move faster, so there are more collisions per second. They also hit each other harder because they have more energy, so there is more chance of each collision causing a reaction.

  Sodium thiosulphate solution ('thio') goes cloudy with dilute acid. If you warm the liquids the reaction will go faster.

look down here
(wear goggles!)

thio and acid
go cloudy

mark on paper
disappears

- Increase the **concentration**. This only works with a solution! Increasing the concentration makes the particles closer together, so there are more collisions per second.

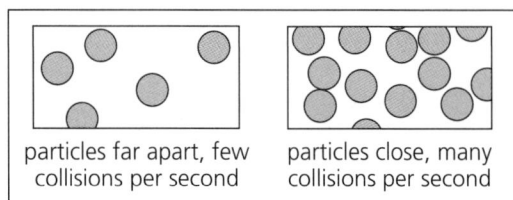

particles far apart, few collisions per second

particles close, many collisions per second

  'Thio' goes cloudy more quickly when it is more concentrated.

- If one of the reactants is a solid, you can break it down into smaller lumps. This increases the **surface area**, giving more places for reactions to happen. There will be more collisions per second.

  Large marble chips react slowly with acid. If you use smaller marble chips with acid the reaction will go faster.

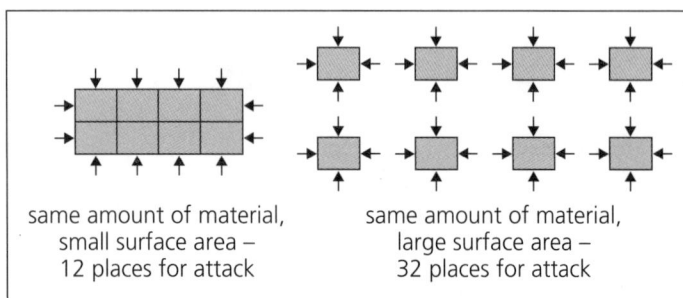

same amount of material, small surface area – 12 places for attack

same amount of material, large surface area – 32 places for attack

- Use a **catalyst**. Catalysts speed up a reaction. They are only needed in small amounts and are not used up by the reaction. Catalysts can be re-used. Different reactions need different catalysts to speed them up.

Hydrogen peroxide slowly breaks down into water and oxygen:

hydrogen peroxide	$\rightarrow$	water	+	oxygen
$2H_2O_2$	$\rightarrow$	$2H_2O$	+	O_2

To speed this up you can add manganese dioxide as a catalyst.
All the manganese dioxide is left in the beaker at the end, and it can be used again.

Measuring the speed of a reaction

The easiest way to measure the speed of a reaction is to find out how fast one of the products is made.

For example, when marble chips react with acid you can measure the amount of carbon dioxide gas given off every minute. You can do this with a large syringe, or by catching the gas in a test tube.

Reactions always start fast, and then slow down as the reactant chemicals are used up.

acid and marble chips

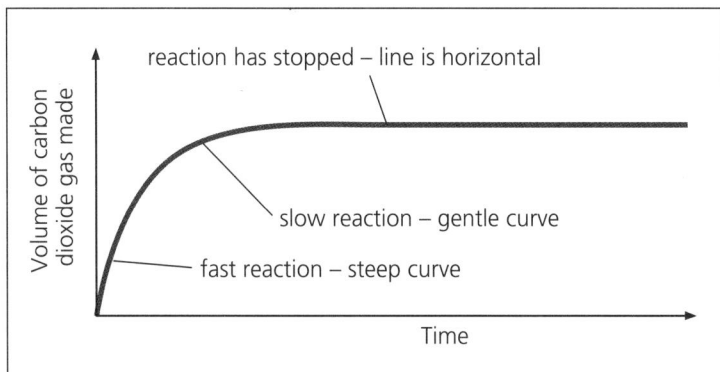

Reactions carry on until one of the reactants runs out.

Making more product?

Increasing the speed of a reaction will not make more product. It just means that the reaction finishes more quickly. The only way to make more product is to use more reactants.

Now do this

1 Give **three** ways of speeding up the reaction between an acid solution and a solid carbonate.

2 Which method will still work for a reaction between an acid solution and a carbonate solution?

This graph shows the way the mass of marble chips changes during a reaction with acid.

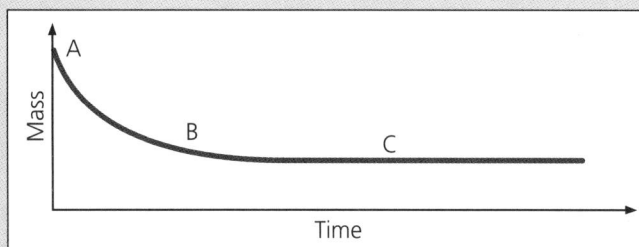

3 Which letter shows where the reaction is fastest? Explain why.

4 Which letter shows where the reaction has stopped?

Energy and reactions

Most chemical reactions transfer energy. The energy can be transferred in different ways: heat and light when something burns; electricity from the chemicals inside a battery; you can even hear the sound when marble reacts with acid.

Exothermic and endothermic reactions

Reactions which get hot are **exothermic**; they are giving out energy. A few reactions take energy in, which makes them feel cold. These are **endothermic**.

Bond making and breaking

When compounds react the first thing that they do is to split into their atoms. Then the atoms join together again to make different compounds. To pull the atoms away from each other the bonds have to be broken. When the atoms join back together, new bonds are made.

Energy has to be put *in* to *break* the bonds – this is an endothermic process. Energy is given *out* when bonds are *made* – this is an exothermic process.

If more energy is taken in than given out, the whole reaction is endothermic. If more energy is given out than is taken in, the whole reaction is exothermic.

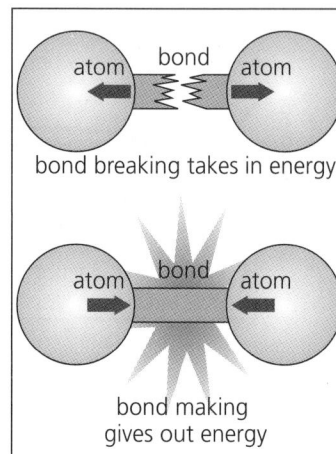

bond breaking takes in energy

bond making gives out energy

Measuring the energy

You can tell how much energy has been transferred in an exothermic reaction by using the reaction to heat up some water. The energy transferred to the water is calculated using the formula

energy transferred = mass × specific heat capacity × temperature change

Remember that the mass, specific heat capacity and temperature change are all for the substance to which you are transferring the energy – the water in the container.

Worked example

Q 3 g of fuel raised the temperature of 500 g of water in a metal container from 20°C to 36°C.
Calculate the energy transferred by one gram of fuel.
(The specific heat capacity of water is 4.2 J/g°C.)

A Temperature rise = 36 – 20   = 16°C
Total energy transfered = 500 × 4.2 × 16   = 33 600 J
Energy transfer per gram of fuel = 33.6 ÷ 3   = 11.2 kJ

water – temperature rises

paraffin – heats up the water

Reactions that produce electricity

If you dip two different metals into a solution the reaction will produce an electric current. You can find out which reaction transfers most energy by using a voltmeter. The higher the reading the greater the energy transfer. The further apart the metals are in the reactivity series, the higher the voltage.

strip of copper

iron nail

salty water

V = voltmeter

Now do this

1 Which bonds are broken and which bonds are made in this reaction?

$$H-\overset{\overset{\displaystyle H}{|}}{\underset{\underset{\displaystyle H}{|}}{C}}-H \ + \ Cl-Cl \ \rightarrow \ H-\overset{\overset{\displaystyle H}{|}}{\underset{\underset{\displaystyle H}{|}}{C}}-Cl \ + \ H-Cl$$

2 Calculate the energy transferred by 2.5 g of fuel if it will raise the temperature of 400 g of water by 4.5°C. (The specific heat capacity of water is 4.2 J/g°C.)

Energy and the environment

Burning hydrocarbon fuels produce two gases that cause a lot of pollution. One is carbon dioxide, the other is sulphur dioxide. Carbon dioxide is a major cause of the greenhouse effect.

The greenhouse effect

Ultraviolet rays from the Sun go through the Earth's atmosphere and heat up the Earth's surface. The heated Earth gives off infra-red radiation, which leaves the Earth. Greenhouse gases in the atmosphere trap some of the infra-red radiation and stop its energy getting out. This means that the Earth gets warmer still.

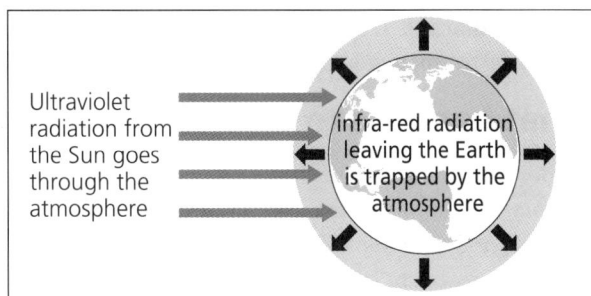

Ultraviolet radiation from the Sun goes through the atmosphere

infra-red radiation leaving the Earth is trapped by the atmosphere

The major greenhouse gas is carbon dioxide. Because we burn millions of tonnes of oil and coal every year carbon dioxide is being produced faster than it is being removed. This is slowly making the Earth warmer. Another greenhouse gas is methane, which is produced by farm animals and rotting vegetation.

Sulphur dioxide and acid rain

Fossil fuels such as coal and oil contain small amounts of sulphur. Sulphur turns into sulphur oxides when the fuel burns. These oxides dissolve in rain water to make several acids, including sulphuric acid. This makes acid rain. Acid rain can corrode buildings. It also changes the soil slightly, which harms animals and plants.

sulphur dioxide

acid rain

Now do this

3 Copy and complete the following sentences:
When carbon compounds burn, _____ gas is formed. This affects the temperature of the Earth, so it is called a _____ gas. It lets _____ radiation from the Sun through the atmosphere but it won't let _____ radiation from the Earth back out again. Fossil fuels also contain small quantities of sulphur. This produces _____ when it burns, which causes acid rain.

Air, oceans and the carbon cycle

Air is a mixture of gases

Oxygen is one of the two most important gases in air, but it does not make up a large amount of the air. The air is made of approximately

- 80% nitrogen – which does very little
- 20% oxygen – a most important gas
- small amounts of other gases, including
- 0.04% carbon dioxide – the other important gas, even though there is only a very small amount of it.

The atmosphere also contains large amounts of water vapour, but the amount changes with the weather.

The amounts of nitrogen and oxygen are approximately constant because they are being made at about the same rate as they are being used up. The amount of carbon dioxide is also approximately constant. We think that it is increasing *very* slowly, because it is being made slightly faster than it is being used up.

What happens to the carbon dioxide?

Carbon dioxide from the atmosphere is taken in by plants during photosynthesis. When the animals eat the plants, carbon goes from the plants to the animals. When plants and animals respire and when plants such as trees burn, carbon dioxide goes back into the atmosphere. If the animals or plants turn into fossil fuels, such as coal and oil, the fuel forms carbon dioxide when it burns. If the animals form rocks, such as chalk, their carbon is locked away in the rock.

Test for carbon dioxide
Carbon dioxide turns lime water milky.

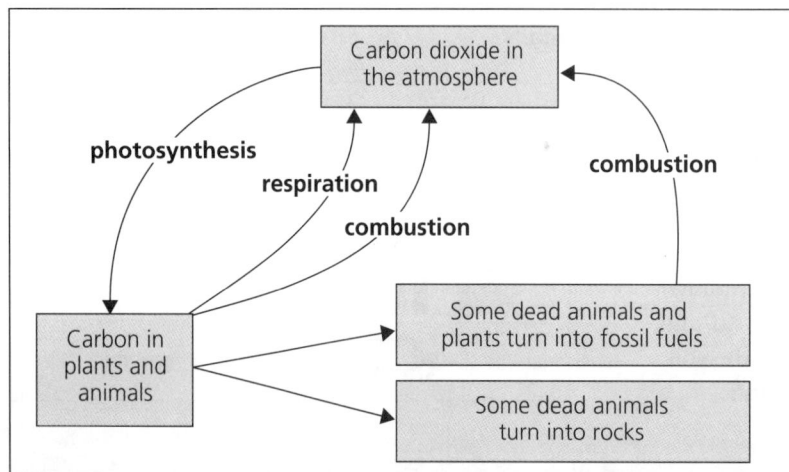

```
            ┌──────────────────────┐
            │  Carbon dioxide in   │
            │   the atmosphere     │
            └──────────────────────┘
   photosynthesis                    combustion
          respiration
          combustion
  ┌──────────┐       ┌────────────────────────┐
  │ Carbon in│──────▶│ Some dead animals and   │
  │ plants and│      │ plants turn into fossil fuels │
  │ animals  │       └────────────────────────┘
  └──────────┘       ┌────────────────────────┐
                     │ Some dead animals       │
                     │ turn into rocks         │
                     └────────────────────────┘
```

Now do this

1   What are the **two** main processes that put carbon dioxide into the atmosphere?

2   What is the main process that takes carbon dioxide out of the atmosphere?

Where did the air come from?

Billions of years ago there was no oxygen in the Earth's atmosphere. Life did not exist. The atmosphere was formed by volcanoes, which were producing ammonia, methane, carbon dioxide and water.

Three billion years ago the first simple plant life appeared. The plants turned the carbon dioxide and water into food and oxygen – photosynthesis had started.

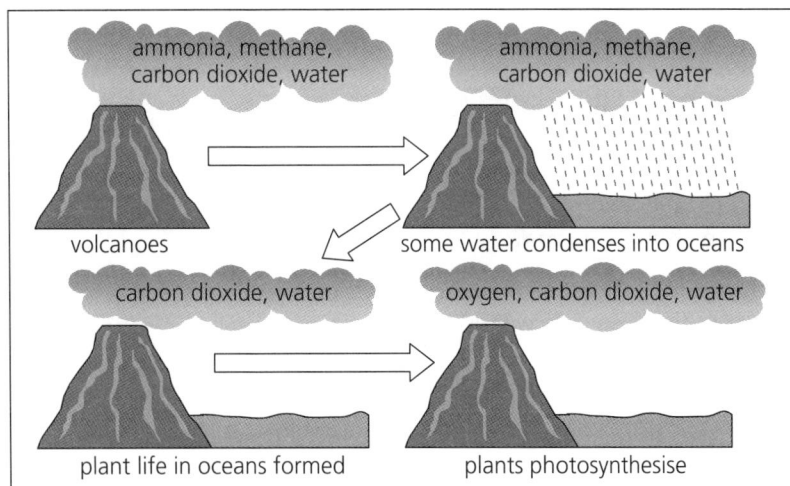

ammonia, methane, carbon dioxide, water

volcanoes

ammonia, methane, carbon dioxide, water

some water condenses into oceans

carbon dioxide, water

plant life in oceans formed

oxygen, carbon dioxide, water

plants photosynthesise

The amount of oxygen in the atmosphere increased, and the different types of living things increased, until the living things were using up the oxygen as fast as it was being made. This now keeps the amount of oxygen constant.

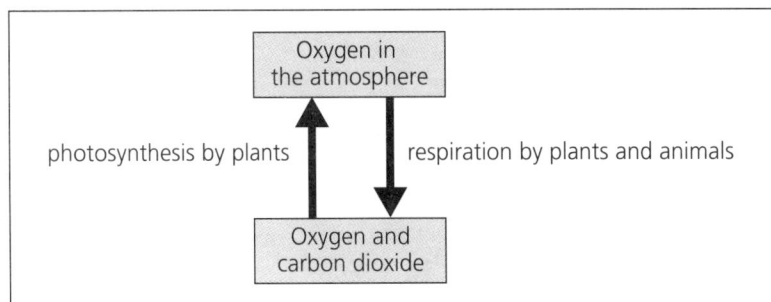

Oxygen in the atmosphere

photosynthesis by plants   respiration by plants and animals

Oxygen and carbon dioxide

Where did the oceans come from?

When the Earth formed there was steam coming out of volcanoes. As the Earth cooled the steam condensed and turned into rain, which formed the oceans. The rain dissolved chemicals out of the rocks, so sea water contains a mixture of different salts dissolved in it.

Now do this

3 Copy and complete the following sentences:

The atmosphere is made of _____% nitrogen, _____% oxygen and _____% carbon dioxide. Plants produce _____ gas during photosynthesis; it is needed for respiration and things burn in it. Respiration is similar to burning because they both produce _____ gas. The amounts of carbon dioxide and oxygen in the atmosphere stay fairly constant because the rate of photosynthesis is balanced by _____ and _____.

The Earth's crust

What is the Earth made of?

The top layer of the Earth is a thin rocky **crust**.

The **mantle** is under the crust. It is made of very hot solid rock that can slowly move.

It can melt into **magma**.

In the middle of the Earth is the **core**. The Earth's core is even hotter and is liquid.

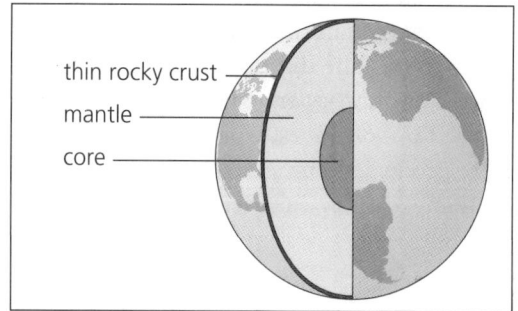

thin rocky crust
mantle
core

Plate tectonics

The shapes of the continents of Africa and South America fit together like a jigsaw. They have similar rocks and fossils on the coasts that face each other. This is because they were once joined together.

The thin rocky crust of the Earth is made up of large sections called **plates** which, because they have a lower density, float on top of the mantle. Heat from the core creates convection currents within the mantle. These currents move the plates slowly across the Earth's surface. Plates travel a few centimetres each year.

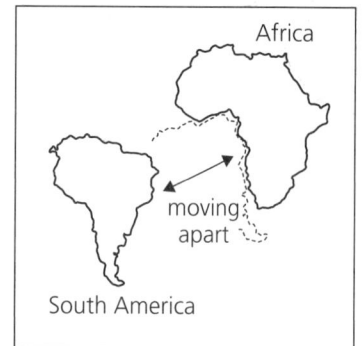

Africa
moving apart
South America

The plates may be moving away from each other, or into each other. The forces created where the plates move against each other are so strong that the edges of the plates are marked by earthquakes, volcanoes and mountain ranges.

North American plate
Eurasian plate
Pacific plate
Ring of fire
Pacific plate
Mid-Atlantic ridge
African plate
Indian plate
South American plate
Antarctic plate

Now do this

The Pacific Plate is surrounded by a ring of volcanoes called 'The ring of fire'.

1 Find the volcanoes on the map.

2 How far are the volcanoes from the edges of the plates?

3 How far are the earthquake zones from the edges of the plates?

Key: ∴ volcanoes   earthquake zones

What happens when plates move together?

When two plates collide, one plate is forced underneath the other; this is called **subduction**. As the plate is pushed down into the mantle the rock melts. This causes earthquakes and volcanoes. Rocks on the surface get pushed up into mountain ranges.

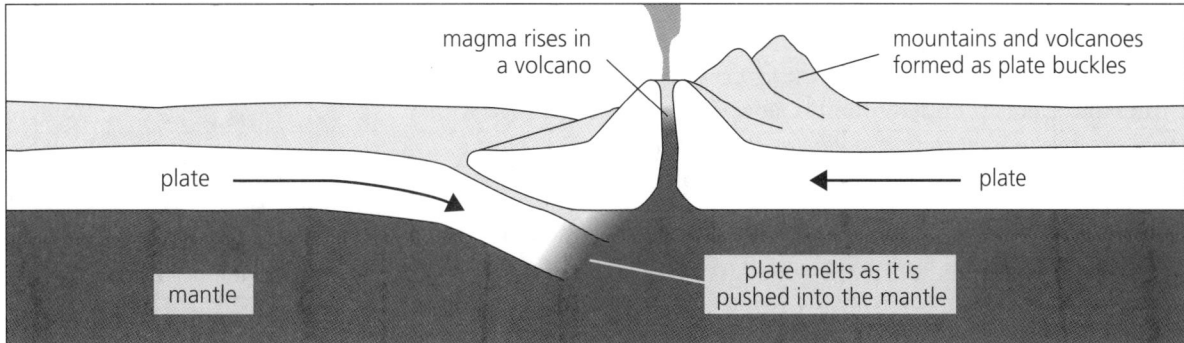

magma rises in a volcano

mountains and volcanoes formed as plate buckles

plate

plate

plate melts as it is pushed into the mantle

mantle

What happens when plates move apart?

The Atlantic Ocean is getting wider by at least a centimetre every year. This is because the plates under the ocean are moving apart, leaving a gap down the centre of the ocean floor. Magma flows into the gap, making a ridge of new igneous rocks. This is called **sea floor spreading**. There are earthquakes and sometimes volcanoes.

ridge

plates moving apart

plates moving apart

magma from the mantle moves into the gap

Scientists first realised that the sea floor was spreading when they found out that as you go further from the ridge the rocks get older.

Now do this

4 When two plates push into each other, one plate stays on the surface and the other plate disappears.
  a Where does this plate go?
  b What happens to the rocks of the plate that disappears?

5 What happens to the age of the rocks as you move away from a place where the sea floor is spreading?

If an oceanic plate collides with a continental plate, the oceanic plate goes underneath because it is more dense.

Rocks and the rock cycle

There are three types of rock – igneous, sedimentary and metamorphic.

Rock forms

Igneous rocks are made from magma which has cooled down and solidified. It usually forms interlocking crystals of different **minerals**. Cooling underground is slow. This produces a rock with large crystals, e.g. granite. Cooling at the surface is rapid. This produces a rock with small crystals, e.g. basalt.

Sedimentary rocks are small pieces of older rock, e.g. sand or mud, which settle and form sediments. The sharp edges of these pieces are usually worn away by the rivers which bring them down to the sea. As layers of sediment build up, the lowest sediments are compressed by the weight of the layers above them, which helps turn the lowest layers into solid rock. Often, chemicals soaking through the sediments will also cement the grains together into a solid.

Examples of sedimentary rock are: shale, which is made from mud; conglomerate, which is made from pebbles; sandstone, which is made from grains of sand. Sedimentary rocks can also be made from bits of animal or plant, e.g. limestone is made from seashells, and coal is made from prehistoric trees. Rock salt is made when seawater evaporates and leaves the salt behind.

Metamorphic rocks are rocks which have changed after they were originally formed. The changes are usually caused by high temperature or by pressure from other rocks. The final rock depends on what you start with and what happened to it. Marble and slate are metamorphic rocks. Both started as sedimentary rocks: marble as limestone and slate as shale.

What to look for

- Igneous – look for interlocking crystals, or glassy rock.
- Sedimentary – look for layers, bits of older rock grains and pebbles; some types may have fossils in them.
- Metamorphic – look for distorted grains, or distorted fossils.

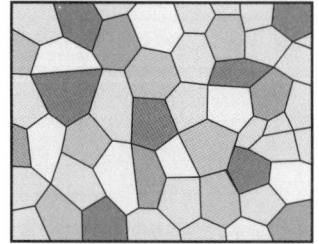

Igneous – slow cooling
large interlocking crystals

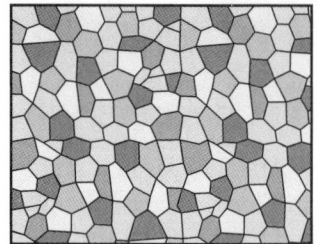

Igneous – rapid cooling
small interlocking crystals

Sedimentary – rounded
grains and fossils

Now do this

1 Copy and complete the following sentences:

Granite rock is made from magma which cools underground. This means that it will have _____ size crystals. It is a _____ type of rock. If rocks are then put under great pressure or temperature they will change to _____ rock.

The rock cycle

Rocks on the surface of the Earth are continually being broken down into pieces. This is called **weathering**. One type of weathering happens when rocks get very hot, then very cold, as in a desert. This makes them expand and contract until they shatter. This is called **exfoliation**.

Another type of weathering happens when water gets into cracks in the rock and freezes. The water expands when it freezes and splits the rock. This is called **freeze-thaw**.

The pieces are then carried away by the wind or by streams and rivers. This is called **transportation**. The pieces hit each other as they move and their jagged edges are rounded off.

Eventually the pieces settle, are buried, and solidify into layers of **sedimentary rock**. Earth movements can then bring the rock back to the surface so that it is weathered all over again.

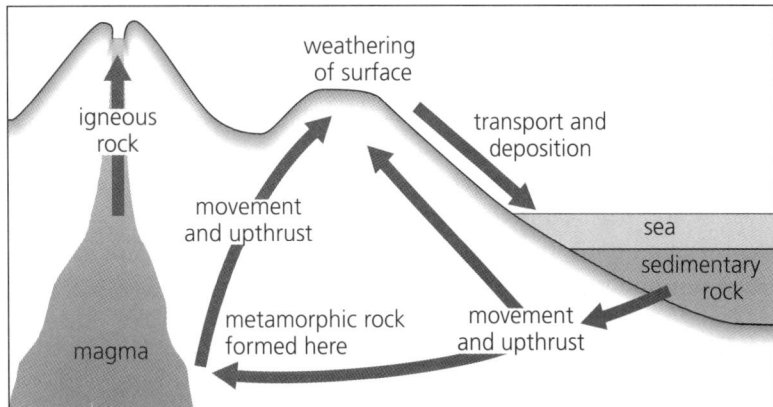

Earth movements can bring any of the three types of rock up to the surface, where they will be weathered and eventually form sedimentary rock.

The age of sedimentary rocks

Usually the oldest rocks form the bottom layer and the youngest rocks form the top layer.

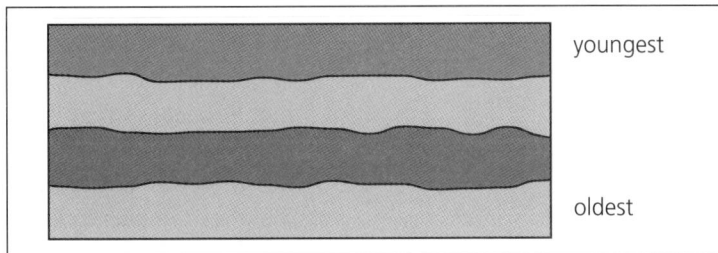

Now do this

2   Copy and complete the following sentences:

Rocks on the surface are slowly broken into small pieces. This is called _____. The pieces are carried to the sea where they settle and turn into _____ rock. If that rock is put under great pressure or temperature it will change into _____ rock. It can appear back on the Earth's surface because of _____.

Rock products – oil

The rocks of the Earth's crust are very useful to us, for example rock formations contain oil and gas.

Oil and natural gas

When microscopic sea creatures die, some of them settle to the sea bed and are covered in sediment, which eventually turns to rock. The solid sediments keep out air, and the pressure and temperature (90–120°C) of the layers of rock forms oil from the dead creatures. The oil soaks up through the rocks until it reaches a layer that it can't soak through (**non-permeable rock**). If that layer of non-permeable rock is the right shape (an oil trap), the oil will stay in the rocks just under the layer.

- surface
- oil collects here in a reservoir
- layer of non-permeable rock
- oil is formed here

Separating oil products

Crude oil is a mixture of liquids which boil at different temperatures. These liquids can be separated by **fractional distillation**. The crude oil is boiled and the mixture of vapours sent up the fractionating column. The column gets cooler nearer the top. As each vapour reaches the part of the column that is just below its own boiling point, that vapour will condense. The highest boiling point liquids condense low down the column where it is hottest, and the lowest boiling point liquids rise up to the cooler part. The column has an exit point for each liquid.

different vapours condense at the different temperatures

20°C cool	gas
100°C	petrol
200°C	kerosene
300°C	diesel
350°C	lubricating oil
hot	bitumen – left at the end

Furnace to turn crude oil into a mixture of vapours

The boiling points of larger molecules are higher because they have more weak forces between them. It takes a higher temperature to overcome these forces and boil the liquid.

Now do this

1   What are the boiling points of diesel, petrol and kerosene?

2   Why does petrol leave the fractionating column higher up than kerosene?

3   Why does diesel have a higher boiling point than petrol?

Burning oil

Crude oil is mainly made of **hydrocarbons**. These are molecules made of hydrogen and carbon only. They have different numbers of carbon atoms inside their molecules.

One group of hydrocarbons is called the **alkanes**. Here are the first five alkanes.

methane, CH_4 ethane, C_2H_6 propane, C_3H_8 butane, C_4H_{10} pentane, C_5H_{12}

Some hydrocarbons are used to make other substances such as plastics, but most are burned as a fuel because they transfer a lot of energy.
• Methane is natural gas – used for heating, cooking and in Bunsen burners.
• Propane and butane are used for heating and for camping gas stoves.
• Paraffin is used for heating and for lamps.
• Petrol and diesel are used as fuels for transport.

What happens in burning

When something reacts with oxygen to make an oxide we say that it has been **oxidised**. This is an **oxidation** reaction.

When a hydrocarbon burns with plenty of oxygen
• the hydrogen atoms form water
• the carbon atoms form carbon dioxide.

The reaction for methane burning in a gas cooker is:

| CH_4 | + | $2O_2$ | $\rightarrow$ | CO_2 | + | $2H_2O$ |
| methane | + | oxygen | $\rightarrow$ | carbon dioxide | + | water |

Beware If there is not enough oxygen in the room, the hydrogen part of the methane molecule reacts as normal but the carbon forms carbon monoxide instead of carbon dioxide. Carbon monoxide is poisonous and will kill you. Gas cookers and some gas fires are only safe if the room is well ventilated.

| CH_4 | + | $1\frac{1}{2}O_2$ | $\rightarrow$ | CO | + | $2H_2O$ |
| methane | + | oxygen | $\rightarrow$ | carbon monoxide | + | water |

A better way of writing this is

| $2CH_4$ | + | $3O_2$ | $\rightarrow$ | $2CO$ | + | $4H_2O$ |

If the oxygen levels drop further, the hydrogen atoms in the methane still react to make water but the carbon stops burning. It forms soot.

| CH_4 | + | O_2 | $\rightarrow$ | C | + | $2H_2O$ |

Now do this

4 Propane is a hydrocarbon. Write a word equation to show what happens when propane burns in oxygen.

5 Propane has the formula C_3H_8. Write a balanced symbol equation to show what happens when propane burns in oxygen.

6 Pentane has the formula C_5H_{12}. Write a balanced symbol equation to show what happens when pentane burns in oxygen.

Rock products – metal ores

We can dig some rocks out of the ground and use them straight away to make useful substances, such as pottery from clay, cement from limestone (calcium carbonate), glass from sand (silicon oxide), and chlorine from salt (sodium chloride).

Minerals and ores

Most rocks can't be used straight away. The useful part of the rock, the **mineral**, is usually mixed in with other bits of rock that we don't want. This combination of mineral and other rock is called an **ore**. Sometimes the mineral is the metal element itself, such as gold, but usually the mineral is a metal combined with other elements such as oxygen or sulphur. For example, iron oxide is the mineral in some types of iron ore.

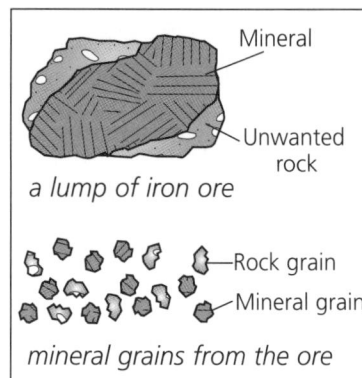

a lump of iron ore

mineral grains from the ore

Reducing the ore

Once the ore has been extracted, we have to get the oxygen away from the metal. Removal of oxygen is called **reduction**. If a metal is not very reactive it is easy to **reduce** the oxide. Reactive metals form bonds with oxygen that are hard to break, so it is difficult to reduce them.

Sodium, calcium, magnesium and zinc are all very reactive. They will all bond tightly with oxygen from the air, they all give off hydrogen with water and with acids. Sodium and calcium are so reactive that it is too dangerous to put them with acids!

Less reactive metals such as copper and silver don't react with water or acids, so copper is used to make water pipes and silver is used for jewellery.

The mineral is made of iron oxide

Metals reacting with other compounds

Aluminium is more reactive than iron, so it can steal oxygen out of iron oxide. It reduces iron oxide.

aluminium + iron oxide → aluminium oxide + iron

Carbon is more reactive than iron and zinc, so carbon will take oxygen out of iron oxide and also out of zinc oxide, it reduces iron oxide and zinc oxide.

Zinc is more reactive than copper, so it can steal the sulphate out of copper sulphate solution and leave the copper behind. This is called **displacement**.

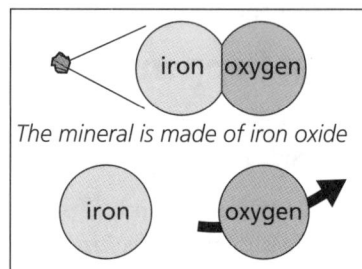

Reactivity of some elements	
sodium	**Most reactive**
calcium	
magnesium	
aluminium	
carbon	
zinc	
iron	
hydrogen	
copper	
silver	**Least reactive**

zinc	+	copper sulphate	→	zinc sulphate	+	copper
grey metal		blue solution		colourless solution		red metal

Now do this

1. Copy and complete the following equation:
   zinc + copper oxide →
   _____ + _____

2. Which of these will hydrogen react with? iron oxide, copper oxide, silver oxide. What will be formed in the cases that do react?

Carbon as a reducing agent

Carbon is a very useful substance for taking oxygen away from (reducing) metal oxides. It is more reactive than iron and copper, which we have to extract in very large quantities. This means that carbon can take copper out of copper ore and also iron out of iron ore. Carbon also has the advantage of being fairly cheap.

Extracting copper

Copper is extracted from copper ore using carbon in a blast furnace. It can also be carried out as an experiment in the laboratory. Copper oxide and carbon are mixed together and then heated over a Bunsen flame.

When the copper oxide and carbon start to react the mixture glows. After it has cooled down there are tiny beads of copper mixed in with the black powder. You can show that the beads are made of a metal by checking that they conduct electricity.

$$C + 2CuO \rightarrow CO_2 + 2Cu$$
carbon + copper oxide → carbon dioxide + copper

Extracting iron

Carbon monoxide is another chemical which will extract some metals from metal oxides. It is mainly used to get iron out of iron ore. It works best at high temperatures, so it is used in a blast furnace.

$$3CO + Fe_2O_3 \rightarrow 2Fe + 3CO_2$$
carbon monoxide + iron oxide → iron + carbon dioxide

There is so much heat given out in this reaction that the iron melts and is run out of the furnace into moulds.

Extracting copper

copper oxide mixed with carbon

Now do this

3 Metal C will take the oxygen from the oxide of metal A.
   Metal B will take the oxygen from the oxide of metal D.
   Metal A will take the oxygen from the oxide of metal B.
   Put the metals in order of reactivity, starting with the most reactive.

4 aluminium + iron oxide → aluminium oxide + iron
   Which substance has been reduced?
   Which substance has been oxidised?

Now do this

5 What do we call the reaction that takes oxygen away from something?

6 Write a word equation for the extraction of copper from copper oxide.

7 How could you show that the coppery coloured beads are made of metal?

8 How can you tell when the carbon is reacting with copper oxide?

9 a Which would you expect to corrode in air more quickly, iron or zinc?
   b Explain why.

Ions and electrolysis

Atoms are neutral. An atom can become electrically charged, but as soon as this happens it is called an **ion**. Atoms turn into ions by gaining electrons or by losing electrons.

If an atom **gains electrons** it becomes a **negative ion**.
If an atom **gives away electrons** it becomes a **positive ion**.

A chlorine atom gains one electron, forming a chloride ion	$Cl + e^- \rightarrow Cl^-$
An oxygen atom gains two electrons, forming an oxide ion	$O + 2e^- \rightarrow O^{--}$
A sodium atom gives away one electron, forming a sodium ion	$Na \rightarrow Na^+ + e^-$
A calcium atom gives away two electrons, forming a calcium ion	$Ca \rightarrow Ca^{++} + 2e^-$

Ionic compounds and electric current – electrolysis

Ionic compounds do not conduct electricity when they are solid but they will conduct electricity if they are melted or dissolved. Ionic solids don't conduct electricity because the particles in a solid are held in one place. In liquids the ions can move, so they can carry the charge through the liquid. Ionic liquids are called **electrolytes**.

Ions are attracted by the oppositely charged electrode. The **cathode** is negative; it attracts positive ions. When the positive ions reach the cathode they pick up electrons from the cathode and turn into neutral atoms.

The **anode** is positive; it attracts negative ions. When negative ions reach the anode they usually give their extra electrons to the anode and turn into neutral atoms.

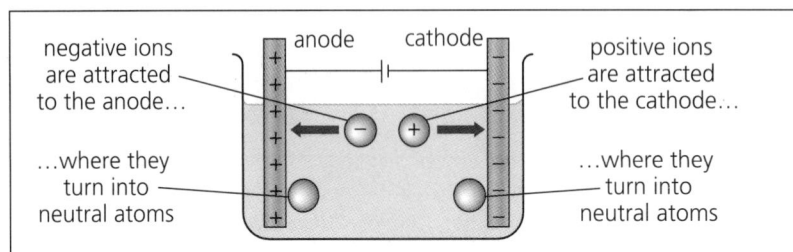

negative ions are attracted to the anode...

...where they turn into neutral atoms

anode   cathode

positive ions are attracted to the cathode...

...where they turn into neutral atoms

Now do this

1   Metals give away electrons. What sort of charges do their ions have?

2   Some non-metals can gain electrons. What sort of charges do their ions have?

3   Magnesium atoms lose two electrons. Write the symbol for a magnesium ion.

4   Solid sodium chloride is ionic. Why doesn't it conduct electricity?

5   Which electrode will metals go towards during electrolysis?

Using electrolysis to extract aluminium

Aluminium ore contains aluminium oxide. Aluminium is very reactive (it bonds tightly to oxygen), so carbon isn't reactive enough to take the oxygen away from the oxide. Instead we melt the aluminium oxide and then electrolyse it. Aluminium oxide melts at a high temperature, so we add a substance called cryolite which lowers the melting point and saves energy.

The sides and the bottom of the tank are lined with carbon. The carbon lining is connected to an electricity supply to make the cathode. The anodes are also made of carbon. They are lowered into the molten mixture of aluminium oxide and cryolite.

Aluminium ions are positive, so they are attracted to the negative cathode and are neutralised. Molten aluminium collects at the bottom of the tank. Oxygen is formed at the carbon anodes and then reacts with the anodes to make carbon dioxide.

Carbon anodes

Carbon cathode lining the cell

Melted aluminium oxide and cryolite

Melted aluminium collects at the bottom

At the cathode	At the anode
$Al^{+++} + 3e^- \rightarrow Al$	$O^{--} \rightarrow \frac{1}{2}O_2 + 2e^-$

Using electrolysis to purify or extract copper

The anode is the impure copper. The cathode is a pure copper plate. During electrolysis the copper dissolves from the impure anode and plates onto the cathode. The pure copper cathode becomes thicker as more copper plates onto it.

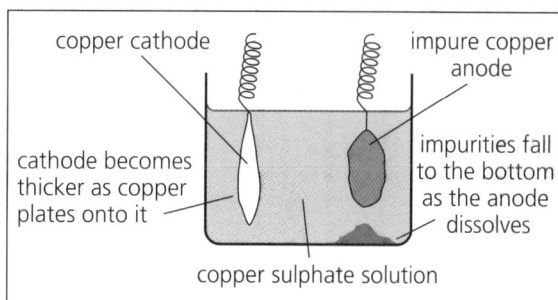

copper cathode

impure copper anode

cathode becomes thicker as copper plates onto it

impurities fall to the bottom as the anode dissolves

copper sulphate solution

At the cathode	At the anode
$Cu^{++} + 2e^- \rightarrow Cu$	$Cu \rightarrow Cu^{++} + 2e^-$

Copper is sometimes extracted from boulders by this method. The impure copper boulder is the anode, a pure copper rod is the cathode.

Now do this

6 What is the charge on
   a an anode?
   b a cathode?

7 Which electrode does aluminium collect at when aluminium oxide is electrolysed?

8 Which electrode does copper collect at when it is purified by electrolysis?

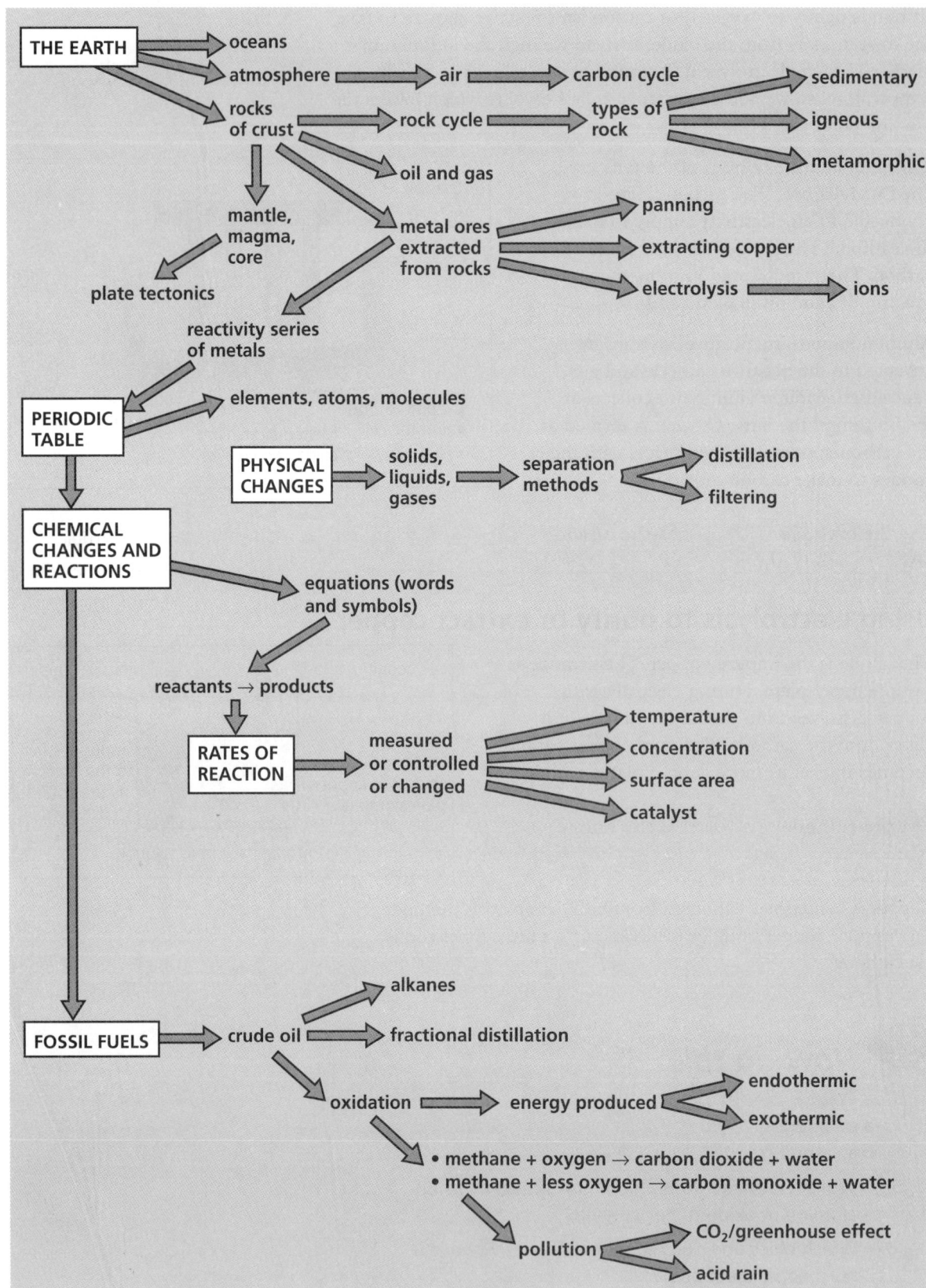

Concept map

THE EARTH → oceans

→ atmosphere → air → carbon cycle

→ rocks of crust → rock cycle → types of rock → sedimentary

→ igneous

→ metamorphic

rocks of crust → oil and gas

rocks of crust → mantle, magma, core

→ metal ores extracted from rocks → panning

→ extracting copper

→ electrolysis → ions

mantle, magma, core → plate tectonics

→ reactivity series of metals

PERIODIC TABLE → elements, atoms, molecules

PHYSICAL CHANGES → solids, liquids, gases → separation methods → distillation

→ filtering

PERIODIC TABLE → CHEMICAL CHANGES AND REACTIONS

CHEMICAL CHANGES AND REACTIONS → equations (words and symbols)

→ reactants → products

→ RATES OF REACTION → measured or controlled or changed → temperature

→ concentration

→ surface area

→ catalyst

FOSSIL FUELS → crude oil → alkanes

→ fractional distillation

→ oxidation → energy produced → endothermic

→ exothermic

oxidation → • methane + oxygen → carbon dioxide + water
• methane + less oxygen → carbon monoxide + water

→ pollution → CO_2/greenhouse effect

→ acid rain

Exam questions

1 Calcium forms calcium oxide, CaO, when you heat it in air.

a Write a word equation for this reaction. [2]

b Write a balanced chemical equation for this reaction. [2]

[4 marks]

2 Crude oil is a mixture of alkane molecules. We can separate these molecules by fractionation (fractional distillation).

a Different hydrocarbons have different boiling points. Explain why. [2]

b Alkanes are made of carbon and hydrogen. When the alkanes such as methane, CH_4, burn they react with oxygen in the atmosphere.

  i What do we call reactions where chemicals combine with oxygen? [1]

  ii Name two chemicals that are made when methane is burned in a plentiful supply of air. [2]

  iii Write a balanced equation for this reaction. [2]

  iv Name two chemicals that are made when petrol is burned in a reduced supply of air. [2]

  v Write a balanced equation for this reaction. [2]

[11 marks]

3 Geologists think that a particular type of rock from South America was made from molten magma which came to the surface and quickly cooled.

a What do we call rocks formed when molten magma solidifies? [1]

b What can you see in the diagram that shows you that both these rocks were formed when molten rock cooled? [2]

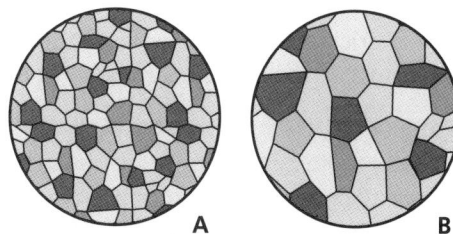

c Which of the rocks in the diagram could have cooled quickly? Explain how you can tell. [1]

d There is an identical type of rock in Africa. Geologists think that the two rocks were formed very close to each other. Use ideas about plate tectonics to explain why they are so far apart. [2]

[6 marks]

4 Aluminium is produced by the electrolysis of aluminium oxide. Aluminium oxide is made up of Al^{+++} and O^{--} particles.

a What do we call Al^{+++} and O^{--} particles? [1]

b Cryolite is added to the aluminium oxide before it is melted. Explain why. [1]

c Explain why melted aluminium oxide will conduct electricity but the solid won't. [1]

d The sides and the bottom of the electrolysis cell are lined with carbon. This is connected to an electricity supply to make the negative electrode. Positive carbon electrodes are dipped into the liquid.

  i What do we call a positive electrode? [1]

  ii What do we call a negative electrode? [1]

  iii What happens to the Al^{+++} particles when the current is switched on? [2]

[7 marks]

Making waves

Jo throws a brick at Sam. The brick (made from **matter**) transfers some **energy** from Jo to Sam.

Sam shouts at Jo. He makes a **sound wave**. The wave transfers some energy to Jo by making the air between them vibrate. There is no transfer of matter from Sam to Jo. There are two different types of wave. Sound is longitudinal and light is transverse.

hand wave — matter
energy transfer
sound wave
energy transfer

Longitudinal waves

Sound is a **longitudinal wave**. It is caused by **vibrations** which squeeze and stretch the air. The pattern of high and low pressure travels through the air as a wave, carrying energy away from the source of the vibrations. The high-pressure regions are called **compressions**. The low-pressure regions are called **expansions** or **rarefactions**.

The **frequency** (in hertz (Hz)) of the wave is the number of vibrations per second. So if the source vibrates 1000 times in 5 s, the frequency is 1000/5 = 200 Hz.

The **wavelength** (in metres (m)) of the wave is the distance from one compression (or expansion) to the next. So if there are 20 compressions in 60 m, the wavelength is 60/20 = 3 m.

This diagram shows a longitudinal wave moving along a spring. Each coil vibrates back and forth in the same direction as the flow of energy. The compressions and rarefactions move from left to right.

Now do this

1 Calculate the frequency of a wave whose source makes 12 000 vibrations in 6 s.

2 Calculate the wavelength of a wave which has 25 compressions in 100 m.

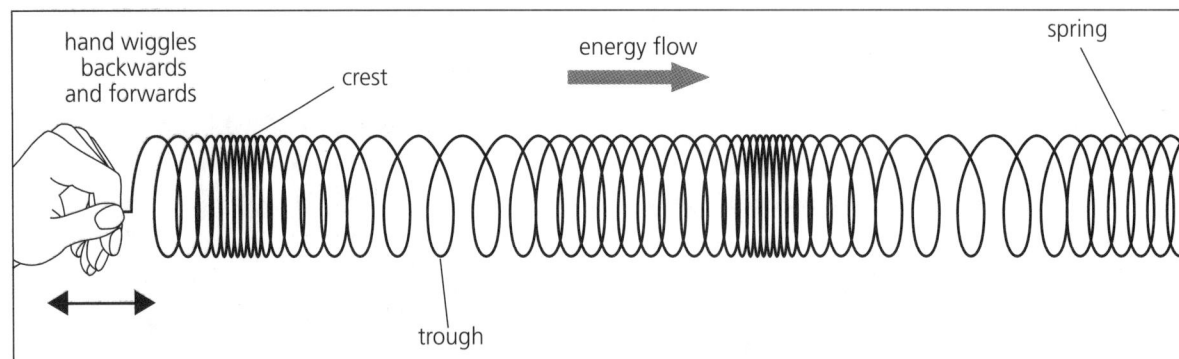

hand wiggles backwards and forwards
crest
energy flow
spring
trough

Now do this

3 Copy and complete the following sentences.

Sound is created by _____. These create regions of high pressure (_____) and low pressure (_____) which move through the air. The number of vibrations per second is the _____ of the wave, measured in _____. The distance between compressions is the _____ of the wave, measured in _____. Sound is a _____ wave. It makes the air vibrate in the same direction as the _____ _____.

Transverse waves

Jo transmits a **transverse** wave to Sam along a stretched rope.
As the wave travels from left to right, it makes each bit of the rope
vibrate up and down. The **amplitude** of the wave is the maximum
distance each part of the rope moves from its rest position.

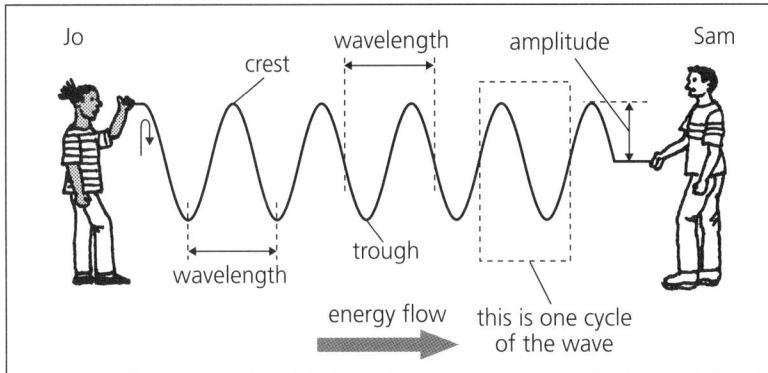

Now do this

4 Calculate values for the number of cycles,
the wavelength and the amplitude of
this wave in a stretched rope.

5 Explain why you can tell that the wave is a
transverse one.

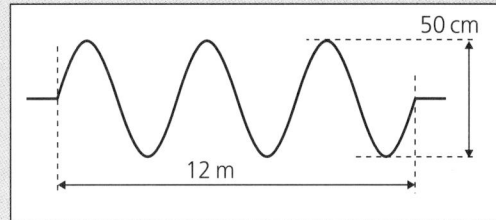

Speed, frequency and wavelength

The speed of a wave is linked to its frequency and wavelength with
this formula.

speed = frequency × wavelength   v = fL

Symbol	Meaning	Units of measurement
v	speed	metres per second or m/s
f	frequency	hertz or Hz
L	wavelength	metres or m

Now do this

6 State the formula linking speed,
wavelength and frequency of a wave.

7 A wave in water has a frequency of 6 Hz and
a wavelength of 4 m. Calculate its speed.

8 A radio wave has a speed of 300 000 000 m/s.
If it has a frequency of 6 000 000 Hz, what
is its wavelength? If its wavelength is 500 m,
what is its frequency?

Worked example

Q Sound has a speed in air of
300 m/s. Calculate the wavelength
of a 1200 Hz sound wave in air.

A v = 300 m/s
f = 1200 Hz $v = fL$
L = ? m

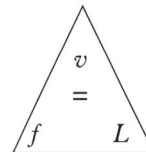

List the data... write the formula...
draw the triangle... change the
formula... insert the data.

$$L = \frac{v}{f} \qquad ? = \frac{300}{1200} = 0.25 \text{ m}$$

Using light waves

Reflection

Light waves travel in straight lines. These are drawn as **rays**.

When light rays reflect off a shiny surface, the **angle of reflection**, r, is the same as the **angle of incidence**, i. Both angles are measured from the **normal**. This is a line at right angles to the reflector at the point where the ray hits it.

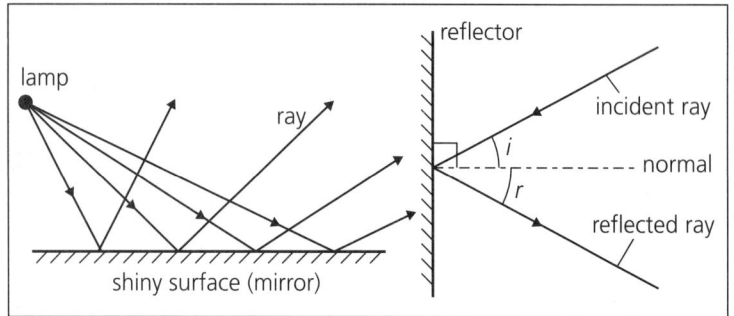

reflector

lamp

ray

incident ray

i

normal

r

reflected ray

shiny surface (mirror)

Now do this

1 What are the values for the angles of incidence and reflection for these rays of light?

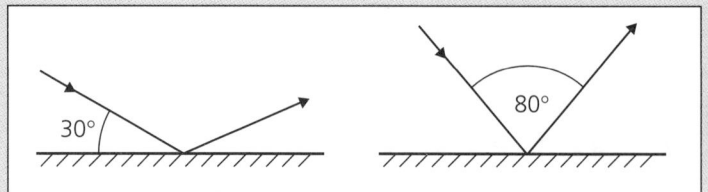

30°

80°

Light reflected from a flat mirror appears to come from behind the mirror. If you look at the reflected light, you see an **image** of the **object** which produced the light. The distance from the image to the mirror is the same as the distance from the object to the mirror.

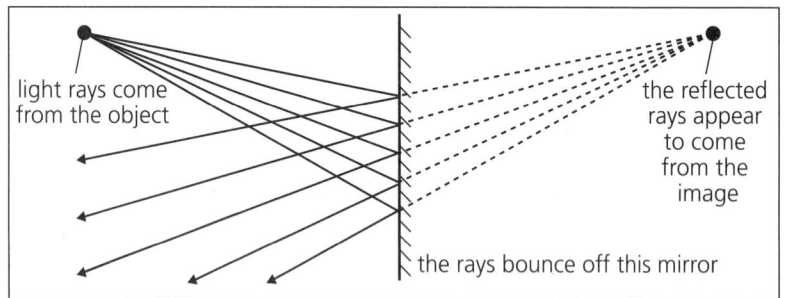

light rays come from the object

the reflected rays appear to come from the image

the rays bounce off this mirror

Curved mirrors can be used to **focus** light from a distant object. All the wave energy which hits the mirror is focused onto a single point, making it easier to detect. Satellite TV receivers use curved mirrors to increase the strength of the TV signal coming from the satellite in space.

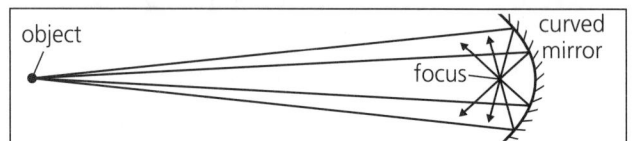

object

curved mirror

focus

Headlamps use curved mirrors to make a beam of light from a lamp. The lamp emits light in all directions. Light which hits the mirror emerges in just one direction.

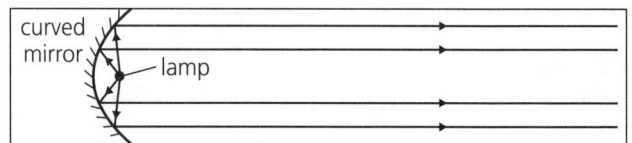

curved mirror

lamp

Now do this

2 A lamp is placed 50 cm in front of a flat mirror. Where will you see the image of the lamp in the mirror?

3 Draw a labelled diagram to show how a satellite TV dish works.

Refraction

When light goes from air into a transparent material (such as glass) it changes direction. It is **refracted**.

On the way into the material the angle of refraction is always smaller than the angle of incidence. Both angles are measured from the normal.

On the way out of the material the angle of refraction is always larger than the angle of incidence.

If the angle of incidence is large enough, rays of light will not refract out. They are **totally internally reflected**. This is used in optical fibres. Light which goes in at one end has to reflect off the edge of the fibre until it gets to the other end.

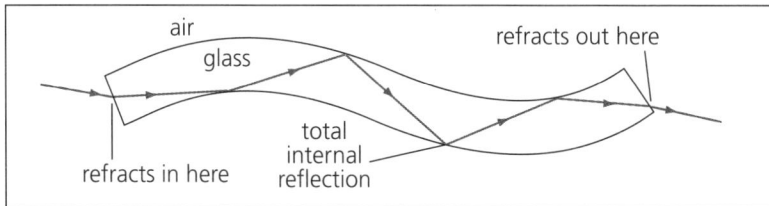

Now do this

4 What are the values of the angles of incidence and refraction for this ray of light?

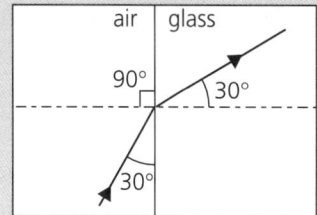

Now do this

5 A ray of light enters a prism. The ray is totally internally reflected at X. In what direction will it emerge from the prism?

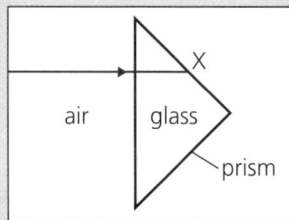

Lenses use refraction to make images. Parallel light rays entering a lens are focused to a point. Cameras and eyes have a light-sensitive surface at the focus point.

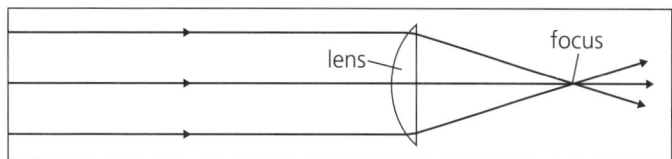

Diffraction

Light is **diffracted** when it goes through a gap which is small enough. The light emerges from the gap with a range of directions. The light is diffracted more as the size of the gap is reduced.

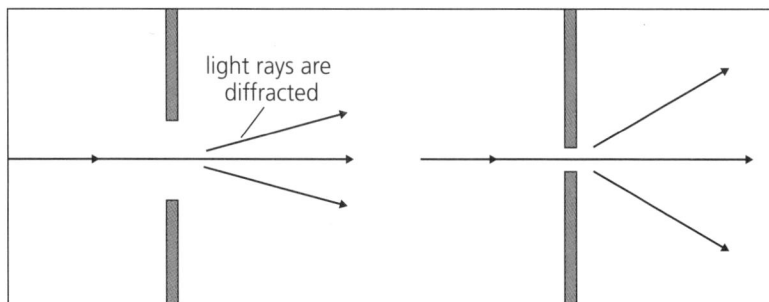

Ultrasound

The highest frequency sound that humans can hear is about 20 000 Hz (or 20 kHz). Sound with higher frequency than 20 kHz is called **ultrasound**. It is very useful.

Ships use **pulses** of ultrasound to detect what is underneath them. Each pulse **reflects** off solid objects in the water. A special microphone under the ship listens for these **echoes**. The time delay between the pulse and its echo is used to calculate the distance to the solid reflector.

Sound travels at 1500 m/s in water. So a time delay of 0.1 s means that the pulse travelled $1500 \times 0.1 = 150$ m. The reflector must therefore be $\frac{1}{2} \times 150 = 75$ m below the ship.

Now do this

2   A submarine sends out pulses of ultrasound. Echoes arrive back 0.05 s after each pulse. How far away is the source of the echoes?

Ultrasound can also be used to look inside the human body without the need for surgery. Pulses of ultrasound are fed in through the skin. Each time a pulse passes from one organ into another, some of it is reflected back to the skin.

These echoes can be used to form a picture of what lies under the skin. Ultrasound is often used to scan babies before they are born.

Now do this

3   Describe a use of ultrasound in medicine.

Seismic waves

Earthquakes produce two different low-frequency waves which travel through the Earth:
- **p-waves** are longitudinal and can therefore travel through both solids and liquids
- **s-waves** are transverse and can therefore only travel through solids.

The Earth has a liquid core which s-waves cannot pass through. The size of this core can be found by finding those places which receive only p-waves from an earthquake.

Now do this

1   Here are the frequencies of five different sound waves. List them in order of increasing frequency. Which of them will be ultrasound?

12 000 Hz   24 kHz   47 Hz
50 000 Hz   900 Hz

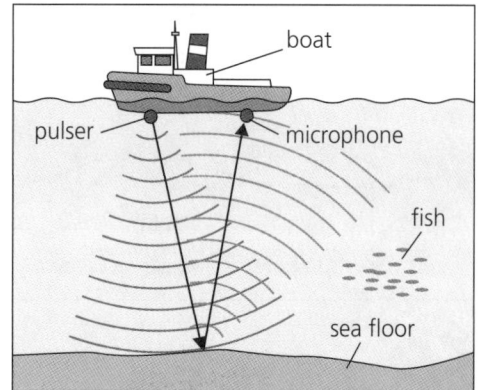

boat
pulser
microphone
fish
sea floor

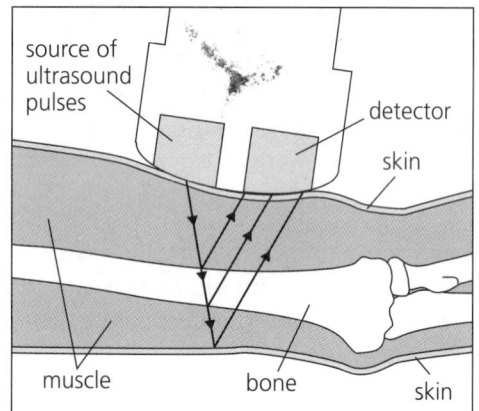

source of ultrasound pulses
detector
skin
muscle
bone
skin

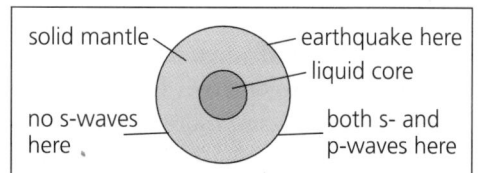

solid mantle
earthquake here
liquid core
no s-waves here
both s- and p-waves here

Now do this

4   Describe the differences between s-waves and p-waves.

Electromagnetic waves

The **electromagnetic spectrum** is a family of waves which can pass through empty space at the colossal speed of 300 000 000 m/s. Here is the spectrum of waves, with the longest wavelength listed first.

We use electromagnetic waves in many different ways. The energy delivered by an electromagnetic wave increases with decreasing wavelength.

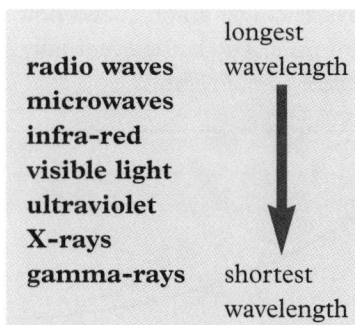

radio waves
microwaves
infra-red
visible light
ultraviolet
X-rays
gamma-rays

longest wavelength

↓

shortest wavelength

Now do this

5   Write down the seven parts of the electromagnetic spectrum in order of increasing wavelength.

Radio waves are used to carry information about sound (music and speech) as well as pictures (TV).

Microwaves can be made into beams by curved reflectors. As well as being used to communicate with satellites in space, pulsed microwaves are used to detect aircraft and ships. Microwaves with one particular wavelength are strongly absorbed by water and can be used to heat up food.

Infra-red waves carry heat energy. They are emitted by hot objects, such as the Sun. They can also carry information down optical fibres and allow hand-held remote controls to communicate with TVs and video recorders.

Ultraviolet waves damage living cells and can cause skin cancer. Dark skin will absorb ultraviolet waves and protect the living cells underneath.

X-rays pass through flesh but are strongly absorbed by bone. They allow photographs to be made of the inside of the body. X-rays also kill living cells and can cause cancer.

Gamma rays can pass through steel and concrete. They are very dangerous, but can be used to destroy cancer cells. Gamma rays are emitted by radioactive atoms. A short-lived radioactive substance can act as a tracer when it is injected into someone – the gamma rays emitted by the tracer can be picked up outside the body, showing the passage of the tracer through the person.

- Radio waves create alternating currents of electrons in electrical conductors.
- Infra-red waves can set whole atoms and molecules vibrating.
- Visible light waves can cause chemical reactions in some substances.
- Ultraviolet waves can damage living cells and knock electrons out of metals.
- X-rays and gamma-rays can knock electrons out of atoms and kill living cells.

Heat energy transfer

A kettle is boiled and then left. The graph shows how its temperature changes with time. The kettle eventually settles to 20°C, the same temperature as the room.

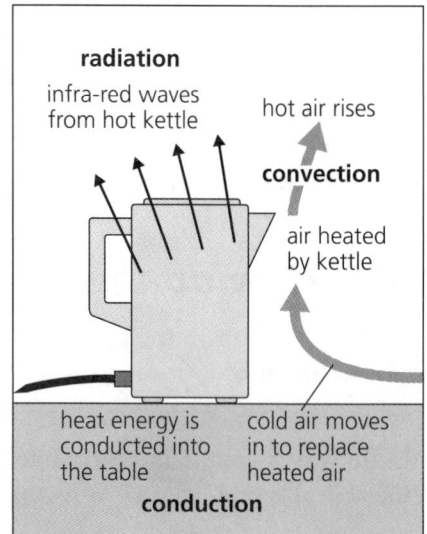

Heat energy flows from the hot kettle to the cold room until they are both at the same temperature.

There are three ways in which the kettle loses its heat energy:
- by **conduction** through the base into the table
- by **convection** as hot air rises from the sides
- by **radiation** as infra-red waves carry energy away.

Conduction

The **heat energy** of the kettle is just the **kinetic energy** of its particles. The particles in the solid kettle walls are always moving. They **vibrate**.

When one end of a solid is hotter than the other, the motion of the particles passes kinetic energy from the hot end to the cold end. The heat energy is **conducted**.

Now do this

1 A mug of coffee at 40°C is placed in a freezer at –20°C. State the final temperature of the mug. State the three ways in which heat energy leaves the mug.

Convection

Air particles which hit the hot surface of the kettle gain extra kinetic energy. So the air around the kettle heats up. This makes the air expand and rise up, carrying the extra heat energy with it. The heat energy is **convected** upwards.

Convection currents are set up around the kettle. There is a flow of cool air towards the kettle to replace the warm air moving upwards.

Now do this

2 Copy and complete the following sentences.

Particles in a solid have _____ energy which makes them _____.

Particles in a hot solid have more _____ than particles in a cold solid.

The process of heat transfer through a solid is called _____ .

3 The cooling element inside a fridge is always at the top. What happens to the air particles when they hit the element? Describe and explain the convection currents inside the fridge.

Radiation

Like all hot objects, the surface of the kettle emits infra-red **radiation**. Black surfaces are much better at radiating heat than shiny ones. So a shiny kettle will lose heat energy less rapidly than a coloured one.

Remember
- **shiny** objects reflect infra-red rays, so they heat up slowly
- **black** objects absorb infra-red rays, so they heat up quickly.

Evaporation

Liquids sometimes lose heat energy by **evaporation**. Particles at the surface of a liquid can escape if they have enough energy. So the particles with the most energy gradually leave the liquid. Only the less energetic particles are left behind, giving a colder liquid. A draught across the top of a liquid speeds up evaporation.

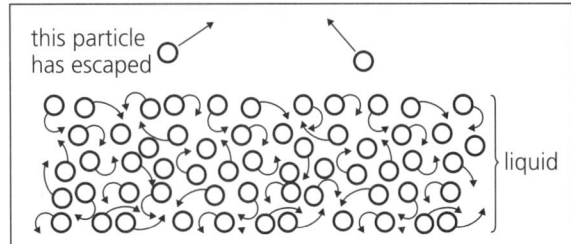

this particle has escaped

liquid

Insulation

Heat energy lost by conduction from a house can be reduced by trapping air in:
- layers of fluffy material in the roof
- cavities in the outside walls
- double glazing in the windows.

Heat energy lost by radiation from a house can be reduced by:
- painting roofs and walls shiny white
- using window glass which does not transmit infra-red radiation.

Heat energy lost by convection from a house can be reduced by:
- sheltering it from the wind
- keeping the surface area small.

Now do this

4 Copy and complete the following sentences with the words GOOD or BAD.

Silver objects are _____ radiators and _____ absorbers of heat radiation. Black objects are _____ radiators and _____ absorbers of heat radiation.

5 What happens to the energy of the particles in a liquid as it cools?

6 Explain how evaporation can cool a liquid.

7 Describe and explain how the rate of heat loss from a house can be reduced.

Space heating

There are two main ways of heating a home. You can either use electricity or you can burn a fuel, such as wood, coal, oil or gas. The heat from the fuel is usually carried to each room in the home by hot water in pipes or by hot air in ducts.

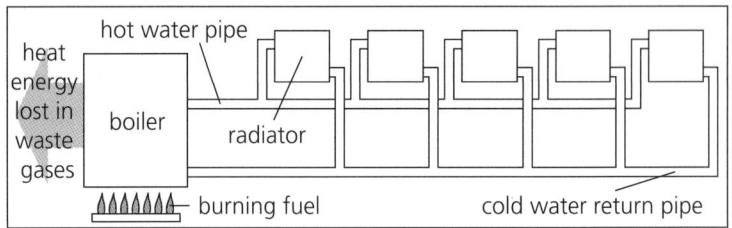

heat energy lost in waste gases

hot water pipe

boiler

radiator

burning fuel

cold water return pipe

This **energy flow diagram** shows how the chemical energy in oil becomes heat energy in a room using a hot water radiator.

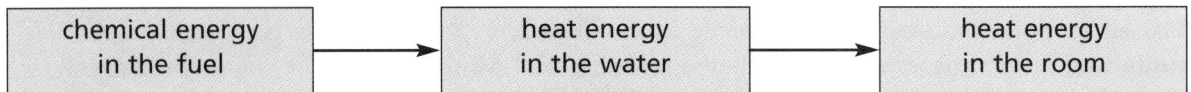

| chemical energy in the fuel | → | heat energy in the water | → | heat energy in the room |

Installing the pipes or ducts is expensive. It is often cheaper to put an electrical heater in each room instead. This also avoids using chimneys to vent the smoke and gases from the burnt fuel. The waste gases from the burnt fuel can **pollute** the environment.

However, making electricity often causes pollution, though it is easier to control this at the power station. Electricity is also expensive.

Now do this

1   Draw an energy flow diagram to show how the energy in gas can become heat energy in a room using hot air ducts.

2   Give two good reasons why electrical heaters should be used.

3   Give one good reason why fuels are better for heating than electricity.

Sources of electricity

Coal, oil and gas are **fossil fuels**. They are **non-renewable** sources of energy, particularly for making electricity. They will eventually be used up, and people are learning to use **renewable** sources, which use energy from the Sun. Energy is continually arriving from the Sun in the form of heat and light radiation.

Renewable sources of electricity include:

- **solar** energy, using solar cells to make electricity directly
- **wind** energy, caused by the heating of air by the Sun. Winds are convection currents, carrying cool air towards hot places
- **wave** energy, transferred to the oceans from the wind
- **plants**, which use **photosynthesis** to convert light energy into chemical energy

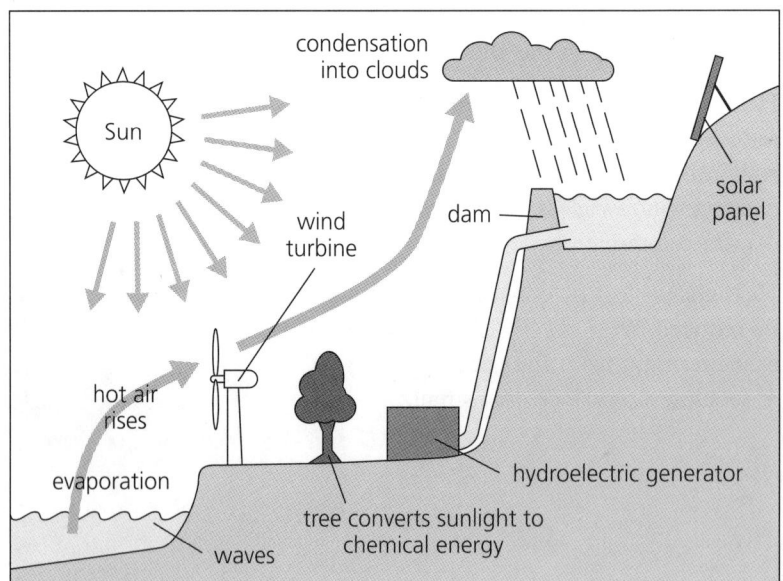

Sun

condensation into clouds

solar panel

wind turbine

dam

hot air rises

evaporation

waves

tree converts sunlight to chemical energy

hydroelectric generator

- **hydroelectric** energy, using rainwater which has fallen on mountains. The Sun evaporates the water from the sea and the wind carries the damp air above the mountains. As the air rises, it cools and the water turns to rain. The water is stored behind a dam. The stored water flows through a turbine to generate electricity.

Now do this

4 Name three non-renewable fuels for heating homes. State two reasons why it might be better to use electricity instead.

5 Name one renewable source of energy for heating a home.

6 Describe five renewable sources of electricity.

Insulation

It can be expensive to keep a building at a comfortable temperature. The only free energy is that which comes directly from the Sun. It pays to build houses which are **insulated**. Although you have to pay for the insulation, it can usually be paid for out of the saving made on buying energy to keep the house warm.

Worked example

Q It costs £5000 to double glaze all of the windows in a house. This cuts the annual heating bill from £750 to £500. How many years will it take before the double glazing pays for itself?

A Money saved in a year = £750 − £500 = £250, therefore pay-back time = $\frac{5000}{250}$ = 20 years.

Now do this

7 The annual cost of heating a house drops from £800 to £600 when £1000 is spent on insulating the roof and walls. Calculate the pay-back time.

Insulators and conductors

A material which is used to cut down the flow of heat energy is called an **insulator**. Most insulators contain a lot of air. Air is a poor conductor so it makes a good insulator when it is trapped. Clothes, curtains and double glazing all use trapped air to cut down heat energy loss.

Metals are good **conductors**. Heat energy flows quickly through them. They feel cold to the touch. Insulators feel warm.

Off-peak electricity

Electricity is produced by most power stations all of the time, night and day. The cheapest way of generating electricity is to keep producing it at a constant rate. However, there isn't much demand for electricity at night when most people are asleep. So electricity producers charge less for electricity at these **off-peak** times, to encourage people to use it. (Electricity is impossible to store directly, even for a few seconds.)

Automatic timers are used to switch on electrical devices at off-peak times, saving the consumer a lot of money. Cheap off-peak electricity can be used to:
- run storage heaters which heat bricks up at night and release their heat energy to air passed over them during the day
- operate washing machines and dishwashers overnight
- heat water overnight to be used during the next day.

Now do this

8 Copy and complete the following sentences.

Wool is an _____ because it contains trapped _____ .
Copper is a _____ because it is a _____ .

Using electricity

Every electrical appliance should be marked with its **voltage** and **power rating**. The voltage rating is usually 230 V in Europe. The power is measured in **watts** (**W**) or **kilowatts** (**kW**).

$$1\,kW = 1000\,W$$

250 W microwave oven

3 kW heater

Calculating the cost

The power rating of an appliance can be used to calculate how much electrical energy it will need when it is switched on.

energy (kilowatt-hour) = **power** (kilowatt) × **time** (hour)

One kilowatt-hour (kWh) of energy is called a **unit** of electricity. It costs about 10p. Off-peak electricity at night costs less.

Worked example

Q A bulb has a power of 200 W. If a unit of electricity costs 8p, calculate the cost of running the bulb for a week.

A Power in kilowatts = $\frac{200}{1000}$ = 0.2 kW

time in hours = 24 × 7 = 168 h

units used = kilowatts × hours = 0.2 × 168 = 33.6 kWh

cost = units × 8 = 33.6 × 8 = 269p.

Now do this

1 A TV is rated at 230 V, 150 W. If a unit of electricity costs 9p, calculate how much it costs to run the TV for 5 hours.

2 If an off-peak unit of electricity costs 6p, calculate how much it costs to run a 2.5 kW water heater for 4 hours at night.

3 Suppose a unit of electricity costs 8p. How much money do you waste by leaving a 100 W bulb on for 10 minutes?

Electrical wiring

Electric currents in metals make them get hot. Thin, high-**resistance** wires get hotter than thick, low-resistance ones. Electrical appliances are connected to the 230 V mains supply by a pair of insulated metal wires. They are called **live** and **neutral**. If the appliance has a metal exterior, there will be a third **earth** wire as well.

metal

water

insulation

heater element

earth

live

neutral

Electrical connections to a kettle

Each wire has a different coloured insulation

Wire	Insulation colour
live	brown
neutral	blue
earth	green and yellow

The live wire carries the energy from the supply to the appliance. The live wire is therefore the one which is most dangerous to touch, so it has the **switch**. The neutral wire completes the circuit for the electric current.

Wiring a plug

4   Name the three wires connecting an electrical heater to the mains supply. State the colour of their insulation.

5   Explain why the wire in the heating element of a water heater is much thinner than the wire in the cable connecting the heater to the mains supply.

Fuses and safety

There should also be a **fuse** or **circuit breaker** in the live wire. This switches off the current automatically if it gets too high.

Large currents in a wire can cause it to get hot and damage its insulation. The fuse is the thinnest wire in the circuit, so it melts (blows) first, before the other wires are damaged.

The earth wire should always be connected to the metal outside of an appliance. This protects anyone using the appliance. If the live wire comes loose and touches the outside, a large current flows in the earth wire and the fuse blows.

Appliances which are **double insulated** do not need an earth wire. Should the live wire come loose, it can't touch any metal which is on the outside of the appliance. Any appliance which has a non-metallic case is definitely double insulated and doesn't need an earth wire.

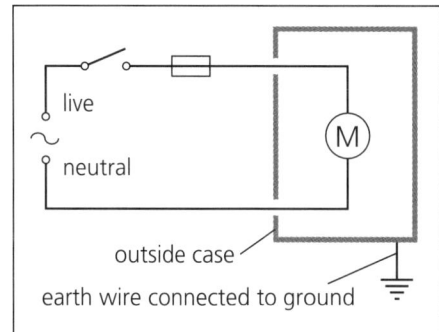

Now do this

6   State the function of each of the three wires connecting an appliance to the mains electricity supply.

7   Explain how a fuse or circuit breaker protects the insulation of mains wires.

8   Explain how a fuse can protect people from electric shock.

9   Where should the fuse and switch be connected?

10 What type of appliance does not need an earth wire?

11 Where should the earth wire be connected to an appliance? Why?

Measuring motion

Joe's car has a top speed of 35 metres per second (m/s). This means that it can move forwards 35 metres in each second, or 70 metres in two seconds.

The following formula can be used to calculate a speed if you know the distance and the time. (You must know this one by heart!)

$$\text{speed} = \frac{\text{distance}}{\text{time}}$$

$$v = \frac{s}{t}$$

Symbol	Meaning	Units of measurement
v	speed	metres per second or m/s
s	distance	metres or m
t	time	seconds or s

(v is for velocity, a word which can mean speed. s is for space, another word for distance. It is easy to get confused – don't!)

Worked example

Q A car at 30 m.p.h. travels 1.2 km in a minute. Calculate its speed in metres per second.

A $v = ?$ m/s
  $s = 1.2$ km $= 1200$ m $\quad v = \frac{s}{t} = \frac{1200}{60} = 20$ m/s
  $t = 1$ minute $= 60$ s

Always make sure that you have the distance and the time in the correct units *before* you calculate the speed!

Now do this

1 Write down the symbols and units for speed, distance and time.

2 Write down the formula for speed using symbols.

Worked example

Q How far will a car with a speed of 15 m/s go in 10 minutes?

A $v = 15$ m/s
  $s = ?$ m $\quad v = \frac{s}{t}$
  $t = 600$ s

  $s = vt \quad\quad ? = 15 \times 600 = 9000$ m

List the data … write the formula … draw the triangle … change the formula … insert the data.

Now do this

3 A car travels 400 m in 20 s. Calculate its speed.

4 Sound can travel 1.2 km in 4 s. How fast does it move?

5 Bill can walk 0.5 km in 5 minutes. How fast can he walk?

6 The legal top speed for a car is 110 km per hour. What is this in metres per second?

Now do this

7 A plane has a speed of 50 m/s. How far will it go in a minute?

8 A cheetah runs at 20 m/s. How long will it take to run 100 m?

Distance–time graphs

Distance–time graphs are a very good way of describing motion.

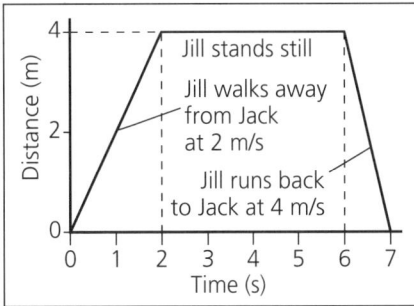

Jill stands still

Jill walks away from Jack at 2 m/s

Jill runs back to Jack at 4 m/s

Now do this

9 Here are three different distance–time graphs. Match each one with a sentence from this list.

a Going away then coming back again.

b Starting off quickly and slowing to a halt.

c Moving at a steady speed.

d Moving away faster and faster.

  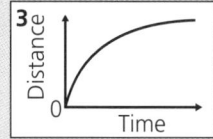

Speed–time graphs

Here are distance–time and speed–time graphs for Paul. He walks away slowly, stops for a while and then runs away quickly.

 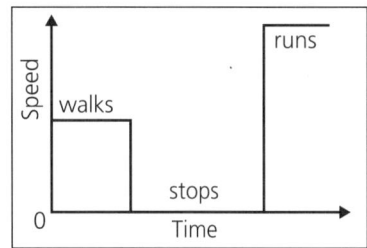

Now do this

10 Here are three speed–time graphs. Match each one with a sentence from this list.

a Speeding up to a steady speed.

b Moving at a steady speed.

c Moving at a steady speed and then slowing to a halt.

  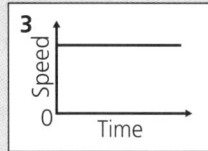

Here is a speed–time graph for Jake as he goes from rest to top speed on his bike.

The distance travelled is equal to the area under the line. The area is triangular in shape, with a base of 10 s and a height of 12 m/s.

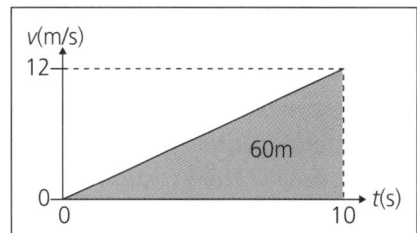

distance = $\frac{1}{2}$ base × height = 0.5 × 10 × 12 = 60 m

Now do this

11 Use the speed–time graph to calculate the distance travelled between

a 0 s and 5 s

b 5 s and 15 s

c 15 s and 25 s.

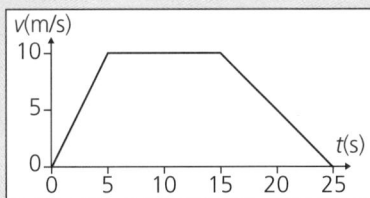

12 Use the distance–time graph to calculate the speed at

a 5 s

b 15 s

c 25 s.

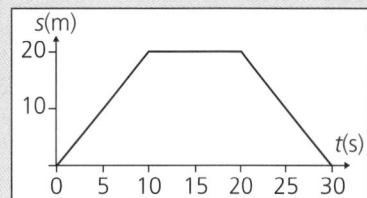

Speeding up and slowing down

Here is the speed–time graph for a bike which is **accelerating**.

Its speed increases as time goes on. The speed increases from 4 m/s to 10 m/s, a change of 6 m/s. This takes a time of 3 s. So the speed changes by 2 m/s each second.

The bike accelerates at 2 **m/s²** (**metres per second squared**).

Here is the formula for calculating acceleration. (You need to know it by heart!)

$$\text{acceleration} = \frac{\text{change of speed}}{\text{time taken}}$$

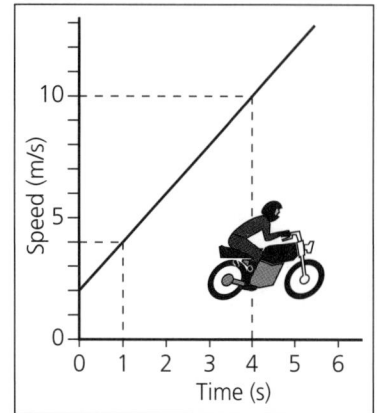

Now do this

1 Write down the formula for calculating acceleration. What are the units of acceleration?

2 A plane takes 4 s to get from a speed of 5 m/s to 45 m/s. Calculate its acceleration.

3 A car accelerates at 5 m/s². How long will it take to get from rest to a speed of 30 m/s?

4 A car at 20 m/s slows with an acceleration of –2 m/s². How fast will it be going after 5 s?

Friction

Jo pedals her bike along a level road. She stops pedalling. The force of **friction** slows her down until she stops. The friction comes from
- the air in front of the bike, which is pushed aside
- the contact between the tyres and the road
- the moving parts of the bike rubbing past each other.

The acceleration of the bike depends on the size of Jo's **thrust** compared with the friction.

Forces on the bike	Motion of the bike
thrust greater than friction	speed increases
thrust and friction the same	speed doesn't change
thrust smaller than friction	speed decreases

Now do this

5 State the sources of friction on a moving car.

6 Describe the motion of these objects:

Mass and acceleration

The acceleration of any object depends on the overall (**resultant**) force and the mass.

force = mass × acceleration $F = ma$

Symbol	Meaning	Units of measurement
F	force	newtons or N
m	mass	kilograms or kg
a	acceleration	metres per second squared or m/s²

Worked example

Q A car has a mass of 800 kg. If the thrust is 600 N and the friction is 200 N, what is the acceleration of the car?

A $F = 600 - 200 = 400 \, \text{N}$

$m = 800 \, \text{kg}$ $\qquad F = ma$

$a = ?$

$$a = \frac{F}{m} \qquad ? = \frac{400}{800} = 0.5 \, \text{m/s}^2$$

Now do this

7 A 1000 kg car accelerates at $-6 \, \text{m/s}^2$ when the brakes are on. Calculate the force needed.

8 A rocket has a mass of 5000 kg and a weight of 50 000 N. It accelerates upwards at $3 \, \text{m/s}^2$. Calculate the upwards thrust from its engines.

9 The thrust on a 600 kg car is 1500 N. Calculate its acceleration when the friction is 300 N.

Road safety

Sam is driving along the road at a steady speed. He notices that there is a tree across the road. He puts on the brakes and stops. Here are speed–time and distance–time graphs for the car as it slows down.

The **thinking distance** is how far the car travels between Sam noticing the tree and the brakes starting to slow down the car.

It will increase if
- Sam is not concentrating
- Sam is tired
- Sam has been drinking alcohol.

The **braking distance** is how far the car travels once the brakes have started to slow it down. It will increase if
- the brakes are not adjusted correctly
- the road surface is wet or loose
- the tyres are inflated incorrectly
- the tyres don't have enough tread.

The gap between cars on the road needs to be more than the thinking distance, otherwise they will collide when the one in front stops suddenly.

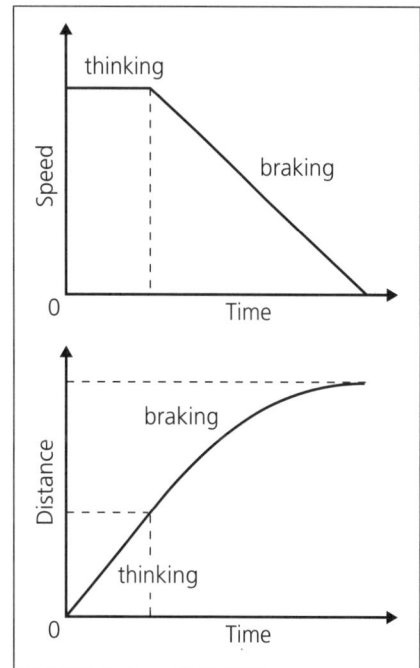

Thinking and braking distances

Now do this

10 Explain what the thinking distance is. State what will increase its value.

11 Explain what the braking distance is. State what will increase its value.

12 Thinking time is 0.7 s. Calculate the thinking distance for a car moving at 30 m/s (70 m.p.h.).

13 The acceleration of a car during braking is $-6 \, \text{m/s}^2$. For a car moving initially at 30 m/s, calculate
a the braking time
b the braking distance.

14 Repeat 12 and 13 for a car moving initially at 15 m/s.

Stretching and squeezing

Jo stretches a rubber band. When she lets go of the band it returns to its original shape. Rubber is an **elastic** material.

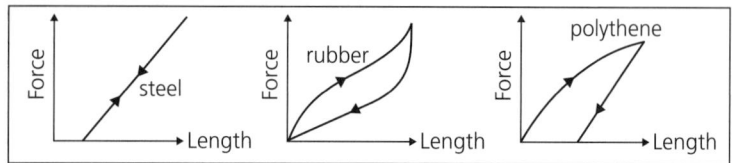

Sam does the same experiment with a polythene bag. When he lets go of it, the bag stays deformed. Polythene is an **inelastic** material.

Now do this

1 Complete the sentences. Choose words from this list.

inelastic   elastic   length   force   smaller   larger

When a _____ is applied to an object its _____ changes. If the object is squashed, its length gets _____ . If the object is _____ , its length returns to its original value when the force is removed. If the object is _____ , its length doesn't change when the _____ is removed.

The force–length graph of many materials (such as springs) is a straight line. Their **extension** is proportional to the force applied.

Now do this

2 A 5 cm spring becomes 15 cm long when a force of 40 N is applied. How long is it for a force of 20 N?

What force is required to give it a length of 20 cm?

Worked example

Q A spring goes from 10 cm to 15 cm when a force of 20 N is applied. What is its length when 30 N is applied?

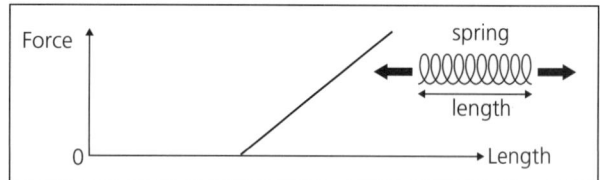

A   20 N gives an extension of 15 − 10 = 5 cm.
1 N gives an extension of 5/20 = 0.25 cm.
30 N gives an extension of 0.25 × 30 = 7.5 cm
So the length will be 10 + 7.5 = 17.5 cm.

Car safety

Inelastic materials are good at absorbing energy in car crashes. The **kinetic energy** of the car is used to squash the metal in the **crumple zone**.

Seat belts are inelastic if they are stretched enough. The kinetic energy of the driver permanently stretches the belt. This weakens the belt, so it should always be replaced after a bad crash. Gases are elastic. Car airbags are filled rapidly with gas in a collision. They provide a soft flat surface which cushions the driver's head.

The pressure of a gas increases as its volume decreases. So the force on the head increases steadily as it squashes the gas in the bag. The gas in the bag obeys this rule:

pressure × volume = constant

for a fixed mass of gas at constant temperature.

Calculating pressure

A material will change its shape permanently if the **pressure** is big enough.

$$\text{pressure} = \frac{\text{force}}{\text{area}}$$

$$P = \frac{F}{A}$$

Symbol	Meaning	Units of measurement
P	pressure	pascals or Pa
F	force	newtons or N
A	area	metres squared or m^2

Worked example

Q A concrete block sits on the ground. The block weighs 5000 N. The base of the block is 0.5 m by 0.5 m. What is the pressure on the ground under the block?

5000N   0.25m^2

Q $P = ?$
$F = 5000\,\text{N}$
$A = 0.5\,\text{m} \times 0.5\,\text{m} = 0.25\,\text{m}^2$

$P = \dfrac{F}{A}$? $= \dfrac{5000}{0.25} = 20\,000\,\text{Pa}$

Now do this

3 Describe three safety features of a car which can protect the driver in a collision. Explain how they provide protection.

Now do this

4 Write down the formula linking pressure, force and area. What are the units used?

5 A paving slab is 0.5 m by 0.8 m by 0.05 m. It weighs 400 N. It can be placed on the ground three different ways. Calculate the pressure for each way the slab can be placed on the ground.

low pressure   medium pressure   high pressure

6 Write down a formula for calculating area from pressure and force.

7 A car weighs 10 000 N. If the pressure on each of its four tyres is 100 000 Pa, what is the area of contact between each tyre and the ground?

Large forces on surfaces can damage them. The pressure can be kept down to a safe value by making the area of contact large enough. Think about pushing on a drawing pin!

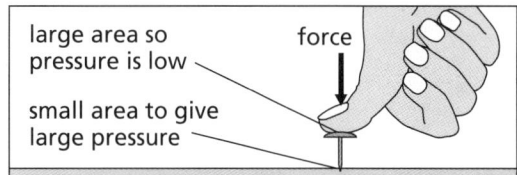

large area so pressure is low   force
small area to give large pressure

Hydraulic brakes

Liquids are **incompressible**. This makes them good at transmitting pressure from one place to another.

In car brakes all of the pressure from the master piston appears at the slave piston. So when the brake pedal is pushed, the brake pads are forced against the brake drum. A small force on the small area of the master piston results in a large force from the large area of the slave piston.

master piston   oil   brake drum   brake pedal   slave pistons   oil   brake pad

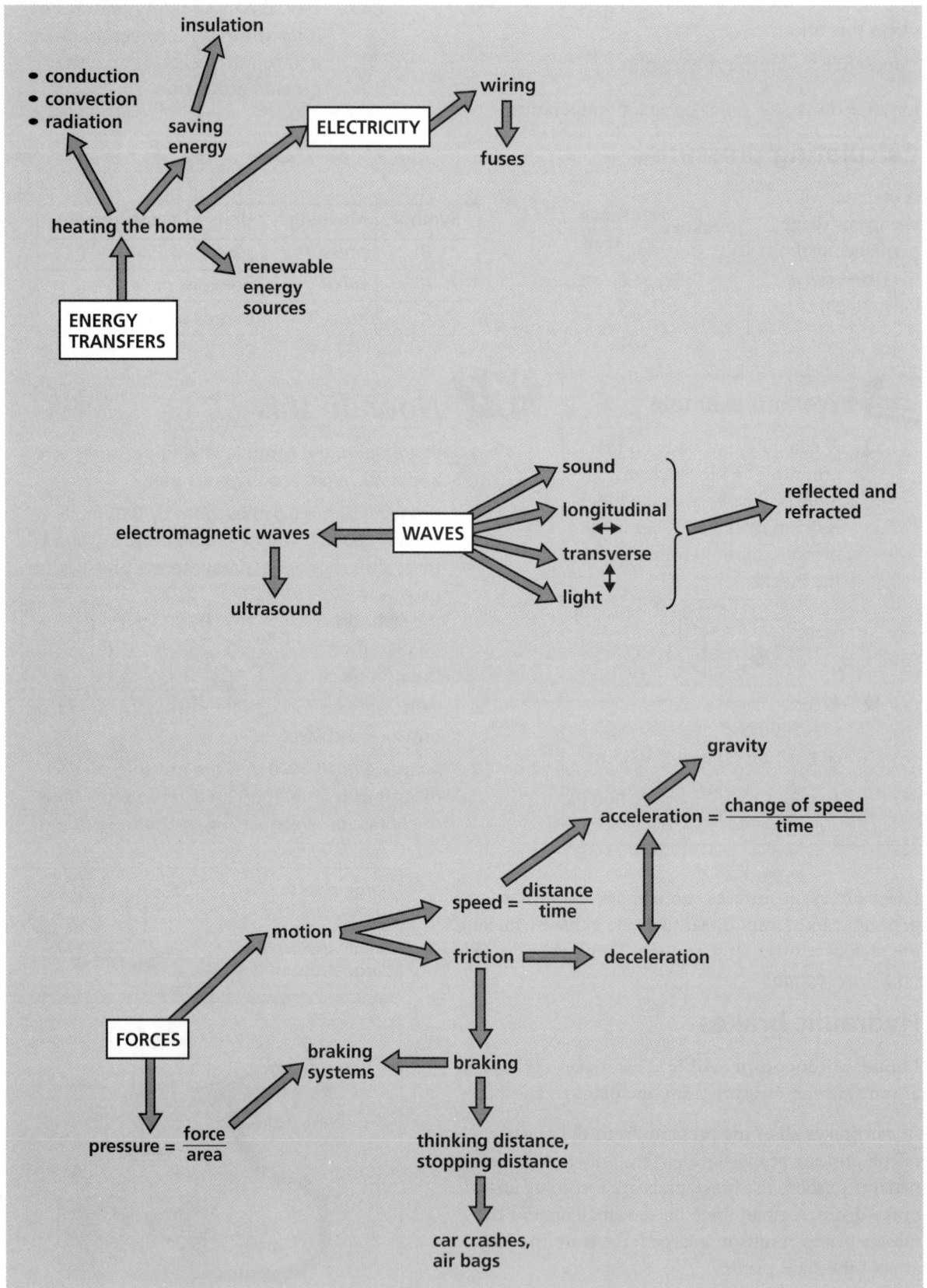

Concept map

insulation

- conduction
- convection
- radiation

saving energy

ELECTRICITY

wiring

fuses

heating the home

renewable energy sources

ENERGY TRANSFERS

electromagnetic waves

WAVES

sound

longitudinal ↔

transverse ↕

light ↕

reflected and refracted

ultrasound

gravity

$$\text{acceleration} = \frac{\text{change of speed}}{\text{time}}$$

$$\text{speed} = \frac{\text{distance}}{\text{time}}$$

motion

friction

deceleration

FORCES

braking systems

braking

$$\text{pressure} = \frac{\text{force}}{\text{area}}$$

thinking distance, stopping distance

car crashes, air bags

Exam questions

1 Tom sends a wave to Jill along a rope. Look at the diagram.

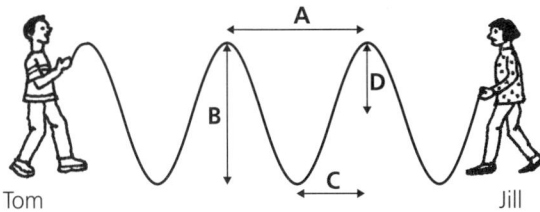

Tom   Jill

a i State the type of wave. Explain how you can tell. [2]

ii Which letter shows the wavelength of the wave? [1]

iii Tom moves his hand up and down six times in two seconds. Calculate the frequency of the wave. [2]

iv The wavelength is 0.5 m. Calculate the speed of the wave. [2]

b Jill uses two paper cups to send a different wave along the rope. Look at the diagram.

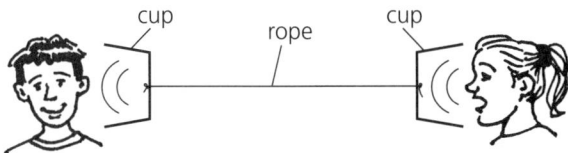

Jill speaks into her cup. Explain why Tom hears a sound from his cup. [3]

[10 marks]

2 Sanjay shines his torch on a mirror. The light reflects off the mirror. Look at the diagram.

a Draw on the diagram the path taken by the ray. [1]

b Some reflected light reaches Susan. Susan sees an image of Sanjay's torch behind the mirror. Explain why she sees the image there. [2]

c Sanjay's torch has a mirror behind the lamp. Look at the diagrams.

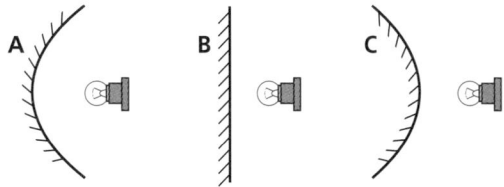

i Which diagram shows the correct type of mirror? [1]

ii Explain why it is the correct type. [2]

[6 marks]

3 Freddie spends £100 a month to keep her house warm. Look at the table.

How the heat escapes	Value
through the windows	£10
through the floor	£15
through the roof	£25
through the walls	£35
by draughts	£15

a The most heat escapes through the walls. Use your idea of particles to describe how the heat travels through a wall. [2]

b Freddie decides to save money by reducing heat lost through the roof.

i What is the best insulating material to put in the loft? Choose from: brick   wood   fibre wool   steel   tile [1]

ii Explain why the material you have chosen is a good insulator. [2]

c Freddie draughtproofs her house.

i What could she could do to stop the draughts? [1]

ii The cost of heat wasted through draughts is now only £5 a month. The draughtproofing cost £80. How long does it take for the money saved to pay for the draughtproofing? [2]

d Freddie wants to save even more money on her heating bills. Explain two ways in which she could do this. [4]

[12 marks]

4 Julie has five electrical appliances in her room. Look at the table.

Appliance	Power in kW
hair dryer	1.2
lamp	0.1
heater	2.0
TV	0.2
computer	0.4

a Julie turns on her computer for 3 hours.

  i Calculate how many units of electricity this uses, in kilowatt-hours. [1]

  ii Each unit of electricity costs 8p. Calculate how much it costs for Julie to run her computer. [1]

b The heater is connected to the mains supply by three wires. Complete the sentences below.
Electrical energy flows to the heater from the mains along the _____ wire. The _____ wire completes the electrical circuit. The _____ wire prevents Julie being electrocuted. [3]

[5 marks]

5 Melissa cycles along the road. Look at the graph below.

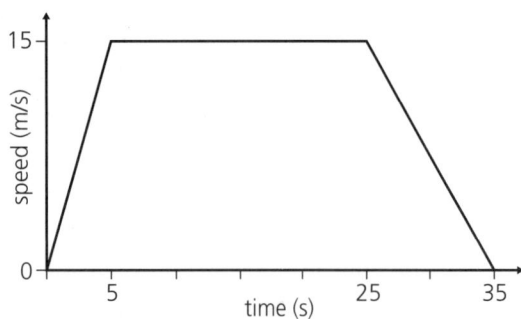

a Melissa starts off by accelerating.

  i Calculate her acceleration. [2]

  ii The overall pushing force on Melissa during acceleration is 180 N. Calculate Melissa's mass. [2]

b Melissa travels at a top speed of 15 m/s. Calculate how far she moves at that speed. [2]

c Melissa stops pedalling after 25 s. Explain why she stops moving at 35 s. Use your idea of forces. [3]

d Melissa wears a cycle helmet. This will protect her if she falls off her cycle. Use your idea of pressure to explain this. [3]

[12 marks]

6 Pete takes some ice cream out of the freezer. He puts it on the table.

a What will happen to the temperature of the ice cream? [1]

b Energy is transferred by **conduction** to the ice cream. Use the idea of particles to explain how. [3]

c Pete wraps the ice cream in shiny foil. This keeps it cold for a long time. Explain how. [2]

d Suggest what else Pete could do to keep the ice cream on the table cold for a long time. Explain your answer. [2]

e The cooling unit of Pete's freezer is at the top. Suggest a reason why it is at the top. [1]

[9 marks]

7 The Highway Code states the distance required to stop an average car in good weather on a normal road. Look at the information.

For a typical driver at an initial speed of 30 m/s:
  thinking distance = 20 m
  braking distance = 85 m
  stopping distance = 105 m

a i Explain what is meant by **thinking distance**. [1]

  ii Use the information to calculate the thinking time of a typical driver. [2]

  iii State two things which could increase the thinking distance. [2]

b A car initially travelling at 30 m/s takes 5.6 s to travel the braking distance.

  i Calculate the acceleration of the car as it is stopped [3]

  ii The braking force on a typical car is 5000 N. Calculate the mass of a typical car. [3]

[11 marks]

Year 11

The working plant

The parts of a plant

flower – used for sexual reproduction

bud

leaf – used for the production of
food by photosynthesis

leaf vein – contains part
of the plant's transport system

stem – for support and transport

root – used for the uptake of water
and to hold the plant in the ground

How do plants produce their food?

Plants **make** their own food by **photosynthesis**. To do this plants use light energy to join water and carbon dioxide, producing carbohydrates. (Photosynthesis comes from 'photo', meaning light, and 'synthesis', meaning to make.)

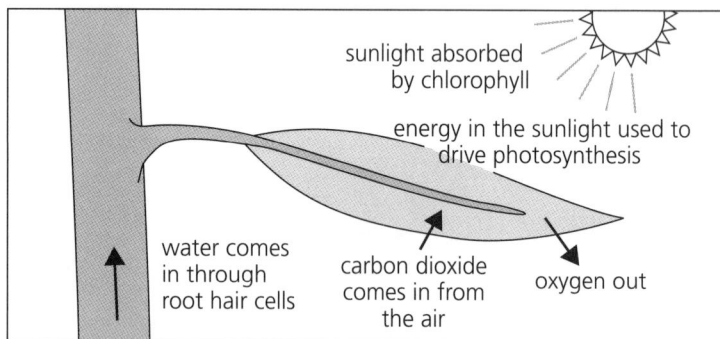

sunlight absorbed
by chlorophyll

energy in the sunlight used to
drive photosynthesis

water comes
in through
root hair cells

carbon dioxide
comes in from
the air

oxygen out

Photosynthesis can be written as an equation:

$$6CO_2 + 6H_2O \xrightarrow{\text{chlorophyll and light energy}} C_6H_{12}O_6 + 6O_2$$

carbon dioxide   water   glucose   oxygen

Carbon dioxide and water are needed for photosynthesis. They are called the **reactants**.

Glucose and oxygen are produced by photosynthesis. They are called the **products**.

What makes plants photosynthesise faster?

- The more carbon dioxide that is available, the faster the photosynthesis, because carbon dioxide is one of the reactants.
- The more light that is available, the faster the photosynthesis, because the energy of the light is used to drive the reaction. The colour of the light is also important. Most plants appear green because they reflect green light. This means green light is not absorbed to be used to drive photosynthesis. Red and blue light are absorbed, therefore these colours are the most important ones for photosynthesis.
- The higher the temperature, the faster photosynthesis will occur.

Now do this

1 Explain, with the help of an equation, how green plants make their food.

2 Explain where a plant gets the reactants for photosynthesis from.

Green plants do not eat, they photosynthesise.

What happens if carbon dioxide, light and temperature are in short supply?

If any of these are in short supply they limit the amount of photosynthesis which can occur. Therefore they are called **limiting factors**.

On a hot, sunny day the temperature is usually high enough and there is plenty of light for photosynthesis to take place. In these conditions the rate of photosynthesis will depend on how much carbon dioxide there is. Carbon dioxide is then said to be the limiting factor.

Therefore a hot, sunny day will allow a plant to photosynthesise more quickly than a cold, dull day. Plants grow faster in the summer because they can produce more food by photosynthesis.

Where do plants make their food?

Plants make their food in their leaves because they are:
- **broad,** so they can catch as much sunlight as possible
- **thin,** so that light reaches all the cells easily
- **full of chlorophyll** to trap light energy
- supplied by a **good transport system (veins)**
- have **stomata** to allow gases (carbon dioxide and oxygen) in and out
- their internal surface area to volume ratio is very large.

One stoma, lots of stomata

Now do this

3   Give **three** ways in which leaves are adapted for photosynthesis.

4   Name **two** substances which pass out through stomata on a sunny day.

5   Do plants photosynthesise at night? Explain your answer.

6   Many offices have lovely pot plants that are illuminated by green lights. The lights make the leaves look attractive and healthy, but the plants do not grow very well. Explain why this happens.

Moving materials around the plant

Plants use glucose produced during photosynthesis to make all the materials they need to live and grow.

Glucose may be:
- moved around the plant
- changed into sucrose to be transported to the growing areas in the roots, shoots, flowers, fruits and buds
- changed into cellulose for new cell walls
- changed into proteins
- changed into large insoluble storage substances such as starch.
- used to release energy (respiration)

??? Now do this

1   Describe **three** uses of glucose in a plant.

Sucrose on the move

The **phloem** is part of the transport system of plants. It carries dissolved sucrose to other parts of the plant and is made of living cells. The movement of materials through the phloem is called **translocation**.

Moving materials in and out of cells

There are three ways of moving materials in and out of cells.
- **Diffusion**

  This is the movement of particles from an area where there are lots of particles (high concentration) to an area where there are very few particles (a low concentration). Substances with small particles, e.g. water, minerals, oxygen and carbon dioxide, pass across cell membranes by diffusion down a **concentration gradient**. It does not require energy and is therefore a **passive** process. It is a consequence of the random motion of the particles.

- **Active transport**

  This is the movement of particles from an area with low concentration to an area with high concentration. It uses energy because it is against the concentration gradient.
- **Osmosis**

  This is a special case of diffusion for water. Osmosis is the movement of water particles from an area of a high water concentration through a **partially permeable membrane**. Cell membranes are partially permeable because they allow some things to pass through, but not others.

??? Now do this

2   Why is a cell membrane considered to be partially permeable?

Water on the move

Plants need water in their leaves for photosynthesis. Water enters the plant by osmosis through the **root hairs**, and travels up to the leaves in the second plant transport system, the **xylem**. The xylem forms long tubes throughout the plant. It is made up of dead cells with no cytoplasm (they look a bit like drinking straws).

soil water containing dissolved minerals

soil particles   root hair cell

→ water moving by osmosis

Root hair cells are good at taking up water because they are:
• long and thin, and therefore have a large surface area
• have thin walls to help water to pass through.

Root hair cells also take up minerals, e.g. nitrates, dissolved in the water. Depending on the concentration gradient, minerals are taken up by diffusion or active transport.

Once in the root hair cell the water and dissolved minerals move by diffusion across the root to the xylem.

Plant minerals

Nitrogen, phosphorus and potassium are the main minerals a plant requires, together with small amounts of magnesium, which is needed to make chlorophyll.

Plants will not grow so well, or as much, if there is not enough of any of these minerals. Fertilisers contain these important minerals.

Now do this

3   Explain why raw potato chips become shorter when left in concentrated sugar solutions, but become longer when left in dilute sugar solutions.

Nitrogen is used to make amino acids, proteins and DNA. Phosphorus is used to make DNA and cell membranes.

Now do this

4   Name the **two** transport systems in plants, and state what each one is used for.

5   Suggest why plants which do not get enough magnesium look yellow and small.

6   Explain why farmers need to use fertilisers if they are going to grow the same crop, in the same field, every year.

7   Explain **two** functions of root hair cells.

Tracking the xylem and phloem

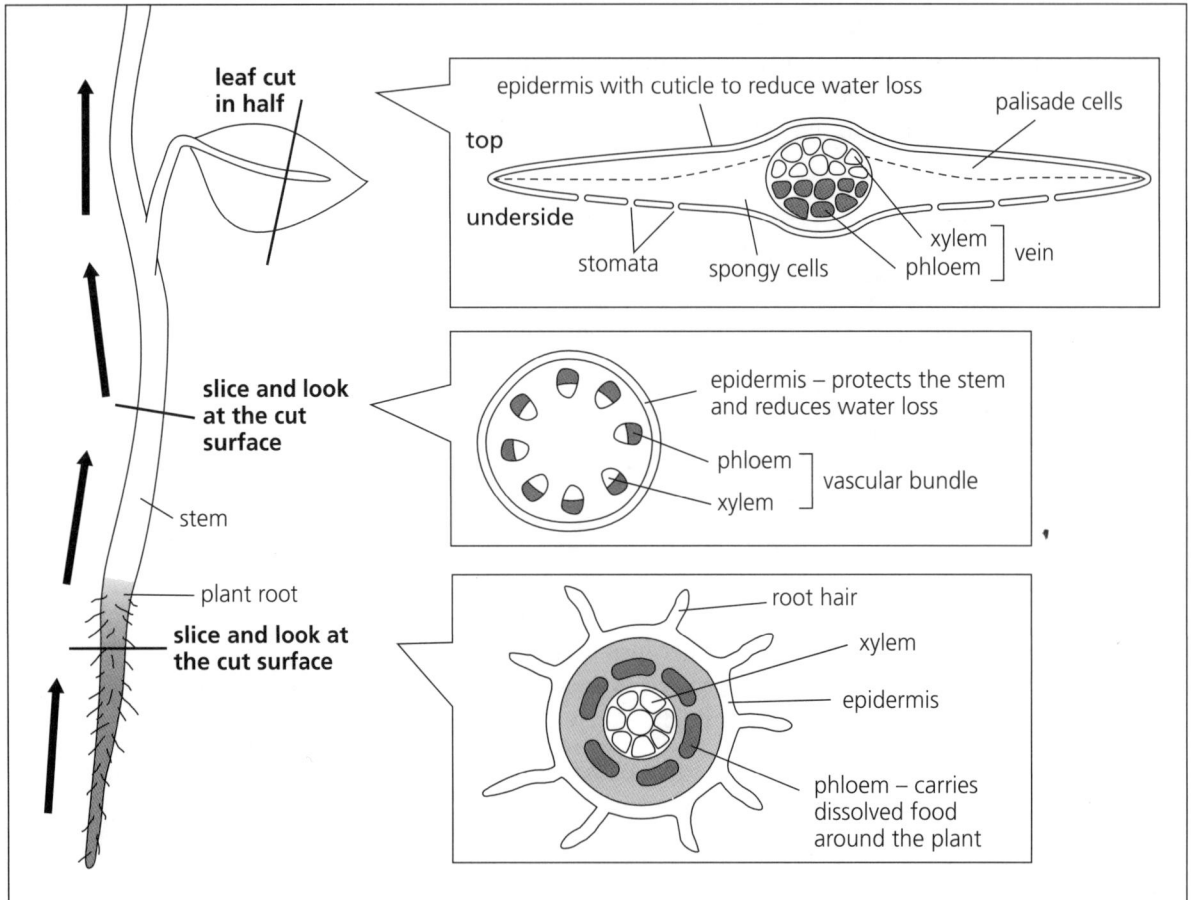

leaf cut
in half

epidermis with cuticle to reduce water loss

palisade cells

top

underside

stomata   spongy cells

xylem
phloem   ] vein

slice and look
at the cut
surface

epidermis – protects the stem
and reduces water loss

phloem]
          } vascular bundle
xylem]

stem

plant root

slice and look at
the cut surface

root hair

xylem

epidermis

phloem – carries
dissolved food
around the plant

Going up!

The xylem transports water and dissolved minerals from the roots to the leaves. They are 'sucked' up the xylem by a process called **transpiration**.

Transpiration is the evaporation of water from inside the leaves to the surrounding air. The water vapour passes out of the leaves by diffusion.

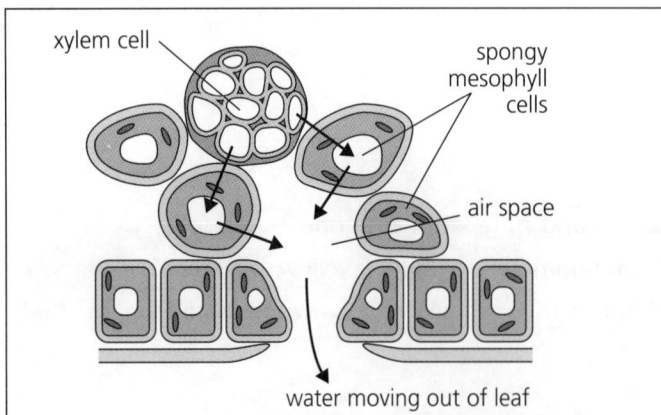

xylem cell

spongy
mesophyll
cells

air space

water moving out of leaf

Transpiration provides
water for:
• photosynthesis
• cooling the plant (it is the
  plant version of sweating)
• movement of minerals
• support.

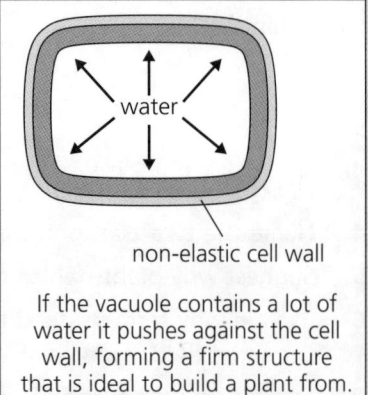

water

non-elastic cell wall

If the vacuole contains a lot of
water it pushes against the cell
wall, forming a firm structure
that is ideal to build a plant from.

This is what happens in transpiration:
- water diffuses from the xylem into the spongy mesophyll cells
- water evaporates into the air space
- water vapour diffuses out of the stomata
- water lost from the spongy mesophyll cells is replaced by more water from the xylem.

What affects the speed of transpiration?

Transpiration is increased by:
- more light, because water is used up as the plant photosynthesises more
- increased temperatures, because photosynthesis and evaporation increase with temperature
- increased air movement increases evaporation
- decreased humidity, because water evaporates more easily into dry air
- the state of the stomata.

Stomata

Stomata can open or close by changing the shape of their **guard cells**.

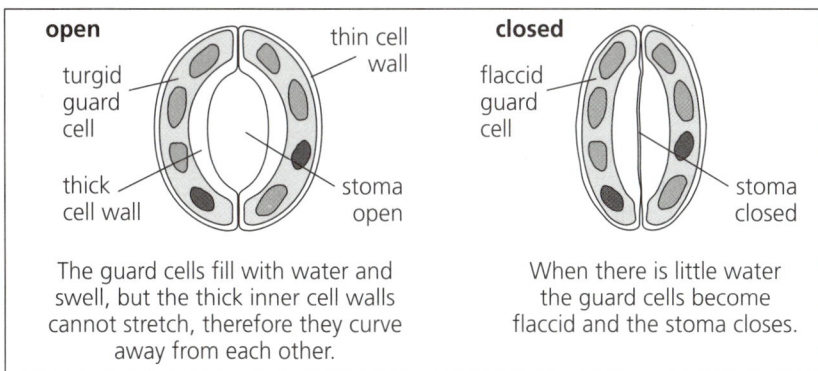

open
- thin cell wall
- turgid guard cell
- thick cell wall
- stoma open

The guard cells fill with water and swell, but the thick inner cell walls cannot stretch, therefore they curve away from each other.

closed
- flaccid guard cell
- stoma closed

When there is little water the guard cells become flaccid and the stoma closes.

cell appears flaccid and limp
- cell wall
- cytoplasm
- cell membrane
- vaculole with little water

cell appears turgid and swollen
- cell wall resisting water pushing against it
- full vaculole
- cell membrane

Stomata can open or close in response to what is going on outside the plant. They may close to prevent excessive water loss, but if they do, carbon dioxide cannot get in for photosynthesis. Stomata tend to be found mainly on the underside of leaves away from direct sunlight. Plant cells are able to survive some water loss by wilting, because the cell wall is too stiff to shrink too much.

Now do this

1. What is a vascular bundle?
2. Stomata are mainly on the underside of a leaf. Suggest why this is advantageous to the plant.
3. Explain what is meant by transpiration.
4. Give **three** reasons why transpiration is so important for plants.
5. Suggest how:
   a the carbon dioxide needed for photosynthesis can get into a leaf
   b the oxygen produced during photosynthesis can leave the plant.

Respiration – releasing energy

Your body needs energy just to stay alive!

You use energy to:
- keep the heart pumping
- work your muscles for movement
- keep your body temperature constant
- grow and repair cells
- actively transport materials

and many, many other activities in the body.

Energy is released from glucose, when it reacts with oxygen in our cells. This is called **aerobic respiration**.

It happens in *all* of our cells *all* of the time.

Aerobic respiration can be written as an equation.

> Plant cells also respire all the time to produce energy.

$$C_6H_{12}O_6 \; + \; 6O_2 \; \rightarrow \; 6CO_2 \; + \; 6H_2O \; + \; ENERGY$$

$$glucose \; + \; oxygen \; \rightarrow \; carbon \; dioxide \; + \; water \; + \; ENERGY$$

Working your muscles requires energy. Therefore, the more you exercise the more energy you need.

This is how the body copes with the need for more energy:
- breathing rate increases to bring more oxygen into the body
- pulse rate increases to speed up blood flow around the body, delivering more oxygen and glucose to the respiring cells
- aerobic respiration in the muscle cells increases.

Running out of oxygen

During vigorous exercise the body cannot get enough oxygen. Therefore the cells respire **anaerobically**, i.e. without oxygen.

Anaerobic respiration can be written as a word equation:

$$glucose \; \rightarrow \; lactic \; acid \; + \; some \; ENERGY$$

Anaerobic respiration releases energy, but much less than aerobic respiration. This is because a lot of the energy remains locked up in the lactic acid.

The lactic acid produced is a mild poison and builds up to cause **muscle fatigue** and **cramp**.

To get rid of the lactic acid the body needs oxygen. Therefore the build up of lactic acid causes an **oxygen debt**. The more lactic acid there is, the more oxygen is needed to get rid of it. This is why we puff and pant after vigorous exercise – we are trying to pay back our oxygen debt!

Now do this

1 What is respiration?
2 Write word equations for
   a aerobic respiration
   b anaerobic respiration.
3 Give **two** differences between aerobic and anaerobic respiration.

Now do this

4 Where does respiration occur?

5 Give **two** ways in which the body changes to cope with increased exercise.

6 Explain how **one** of these changes helps the body when it is exercising actively.

7 Explain what is meant by oxygen debt.

Sample examination question

Question Look at the diagrams. They show how an experiment was set up. Each tube contains red hydrogencarbonate indicator. It turns yellow with carbon dioxide.

a What colour does the indicator turn if carbon dioxide is present?
After 30 minutes the indicator in some of the tubes has changed colour.

b The indicator in tubes A and B was yellow. Explain what had happened.

c The indicator in tube C was reddish-orange. Explain what had happened.

d The indicator in tube D stayed red. Why was this?

e Why was tube D included in the experiment?

Answer

a It turns yellow.

b Yellow indicates there was carbon dioxide present in tubes A and B. This was produced by the snails respiring.

c The reddish-orange colour indicates there was some carbon dioxide in tube C but not as much as in A and B. This is from the pond weed respiring though not producing as much carbon dioxide as the snails. The pond weed is also photosynthesising and using up carbon dioxide.

d There was no carbon dioxide in tube D.

e D is the control and it shows the pond water and indicator will not change colour on their own.

Advice:
Link colour changes to the behaviour of the indicator. Explain where the carbon dioxide has come from. Plants are living things and they respire. Any part of an experiment which shows no change is likely to be a control.

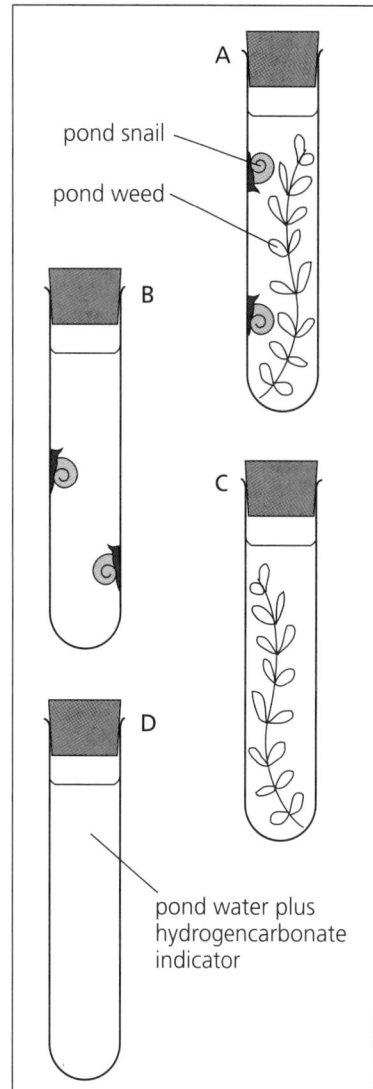

A

pond snail

pond weed

B

C

D

pond water plus hydrogencarbonate indicator

Homeostasis

Homeostasis literally means keeping conditions inside your body more or less constant, to enable your cells to work most efficiently.

What conditions need controlling?

In the human body the following conditions need controlling:

- blood glucose concentration
- blood water and salt concentration
- blood carbon dioxide level
- blood temperature
- waste products in the blood, such as urea
- the composition of body tissue fluid.

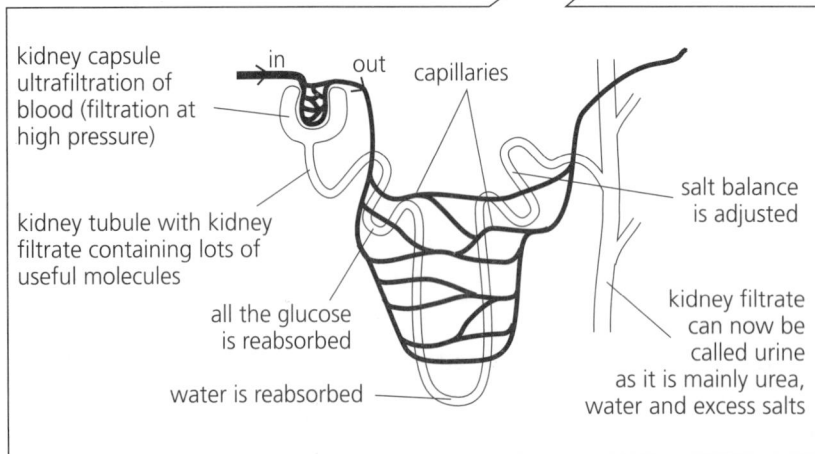

skin – helps to control body temperature

lungs – control carbon dioxide level

control blood glucose level { liver, pancreas

kidneys – filter urea, excess water and excess salt out of the blood at high pressure

ureter – takes urine to the bladder

bladder – stores urine

urethra – takes urine to the outside of the body

kidney capsule ultrafiltration of blood (filtration at high pressure)

in   out   capillaries

kidney tubule with kidney filtrate containing lots of useful molecules

all the glucose is reabsorbed

water is reabsorbed

salt balance is adjusted

kidney filtrate can now be called urine as it is mainly urea, water and excess salts

The water balance

If the balance of water in the body is upset we either dehydrate (dry out) or swell up with excess fluid.

food and drink (water in)	urine, sweat and breath (water out)

We cannot survive either extreme for long. The water content of the blood is monitored by the brain. If the water content of the blood is low, the brain causes the kidney to reabsorb more water. If the water content of the blood is high the brain causes the kidney to reabsorb less water, therefore more watery urine is produced and the water content of the body begins to return to normal.

Now do this

1. What does homeostasis mean?

2. Which **two** body organs are used to control blood glucose level?

3. What is passed out of the bladder down the urethra?

4. Suggest why high levels of carbon dioxide in the blood are harmful to the body.

Controlling body temperature

When our cells respire, some of the energy released is heat energy. We use this to keep us warm.

Think about what you do when you feel cold. You might stamp your feet or rub your hands together, or even shiver. All of these actions involve respiration, which releases energy, therefore heat energy is also released to warm you up. The liver has a lot of reactions going on all the time, therefore it releases a lot of heat energy. It is like the boiler in your central heating system.

If the core body temperature increases, it causes the blood temperature to increase. If the core body temperature goes above 37 °C cells in the brain notice and switch on **cooling mechanisms** (e.g. sweating) to reduce the temperature. If the blood temperature goes below 37 °C the brain switches on **warming mechanisms** (e.g. shivering).

```
                    blood becomes too warm
                    (detected by the brain)
                                              cooling mechanisms
                                              switched on
    normal
    blood                                         normal blood
    temperature                                   temperature (37°C)
    (37°C)
                                              warming mechanisms
                                              switched on
                    blood becomes too cool
                    (detected by the brain)
```

The mechanisms

Cooling mechanisms	Warming mechanisms
• Sweating – heat from the body is used to evaporate sweat from the skin surface.	• Shivering – muscles make heat by respiration to warm us up.
• Vasodilation – blood vessels near the skin surface open to allow blood to flow near to the surface of the body and lose heat by radiation to the air.	• Vasoconstriction – blood vessels running near the skin surface close, diverting the blood back to the warmer parts of the body.
• Behavioural – take some clothes off.	• Behavioural – put some extra clothes on.

Homeostasis is achieved by **negative feedback**. This means that:
1 a change is detected by the body, e.g. the blood carbon dioxide concentration increases
2 the body responds to the change, e.g. the brain brings about an increase in the breathing rate
3 the situation returns to normal, e.g. blood carbon dioxide concentration decreases back to normal
4 the body response stops, e.g. the breathing rate returns to normal.

Now do this

5 Explain why you produce less urine on a hot sunny day than on a cold day.

6 Which part of the body checks the temperature of the blood?

7 Explain how sweating helps to cool us down.

Defence against disease

Your body has to defend itself against microbes which are able to attack it and cause disease. The body has a number of ways of stopping microbes getting in.
- The eyes: tears contain a substance that destroys microbes.
- The nose and breathing passages are protected by mucus and cilia.
- The mouth leading to the digestive system: relies on the stomach acid to destroy microbes.
- The skin: provides a barrier to entry.

Fighting back

If the skin is damaged, blood forms a second line of defence by:
- forming a clot and scab to block entry to microbes
- allowing white blood cells to escape from blood vessels to attack any invading microbes.

There are two types of white blood cell.

> Another word for microbes and other foreign materials in your body is **antigens**.

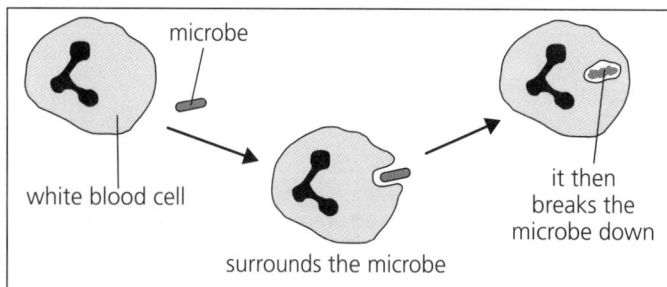

white blood cell — microbe — surrounds the microbe — it then breaks the microbe down

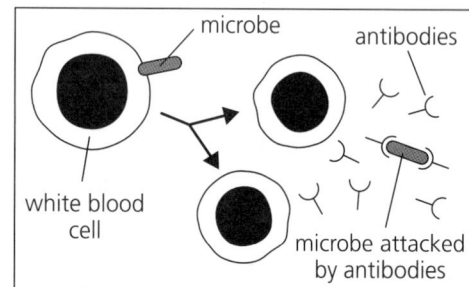

microbe — antibodies — white blood cell — microbe attacked by antibodies

One type engulfs (eats) the microbes. The other type produces chemicals called **antibodies**, which attack the microbes and destroy them. The white blood cell makes contact with the microbe and identifies it. It then divides to produce a lot more white blood cells, all capable of releasing the right antibody. Each disease has its own antigens, therefore each one can be attacked by its own **specific antibodies**.

Immunity

Once your body has met a microbe and made antibodies against it, it does not forget. When you meet the same type of microbe again, your body is waiting. It quickly produces lots of antibodies, so you are unlikely to get the disease again. This is called **immunity**.

Unfortunately it does not work very well with colds and flu, because there are so many different strains of them. Antibodies to cold strain A will not give you immunity to any of the other cold strains!

Now do this

1 How are the eyes protected from microbe invasion?

2 If the skin is damaged, how does the body continue to protect itself?

3 What is an antibody?

4 Why is it important that white blood cells can escape from blood vessels?

Immunisation is a means of giving the antigen without the disease. For example, a vaccine contains dead or inactive microbes which will enable your body to make antibodies against them without the risk of developing the disease. This is a way of protecting the population from serious diseases such as polio or smallpox.

Treatment

If you do become ill, you may need medicine to make you feel better. Medicines contain drugs. A **drug** is a substance that changes the way in which your body works.

When taken as painkillers or antibiotics drugs can be very useful. Unfortunately some drugs have side effects and some produce sensations which encourage people to misuse them.

Problems with drugs

Many drugs work either by speeding up brain activity or by slowing it down.

Stimulant – speeds up brain activity by increasing the activity of brain synapses.

Depressant – slows down brain activity by blocking some of the brain synapses.

Drug	Action	Negative effects
caffeine	stimulant	can cause sleeplessness
nicotine	anaesthetic	can stop cilia in the trachea beating, leading to a build up of mucus and a smokers' cough bacteria thrive in the mucus, causing lung infections
alcohol	depressant	may slow down brain activity to the point of passing out, reduces ability to make judgements prolonged use may result in damage to the brain it poisons the liver, leading to liver damage
solvents	depressants	may slow down brain activity so much that the brain stops

Some drugs are **addictive**, meaning that they produce a dependence in the person taking the drug. The person then has to keep taking the drug.

Some drugs produce **withdrawal symptoms** if the user stops, or is prevented from, taking the drug. These vary in severity from a headache if you are deprived of coffee for the day, to sickness, blinding headaches and an inability to sleep, eat or do anything.

The body gets used to some drugs, which means that the drug user needs larger and larger doses to get the same effect. This is called **drug tolerance**.

Now do this

5 What is a drug?

6 Explain why smoking may make someone more likely to get lung infections.

7 What is the difference between a depressant and a stimulant? Give an example of each.

Reproduction

When plants and animals **reproduce** they make new plants and animals (offspring) like themselves. There are two main ways of reproducing.

Asexual reproduction takes place when one parent produces offspring which are identical to the parent. For example, spider plants and strawberries grow runners with new plants on them, potatoes produce tubers and tulips reproduce by forming bulbs.

In **sexual reproduction** two parents produce male and female sex cells called **gametes**. In animals, male gametes are called **sperm** and female gametes are called **eggs**. These join together at **fertilisation** to form a **zygote**. This develops into an embryo and then, in humans, into a baby. The result of sexual reproduction is offspring who are *not* identical to their parents but are similar to them. They inherit a mix of characteristics from their parents.

Passing on characteristics

The characteristics of every plant or animal are determined by **chromosomes** in the nucleus of their cells. Chromosomes are long molecules of the chemical **DNA**. Every chromosome carries thousands of **genes** and each gene controls some characteristic of the organism, e.g. eye colour or petal shape. These characteristics are passed on from parents to offspring during reproduction.

Spider plant

new plant

runner   -new plant growing

Strawberry plant

male
penis – enables sperm to reach the cervix

urethra – carries urine and sperm out of the body

sperm tube – carries sperm to urethra

bladder

testes – produce sperm

scrotum – sac holding both testes

female
ovary – produces eggs

oviduct – area where fertilisation usually occurs

uterus – where embryo grows

cervix – where sperm is deposited

vagina – area to receive penis

Mitosis

In asexual reproduction exact copies of the chromosomes are passed on. This is done by **mitosis**. The chromosomes in one cell are copied exactly and then one copy moves to each end of the cell. The cell divides into two, producing two genetically identical cells.

Parent cell contains four chromosomes

Each chromosome is copied exactly

Two identical cells are formed, each containing four chromosomes

Meiosis

In sexual reproduction, gametes have half the usual number of chromosomes. Gametes are produced in the sex organs of the parents by **meiosis**. When male and female gametes join together at fertilisation the zygote has a full set.

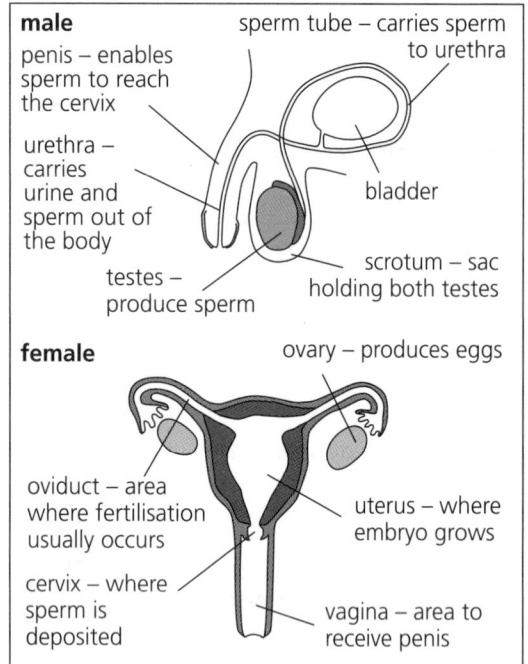

Parent cell contains four chromosomes which have made copies of themselves

The chromosomes line up in their pairs

One from each pair goes into the two daughter cells which then divide again

Most human cells have 46 chromosomes arranged in pairs. One of each pair came from your mother and the other from your father. Most of your characteristics depend on which of your parents' genes were carried by the gametes which formed you. So you may have similar characteristics to your parents, but in different combinations. These differences are called **variation**.

One pair of chromosomes determines your sex. There are two types of sex chromosome: the **X chromosome** and the **Y chromosome**. Female gametes, eggs, have X chromosomes. Male gametes, sperm, have either an X or a Y chromosome. If two gametes with X chromosomes fuse, the offspring is female (**XX**). If a gamete carrying an X and one carrying a Y fuse, the offspring is male (**XY**).

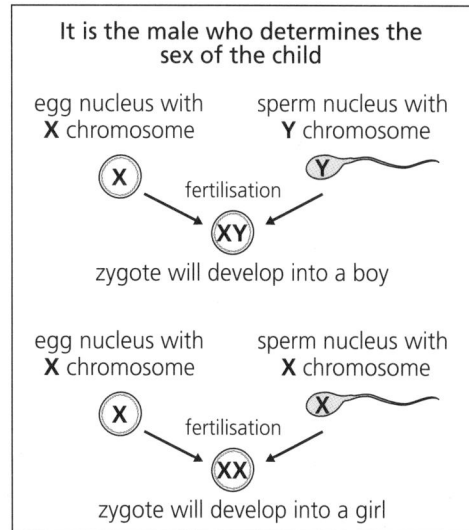

It is the male who determines the sex of the child

egg nucleus with **X** chromosome — sperm nucleus with **Y** chromosome — fertilisation — **XY** — zygote will develop into a boy

egg nucleus with **X** chromosome — sperm nucleus with **X** chromosome — fertilisation — **XX** — zygote will develop into a girl

Now do this

1 When plants or animals grow, their cells increase in number by mitosis. Why does this growth use mitosis and not meiosis?

Mutations

Sometimes there are changes (or **mutations**) to the genetic code or the number of chromosomes. This has serious effects. For example, when a human egg has 24 instead of the normal 23 chromosomes the baby formed from the egg will have Down's syndrome.

Other changes can be caused by: chromosomes not being copied correctly in cells; exposure to radiation; exposure to certain chemicals.

Making use of mitosis

We can use mitosis to produce **clones**. A clone is an individual which is genetically identical to its parent, and cloning plants is big business. When we take **cuttings** of plants to grow we are producing clones. Commercially much smaller pieces of plant material are used. This is therefore called **micropropagation** or **tissue culture**.

A plant with the desired characteristics is divided into large numbers of small pieces of tissue. These are grown in a suitable growth medium using an **aseptic** technique, which prevents any microbes growing and spoiling the culture. When ready, the small plantlets are transferred to pots and sold.

Advantages of cloning	Disadvantages of cloning
All the desirable parental characteristics are transferred to the clones.	Any genetic weaknesses or defects will be passed on to all offspring.
A relatively quick and cheap way to obtain large numbers of offspring.	No genetic variation to overcome environmental change, e.g. a new disease could wipe out all the clones.

Now do this

2 Make a table comparing mitosis and meiosis.

3 Name **one** condition caused by a chromosome mutation.

4 What do you understand by the word clone?

5 What sort of cell division produces a clone?

Inheritance

Many genes have several different versions, called **alleles**. For example, there are blue and brown alleles for eye colour. If you inherit a blue one from each parent you will have blue eyes. But if you inherit one blue allele and one brown you do not have stripy eyes, you have brown eyes. Some alleles are stronger than others.

Strong alleles are called **dominant** and weak alleles are called **recessive**. We show a dominant allele by a capital letter and a recessive allele by a small letter.

The allele for brown eyes is dominant (**B**), the one for blue is recessive (**b**). If you inherit a **B** allele from one parent and a **b** allele from the other parent, you will have brown eyes because the brown allele is dominant. If you inherit a **b** allele from each parent you will have blue eyes.

The alleles you inherit are called your **genotype**. How you look because of these alleles is called your **phenotype**. A person with the phenotype of blue eyes can have only one genotype, **bb**. A person with the phenotype of brown eyes could have a genotype of **BB** or **Bb**.

If you know the genotype of the parents you can work out what their offspring are likely to be.

For example, if one parent is **BB** for brown eyes and the other is **bb** for blue, we can work out the possible combinations of their alleles with a diagram like this:

If one of these children has offspring with another **Bb** individual the combination of offspring would be this:

genetic diagram for cross of
two parents homozygous
for brown and blue eyes

Gametes	B	B
b	Bb	Bb
b	Bb	Bb

all offspring have brown eyes

genetic diagram for cross of
two parents heterozygous
for brown eyes

Gametes	B	b
B	BB	bB
b	Bb	bb

three brown-eyed, one
blue-eyed offspring

If both the alleles are the same, **BB** or **bb**, the individual is called **homozygous**. If the alleles are different, **Bb**, the individual is called **heterozygous**.

Some diseases are caused by faulty genes inherited from the parents. Examples are sickle-cell anaemia, cystic fibrosis, muscular dystrophy and haemophilia. Many of these are caused by recessive genes.

Inheritance of cystic fibrosis

Gametes	F	f
F	FF	fF
f	Ff	ff

Both parents are heterozygous Ff. Cystic fibrosis is controlled by the recessive allele f.

A child with homozygous ff will suffer from cystic fibrosis.

A child with heterozygous Ff will be a carrier like its parents.

A child with homozygous FF will not have the abnormal allele at all.

Working out the probabilities

The way a characteristic is inherited can be studied by breeding two individuals and observing the characteristics in their offspring. This is called a **monohybrid cross** because it only follows the inheritance of one characteristic. We can make predictions about the probable outcome of a monohybrid cross.

The probability of two heterozygous brown-eyed parents producing a blue-eyed child is 1 in 4, or 25%. This means that when they have a child, there is a 25% chance that it will have blue eyes.

Now do this

1   Explain what ratio of offspring would be expected from a cross between a blue-eyed parent and a heterozygous brown-eyed parent.

2   Tongue rolling is an inherited characteristic. The 'tongue rolling' allele is dominant (**T**). What ratio of tongue rolling offspring would you expect from a heterozygous tongue rolling mother and a non-rolling father?

Sex linkage

Some inherited human disorders such as red-green colour blindness and haemophilia are caused by a recessive allele which appears only on the X chromosome. These are called **sex-linked** disorders.

A female can carry a recessive allele on one of her X chromosomes without being affected. However, if a male has the allele on his X chromosome there is no corresponding allele on the paired Y chromosome, so he will have the disorder. For example, a normal-sighted woman carrying one allele for colour blindness (X^cX) and her unaffected husband (XY) can have a colour blind son.

Gametes	X	X^c
X	XX	X^cX
Y	XY	X^cY

X Normal X chromosome

X^c Chromosome with allele for colour blindness

Y Normal Y chromosome

Environmental variation

Some of your characteristics are also affected by your environment. For example, your genes may make you tall, but if you are well fed as a child you may be even taller. A child's weight at birth is partly determined by genes but partly by its mother's health and age. Very hot sun can make fair skin brown and brown hair fair. And you can change your hair colour and shape with chemicals any time you like!

Plants are also affected by their environment. For example, wind can affect the shape of a tree, and soil can affect the growth of crops.

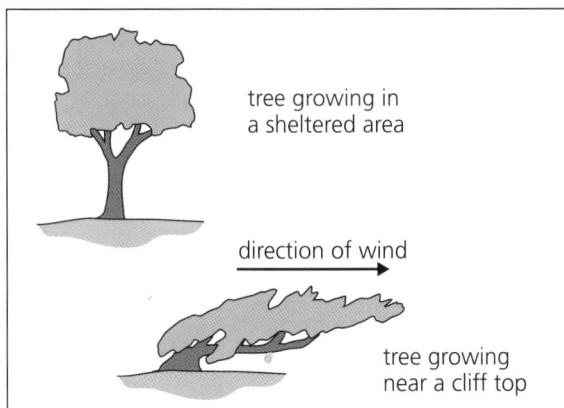

tree growing in a sheltered area

direction of wind

tree growing near a cliff top

Now do this

3   Girls can be born colour blind, although this is rare. Draw a genetic diagram showing how a girl could inherit two recessive alleles for colour blindness.

4   Which of these characteristics can be affected by environment as well as genes: eye colour, weight, fingerprints, body shape?

Natural selection and evolution

Animals and plants have gradually developed (**evolved**) from much simpler forms over many millions of years. This process is called **evolution**.

We only know about evolution from the fossils that have been found. **Fossils** are the remains of dead organisms which have become preserved in rock.

Fossil formation

An organism dies by the water's edge.

The water level rises and the dead organism gradually becomes covered in silt.

The soft parts decay, but the hard bits (bone and cellulose) survive long enough to absorb minerals from the water.

As layers of sediment build up on top of the fossil, it becomes embedded in a layer of sedimentary rock.

The fossil record

The fossil record shows that the variety of living things in the world today did not appear all at once many years ago. This happened very gradually over millions of years, with some things dying out while new ones evolved.

Dinosaurs existed until 65 million years ago, but we only know about them from fossils. Human beings are relative newcomers to the world, with our earliest ancestors making an appearance only 6 million years ago.

However, what we know about evolution from fossils is not the whole story. There are reasons for this:
- some body parts may not have fossilised
- fossilisation was a comparatively rare event
- we have not yet discovered all the fossils.

This means that what fossils show can be interpreted in different ways, according to the views at the time. It is possible to argue that dinosaurs and humans were created together, but we just have not found the fossil evidence yet!

Natural selection

Charles Darwin explained evolution as the result of **natural selection**. This is the idea that those animals and plants best adapted to their surroundings (environment) will have the best chance of surviving and reproducing.

The genes of animals and plants determine how well they are adapted to their surroundings. These genes can then be passed on to the next generation. So, over a very long time a population can become better adapted to its surroundings. This happens because some alleles become more common and some (the less desirable ones) become less common.

Charles Darwin's theory was based on:
- the presence of natural variation within a population
- the inheritance of some of the variations
- the fact that all organisms potentially over-reproduce and yet population numbers tend to remain fairly constant over long periods of time
- the fact that the best adapted individuals are more likely to survive – this is **survival of the fittest**.
- the extinction of species unable to compete.

Now do this

1 Suggest why fossils do not provide a complete record of evolution.

Natural selection in action!

1 Before the Industrial Revolution trees had pale bark, so the pale speckled peppered moth was camouflaged.

2 Chance mutation produced a black (melanic) version.

3 As the Industrial Revolution progressed, the landscape became coated with smoke and soot and the trees turned black.

4 By the start of the 20th century, 98% of the peppered moths were black. They were more numerous because they were better adapted to the environment and the pale ones were easier for the predators to spot.

At the time, Darwin's theory was greeted with hostility. This was because most people believed in the idea of creation, which was the belief that all living things had been created at the same time. Darwin's theory was difficult to understand because most people knew little or nothing about inheritance.

Now do this

2 Explain what is meant by the term natural selection.

3 Use the peppered moth as an example to explain what is meant by survival of the fittest.

4 Why have some species become extinct?

Artificial selection

We take advantage of variation when we **selectively breed** animals and plants. We pick individuals with the characteristics we want and breed them. Their best offspring are selected and bred. This is repeated over many generations.

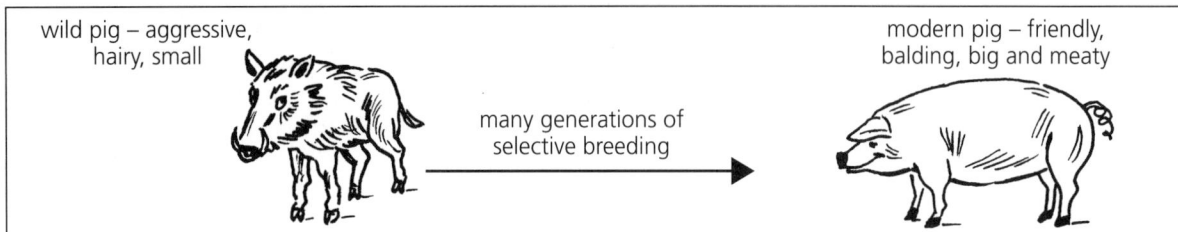

wild pig – aggressive, hairy, small

many generations of selective breeding

modern pig – friendly, balding, big and meaty

We selectively breed for many reasons. In animals we may want better yields of meat or milk, less aggression or a more attractive appearance. In plants we may want better yields of grain or fruit, better flavour or resistance to disease.

Now do this

1 a What characteristic would you want to breed into racehorses?

b How would you do it?

Genetic engineering

Selective breeding takes a long time. It is unreliable because we cannot control exactly which genes are passed on, and is limited to living things within the same species. So, for example, you cannot breed a cow with a giraffe to produce a long-necked cow able to feed over hedges!

Genetic engineering gets round these problems by transferring genes directly from the cells of one living thing to the cells of another. The desired gene is first identified in an organism and then removed and isolated. It is replicated to make lots of copies and then inserted into the genetic material (the DNA) of the host organism.

For example, inserting the gene for human insulin into microbes has led to microbes capable of producing large amounts of human insulin for use in treating diabetes, which would otherwise be very difficult to produce.

Genetic engineering has a number of possible drawbacks. It is expensive to set up and develop. There are also worries about transferred genes finding their way into other species, and about eating food which has been genetically engineered. Finally, there is a lot of concern about possibly engineering humans in the future for 'desirable' characteristics.

Now do this

2 Explain why selective breeding is still used a lot for animals nowadays, but not so much for plants.

3 Make a table showing the advantages and disadvantages of genetic engineering and selective breeding.

Concept map

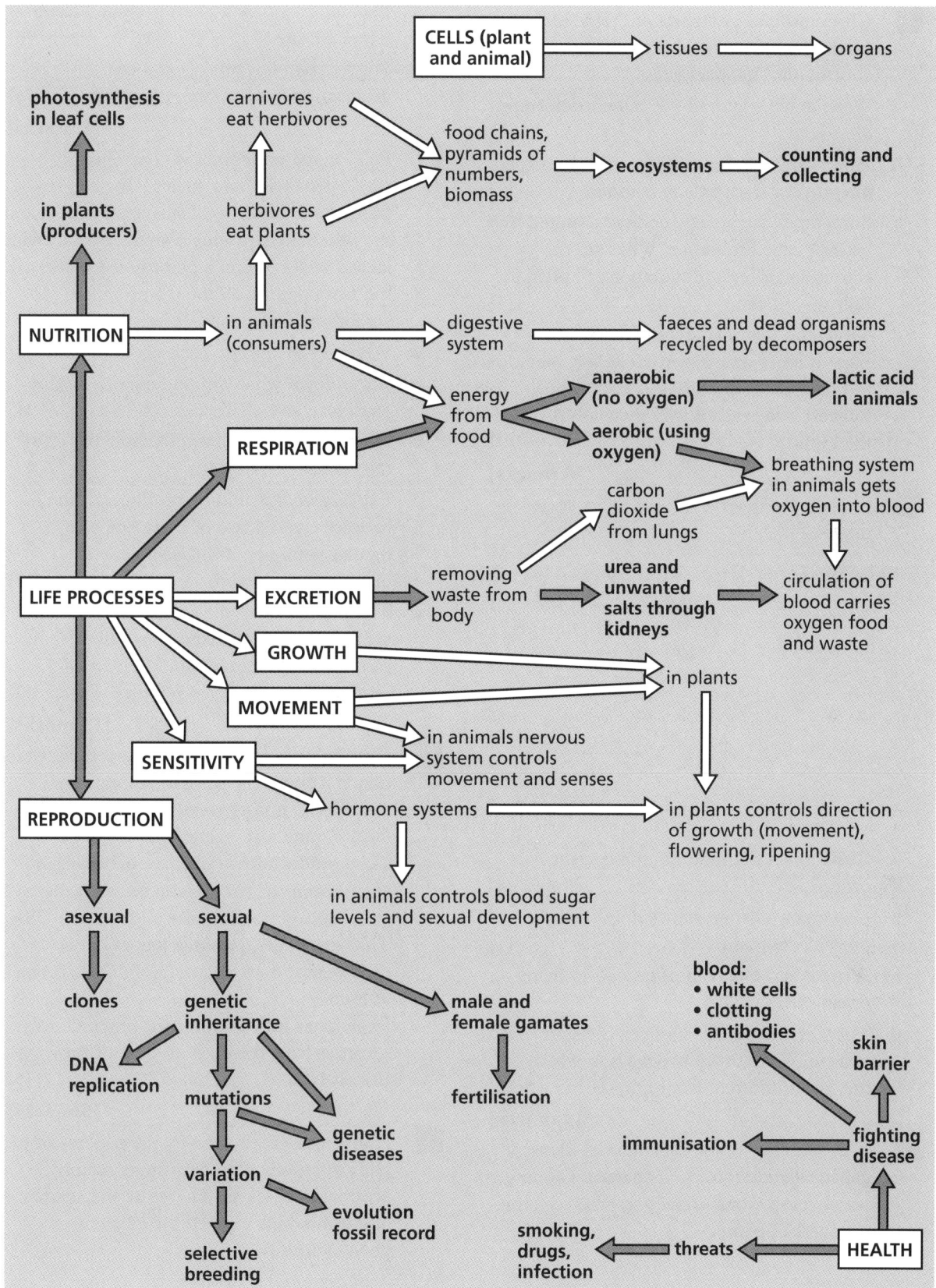

CELLS (plant and animal) → tissues → organs

photosynthesis in leaf cells

carnivores eat herbivores → food chains, pyramids of numbers, biomass → ecosystems → counting and collecting

in plants (producers)

herbivores eat plants

NUTRITION → in animals (consumers) → digestive system → faeces and dead organisms recycled by decomposers

in animals (consumers) → energy from food

RESPIRATION → energy from food → anaerobic (no oxygen) → lactic acid in animals

aerobic (using oxygen) → breathing system in animals gets oxygen into blood

carbon dioxide from lungs

LIFE PROCESSES → EXCRETION → removing waste from body → urea and unwanted salts through kidneys → circulation of blood carries oxygen food and waste

GROWTH → in plants

MOVEMENT → in plants

SENSITIVITY → in animals nervous system controls movement and senses

hormone systems → in plants controls direction of growth (movement), flowering, ripening

REPRODUCTION

in animals controls blood sugar levels and sexual development

asexual → clones

sexual → genetic inheritance

sexual → male and female gametes → fertilisation

genetic inheritance → DNA replication

genetic inheritance → mutations → genetic diseases

mutations → variation → evolution fossil record

variation → selective breeding

blood:
• white cells
• clotting
• antibodies

skin barrier

immunisation ← fighting disease

smoking, drugs, infection ← threats ← HEALTH

Exam questions

1 Chromosomes are made of DNA. DNA carries the genetic code (genes) for cells to control our characteristics.

a Write down where in the cell chromosomes are found. [1]

b How many chromosomes would you expect one of your liver cells to contain? [1]

c Sometimes the genetic code is changed by a process called mutation. What are the causes and effects of mutation? Explain as fully as you can. [4]

d Sarah and Gemma are sisters with the same mother and father. However, they do not have the same DNA as each other. Suggest **two** reasons why their DNA is not the same. [2]

[8 marks]

2 Look at the diagrams. They show stages in mitosis.

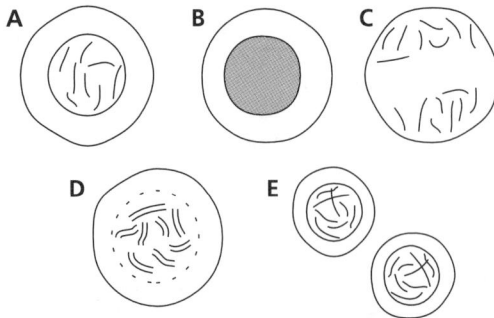

a Write down the stages in the correct order. [4]

b How many chromosomes does the cell normally contain? [1]

c Write down **two** uses of mitosis in living organisms. [2]

d There is another form of cell division called meiosis. Write down two ways in which meiosis is different from mitosis. [2]

[9 marks]

3 This question is about cloning. A clone is genetically identical to its parent. Cloning is widely used commercially to produce large numbers of plants.

a Explain fully how a plant is cloned using tissue culture. [4]

b Suggest **two** advantages and **two** disadvantages of cloning plants. [4]

[8 marks]

4 Petal shape in poppies is controlled by a single gene with two alleles. One allele produces smooth regular-shaped petals, and the other allele produces smaller petals with jagged edges. When a plant breeder crossed the two poppies, all the offspring had smooth regular petals.

a Which of the poppy alleles is dominant? [1]

b Write down what you understand by the term recessive allele. [1]

c Draw a genetic diagram to show the cross the breeder carried out. [4]

d Explain what would be produced if the breeder crossed two of these smooth regular petal poppies. Use a genetic diagram to help you. [4]

e The poppies with the jagged edged petals are very attractive. Explain as fully as you can how the breeder could be sure of producing more jagged poppies. [3]

[13 marks]

5 Until the early twentieth century there were only red squirrels living in Britain. They were small, non-aggressive animals which lived in pine forests and ate pine cones. They produced two or three babies each year. About the turn of the century, the grey squirrel was introduced from the USA. They are larger, produce lots of babies each year and eat a variety of different types of food.

Explain, as fully as you can, why red squirrels have died out in most of the British Isles. [5]

[5 marks]

6 Plants make their food by the process of photosynthesis. Photosynthesis mainly occurs in the leaves. Therefore the structure of a leaf is well adapted for efficient photosynthesis.

a Explain **three** ways in which the leaf is adapted for photosynthesis. [3]

b On a warm, sunny day, what is most likely to be the factor limiting the rate of photosynthesis? [1]

[4 marks]

7 Look at the drawing of Max swimming.

He needs lots of energy to swim. The energy is released by the process of respiration.

a Where does respiration occur? [1]

b Write down the symbol equation for aerobic respiration. [3]

When Max gets out of the water, he sits by the side of the pool talking to his friends. Although it is a hot, sunny day, Max is surprised to feel cold.

c Explain why the wet Max is feeling cold, but his friends are not. [2]

[6 marks]

8 Caffeine is a stimulant and is present in coffee and chocolate.

a Explain what is meant by the term stimulant. [1]

b Some people claim to be addicted to chocolate and if they try to give it up, they can suffer from headaches, bad temper and loss of concentration.

 i Write down what is meant by the terms addiction and withdrawal symptoms. [2]

 ii Explain what is meant by drug tolerance, and suggest how it can lead drug addicts into deeper and deeper troubles. [2]

[5 marks]

9 Max cut 50 cylinders of beetroot each 50 mm long. He then put 10 in each flask of sugar solution and after 30 min he remeasured the length of each cylinder. This is a table of his results.

Sugar concentration (mol/dm³)	Mean length after 30 min (mm)	Change in length (mm)
0.0	54	+4
1.0	51	
2.0	48	
3.0	46	
4.0	45	

a Calculate the change in length and complete the end column of the table. [4]

b Use your calculated values to draw a graph on the grid below. The first point has been plotted for you. [3]

c Use the graph to determine the concentration of cell sap in beetroot cells. [2]

d Explain fully why the beetroot gets smaller in the high-concentration sugar solutions. [4]

[13 marks]

10 The kidneys help the body to maintain conditions at a favourable level for cells to work efficiently.

a What is the name given to this type of control process? [1]

b List three conditions which the body needs to control. [3]

c Briefly explain how the kidney produces urine. [4]

d Explain the difference between the urine you would produce after a game of tennis on a hot summer's day, and that which you would produce watching a rugby match on a cold winter day. [3]

[11 marks]

Bonding

Ionic bonding

Ions with opposite charges will hold each other together. This is **ionic bonding**.

We can use 'dot and cross' diagrams to show how these ions are made – this one is for sodium chloride, salt.

| a sodium atom | gives its outer electron | to a chlorine atom | to make | a sodium ion, **Na⁺** | and | a chloride ion, **Cl⁻** |

Ionic bonds are very strong forces. Substances with ionic bonds form enormous groups called **ionic giant structures**. Giant structures have high melting and boiling points because all the strong forces holding the particles together are dificult to overcome. Salt has a giant structure.

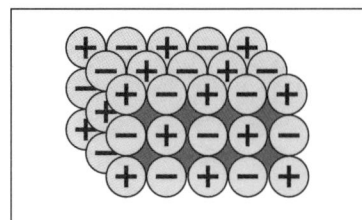

Covalent bonding

When non-metals react with each other they don't form ions, they share electrons instead. This is **covalent bonding**, and it is just as strong as ionic bonding.

The hydrogen molecule, H_2, has a single covalent bond. The outer shell of each hydrogen atom needs two electrons to make it stable.

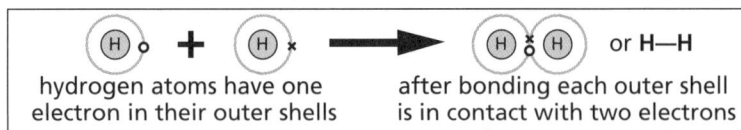

hydrogen atoms have one electron in their outer shells

after bonding each outer shell is in contact with two electrons

The chlorine molecule, Cl_2, also has a single covalent bond. The outer shell of each chlorine atom needs eight electrons to make it stable.

chlorine atoms have seven electrons in their outer shells

after bonding each outer shell is in contact with eight electrons

The oxygen molecule, O_2, has a double covalent bond. The outer shell of each oxygen atom needs eight electrons to make it stable.

oxygen atoms have six electrons in their outer shells

after bonding each outer shell is in contact with eight electrons

Now do this

1   Draw 'dot and cross' diagrams for the bonds in the following molecules:

water, H_2O methane, CH_4 carbon dioxide, CO_2 nitrogen, N_2

Molecules and giants

Covalent compounds can form giant structures or they can form small molecules.

Covalent molecules

Molecules have strong covalent bonds inside them, but only very weak forces holding one molecule to another. The weak forces between molecules make it easy to separate molecules from each other; in other words they have low melting and boiling points.

weak forces between each molecule

strong covalent bonds inside each molecule

Covalent giant structures

Sometimes all the atoms inside a structure are held together with covalent bonds, there are no weak forces. This makes a **covalent giant structure**. As the covalent bond is just as strong as the ionic bond, the structure will have very high melting and boiling points.

Carbon is special because it is an element that has three different forms; diamond, graphite and Buckminster Fullerene. Diamond and graphite are both covalent giant structures.

Diamond
covalent giant structure
hard
does not conduct electricity

Graphite
covalent giant structure
soft
conducts electricity
weak forces *between* the layers allow the layers to slide

Buckminster Fullerene
Carbon atoms joined to make a microscopic football. This was only discovered in 1983

Covalent giant structure

- strong forces between molecules
- high melting/ boiling points

Ionic giant structure

- strong forces between molecules
- high melting/boiling points
- solid won't conduct electricity, liquid will

Molecular structure

- weak forces between molecules
- low melting/boiling points
- doesn't conduct electricity

Now do this

2   A solid melts at 100°C. What type of structure has it got?

3   A solid melts at 1000°C. What sort of structure has it got?

4   What sort of forces hold the atoms together inside a molecule of hydrogen?

5   What sort of forces hold one molecule of hydrogen to another molecule of hydrogen?

Alkanes, alkenes and plastics

There are millions of carbon compounds. Some of them are very similar, so we put them into groups. The two groups that you need to know are the **alkanes** and the **alkenes**. Both groups are made of carbon and hydrogen only, so they are both hydrocarbons.

Alkanes

The first alkanes in the group are:

The carbon atoms in the alkane molecules are linked by single covalent bonds only, so we say that they are **saturated**.

As the alkane molecule gets bigger, there are more weak forces between the molecules. The melting points and boiling points of the alkanes increase as they get bigger.

The alkanes all burn well with a clean blue flame.

$$CH_4 + 2O_2 \rightarrow CO_2 + 2H_2O$$

Larger alkane molecules are 'cracked' into smaller alkanes and into alkenes using a catalyst, high temperatures and high pressure. Cracking also produces hydrogen, which is used in the Haber Process.

Alkenes

The simplest alkene is ethene, C_2H_4. Its structure is

.

It has a double bond between the carbon atoms so we say that it is **unsaturated**. Alkenes are often used to make plastics.

Plastics

Plastics are made of small molecules which are joined together into long chains. The small molecules are called **monomers**, the large molecule is a **polymer**. Polymerisation often needs high pressures and a catalyst.

Now do this

1 How many C—C bonds are present in ethane?

2 How many C—H bonds are present in ethane?

3 Draw a dot and cross diagram to show the covalent bonds inside an ethane molecule.

4 Why is octane a liquid at room temperature?

| monomer | + | monomer | + | monomer | + | monomer | → | polymer |

Alkenes make excellent monomers. The double bond allows the alkene molecules to add on to each other to make the chains – this is **addition polymerisation**. Ethene is the monomer used to make poly(ethene), or polythene.

ethene + ethene + ethene → poly(ethene)

Different alkene monomers make different types of plastic which do different jobs. Polythene is cheap and flexible, so it is used to make polythene bags. Vinyl chloride is the monomer used to make poly(vinyl chloride), PVC.

vinyl chloride + vinyl chloride + vinyl chloride → poly(vinyl chloride) (PVC)

PVC is not as cheap as polythene but it lasts better outdoors, so it is used for drainpipes and window frames as well as clothing and vinyl records.

Some plastics bend easily, especially when warmed. The weak forces between their molecules allow the molecules to slide past each other. These are called **thermosoftening plastics**. Other plastics will not bend; they have strong 'cross-links' between their molecules which hold the molecules together. These are the **thermosetting plastics**. Forces between molecules are **intermolecular forces**. Forces inside the molecules – the bonds which hold it together – are **intramolecular forces**.

One problem with plastics is that when they are thrown away they are not attacked by decomposers in the soil, so they do not rot like most rubbish. Plastics are **non-biodegradable**. Some modern plastics have now been produced which will rot when they are thrown away, so these are **biodegradable**.

thermosoftening plastic
long chain molecules

strong forces within the molecules   weak forces between the molecules

thermosetting plastic
long chain molecules

strong covalent bonds between chains

- Vegetable oils are unsaturated; they have C=C bonds.
- Fats are saturated; they have only C-C single bonds.
- Margarine makers use hydrogen to turn vegetable oils into fats. The hydrogen changes the double bonds to single bonds; it saturates the oils. If there are some C=C bonds left, the margarine is polyunsaturated.

Unsaturated hydrocarbons have a C=C bond. They turn orange/brown bromine water colourless.

Saturated hydrocarbons have no C=C bond. They do not affect bromine water.

Now do this

5 Propene is $\overset{H}{\underset{H}{C}} = \overset{CH_3}{\underset{H}{C}}$. Show three links of a poly(propene) molecule.

6 'Orlon' is a plastic used to make clothes.
Part of an Orlon molecule looks like this:

Draw a monomer of Orlon.

Making food

Using yeast

Catalysts are important in a wide range of industrial processes. In the food industry the catalysts used are often **enzymes**. Enzymes are biological catalysts; they are produced inside living things.

Unlike other catalysts, enzymes have a very delicate structure, and are quickly damaged by temperatures that are too high for them. All reactions go faster as they get hotter, but if an enyme is involved the reaction will only get faster up to a certain temperature, then it will slow down or stop due to damage to the enzyme. As the temperature increases, all the molecules move about more and more. The molecules also vibrate, and the vibrations inside the enzyme molecules become so great that the delicate structure is destroyed. We say that the enzyme has been **denatured**.

Yeast is used in both baking and brewing because the yeast cells contain enzymes which convert sugar into carbon dioxide and alcohol during **fermentation**.

sugar → alcohol + carbon dioxide

Brewers use yeast for the alcohol, bakers use it for the carbon dioxide. In each case the yeast needs sugar, moisture and warm conditions to work.

Baking

Sugar and yeast are added to bread dough so that the enzymes in the yeast can produce bubbles of carbon dioxide. When it is cooked the dough solidifies round the bubbles, giving bread an open texture. The high temperature of the cooking kills the yeast and drives off the carbon dioxide and the alcohol.

Brewing

Yeast is added to grape juice to make wine, and to barley grains to make beer. The enzymes in the yeast convert sugars from the grapes and barley into alcohol during fermentation. The carbon dioxide bubbles out of the liquid. The alcohol inside a bottle of wine will slowly change to vinegar, an organic acid, if you leave the bottle open to the air.

Other useful chemicals in food

- **Sugars** are used as sweeteners and for preserving food as well as for making alcohol. They are also an important source of energy in our diet.
- **Alcohol** is not just a drink but also a solvent. We dissolve some medicines in alcohol.
- **Organic acids and esters.** When alcohols react with **organic acids** they form sweet-smelling compounds called **esters**. Esters are natural flavouring compounds in food; we add esters to some foods to increase the flavour. **Organic acids** occur naturally in most fruit and give the fruit its 'tangy' taste. Vinegar is a solution of an organic acid and is used to preserve food.

> Some sugars are called **reducing sugars** and form a red-brown precipitate when warmed with Fehling's solution. This is a way of testing whether sugars are present in a substance.

Functional groups

The reactions of organic compounds such as those in foods depend on a small part of the molecule called the functional group.

Functional group	Found in
$-O-H$	alcohols
$-C=O$ with H	aldehydes (reducing sugars)
$-C=O$ with $O-H$	acids
$-C=O$ with O, C	esters

![icon] **Now do this**

1. What happens to the speed of a reaction involving an enzyme:
   a if you start to heat it up
   b if you heat it further?

2. What happens to the enzyme in **1a**?

3. a When yeast ferments it converts sugar into two chemicals. What are they?
   b One of the chemicals in **a** will turn into vinegar, an organic acid. Which one?
   c Which of these formulae could be vinegar?

   A
   $$H-\overset{\overset{\displaystyle H}{|}}{\underset{\underset{\displaystyle H}{|}}{C}}-O-H$$

   B
   $$H-\overset{\overset{\displaystyle H}{|}}{\underset{\underset{\displaystyle H}{|}}{C}}-C=O$$

   C
   $$H-\overset{\overset{\displaystyle H}{|}}{\underset{\underset{\displaystyle H}{|}}{C}}-\overset{}{\underset{\underset{\displaystyle O-H}{|}}{C}}=O$$

4. Give **one** use for an ester.

Acids and pH

Natural acids are all around us. Acids in orange juice and vinegar give a sharp taste; acids in nettles and bee stings hurt us; acids in our stomach help digest our food. Acidity is caused by the presence of hydrogen ions, H^+.

How acidic is it?

The pH scale tells us how strongly acidic something is. The lower the number, the greater the hydrogen ion concentration.

		NEUTRAL		
very acidic	slightly acidic	↓ slightly alkaline		very alkaline
0 1 2 3	4 5 6	7	8 9 10 11	12 13 14

Acids from the lab such as hydrochloric acid or sulphuric acid have a pH of about 1. Lemon juice and vinegar are much less acidic, with a pH of around 4. Sodium hydroxide is at the other end, with a pH of about 14, but baking soda is around pH 8.

Bases, alkalis and neutralisation

Anything that reacts with an acid is called a **base**. A base which will dissolve in water (such as sodium hydroxide) is an **alkali**. Metal oxides and hydroxides are usually bases and alkalis. Non-metal oxides are usually acidic.

Acids contain hydrogen ions, H^+; alkalis contain hydroxide ions, OH^-.

When an acid and a base react they **neutralise** each other. The hydrogen ions react with hydroxide ions to form water.

$$H^+(aq) \quad + \quad OH^-(aq) \quad \rightarrow \quad H_2O(l)$$

If you add acid to a beaker of alkali the pH of the liquid in the beaker will start at a high number and drop to pH 7 once the acid and alkali have neutralised each other. If you add too much acid you will go too far. The pH will go below 7.

When acids react with alkalis they produce a **salt** and water. The salt is the substance left over after the hydrogen ions have reacted with the hydroxide ions.

acid	+	alkali	→	salt	+	water
HCl	+	**NaOH**	→	**NaCl**	+	**H₂O**
hydrochloric acid		sodium hydroxide		sodium chloride		water

Acids always form salts when they react.

Acids and metals

If a metal reacts with an acid, the metal is behaving as a base.
The hydrogen ions from the acid are converted to hydrogen gas
and a salt is left behind.

acid	+	metal	→	salt	+	hydrogen
H_2SO_4	+	Mg	→	$MgSO_4$	+	H_2
sulphuric acid		magnesium		magnesium sulphate		hydrogen

Not all metals react with acids. Metals such as copper and silver
are not reactive enough to be attacked by acids.

Using a neutralisation reaction to make fertilisers

Ammonia (NH_3) should make a good fertiliser, but when it
dissolves in the water in the soil it forms a solution of ammonium
hydroxide. Ammonium hydroxide solution is alkaline, and damages
the crops. If the ammonium hydroxide is neutralised with an acid it
will form an ammonium salt. This salt can be used as a fertiliser.

acid	+	alkali	→	salt	+	water
sulphuric acid		ammonium hydroxide		ammonium sulphate		water

Ammonium salts make good fertilisers because they contain
nitrogen, which is used for growth. This makes crops produce more
– it increases their yield.

Sometimes the fertilisers are washed into lakes and ponds by
rainwater. Microscopic plants then grow on the surface of the
water, cuting off light to the rest of the pond so the rest of the
plants die. As the dead plants rot the microbes use up the oxygen
in the water, so everything else dies. This is called **eutrophication**.

Now do this

1 If the acidity of something increases, does the pH rise, fall or stay constant?

2 Bee stings are acidic. Choose the best substance to neutralise a bee sting from those described under the pH scale.

3 Name the salt produced when sulphuric acid reacts with iron.

4 Magnesium reacts with hydrochloric acid (HCl).
   a Name the two products.
   b Write a balanced equation for the reaction.

Reversible reactions and ammonia

Some chemical reactions will go in both directions. If you put acid
with pH indicator, the indicator will turn red. If you now add alkali
the indicator changes to blue. Add acid again, and it goes back to red.

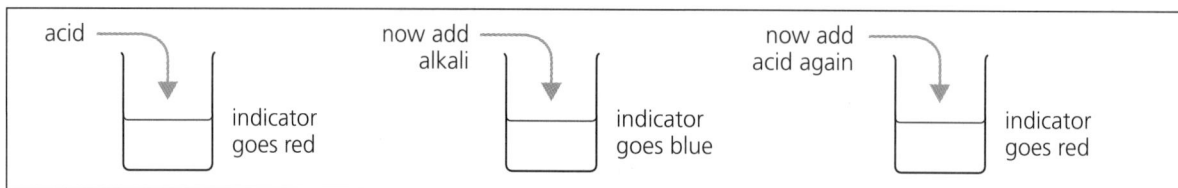

acid	now add alkali	now add acid again
indicator goes red	indicator goes blue	indicator goes red

You can do this as many times as you want. The reaction will go in
either direction just as easily.

Usually it is very difficult to make a reaction go backwards, but in
this case it is very easy. We call this type of reaction a **reversible
reaction**.

Ammonia is made by a reversible reaction

Millions of tons of ammonia are produced every
year so that we can make fertiliser. The method
of making ammonia is called the **Haber Process**
after the man who discovered it. Ammonia is
made by the reversible reaction between nitrogen
and hydrogen.

When nitrogen and hydrogen meet they start to
react to form ammonia. The ammonia
immediately starts to turn back to nitrogen and
hydrogen. The reaction goes in both directions at
the same time.

this is a
'forward reaction'

$$N_2 + 3H_2 \longrightarrow 2NH_3$$
$$N_2 + 3H_2 \longleftarrow 2NH_3$$

this is a
'backward reaction'

$$N_2 + 3H_2 \rightleftharpoons 2NH_3$$
nitrogen + hydrogen   ammonia

Eventually the forward reaction is going at the
same speed as the backward reaction. From this
point onwards there will not be any change in the amount of
chemicals; they have reached **equilibrium**. The symbol for an
equilibrium reaction is $\rightleftharpoons$.

The Haber Process

Hydrogen is made by cracking hydrocarbons from crude oil and
nitrogen is taken from the air. High pressure pushes the balance
point of the equilibrium further to the right, so that more ammonia
is made. Low temperature also pushes the equilibrium to the right,
but a high temperature makes the reaction go faster, so we use an
in-between temperature as a compromise.

Ammonia is removed as fast as it is made to stop it reacting back
into nitrogen and hydrogen. A catalyst of iron, a transition metal,
speeds up the reaction. Catalysts in equilibrium reactions speed up
both the forward and the backward reactions, so the reactions get
to their balance point more quickly.

Now do this

1   What is a reversible
    reaction?

2   What is produced if
    you put an iron
    catalyst with
    ammonia?

Keeping the costs down

Making new substances can often be expensive. The total cost depends on:
- the cost of the equipment needed
- the cost of the energy needed
- the cost of the starting materials
- operators' wages
- how fast it can be made – the quicker you make it, the cheaper it is.

Keeping costs down for the Haber Process

We can keep costs down by getting the nitrogen for the Haber Process from the air. The air is an important natural resource. However, the process is still not cheap to run. It needs
- high temperature
  The reaction works at about 450°C. This means high energy costs for the fuel.
- high pressure
  This means money has to be spent on compressors and also on extra-thick reaction vessels and pipes, which won't explode under the pressure.

Two ways of saving money are to
- make the ammonia as quickly as possible. We use the catalyst to do this
- recycle any unused nitrogen and hydrogen back through the reaction vessel so that none of it is wasted.

Keeping costs down for the industrial production of alcohol

Large amounts of alcohol are made every year for making and dissolving chemicals in industry. Alcohol is made by reacting steam with ethene at a high temperature and pressure, using a catalyst.

steam + ethene → alcohol

This process is expensive to run, for the same reasons that the Haber Process is expensive. The costs can be reduced in the same two ways as in the Haber Process.

This reaction uses water, which is another very important natural resource.

??? Now do this

3   Use the list at the top of the page to decide on **one** thing that makes the industrial production of alcohol expensive.

4   Use the list at the top of the page to decide on **one** way of saving money in the industrial production of alcohol.

5 a Give **two** ways to keep the cost of ammonia down.
  b Give **two** things that push costs up.

Chemical calculations

How much do we need?

If you want to carry out a chemical reaction without wasting any of the chemicals you need to know precisely how much of each reactant to use. To measure out chemical reactions we weigh them. We weigh out atoms in 'pre-packed' quantities called moles. Moles of different elements weigh different amounts. The mass of a mole of atoms of an element is its **relative atomic mass** in grams.

hydrogen ram = 1	carbon ram = 12	oxygen ram = 16
1 mole of hydrogen atoms weighs 1 gram	1 mole of carbon atoms weighs 12 grams	1 mole of oxygen atoms weighs 16 grams

ram = relative atomic mass

For example, the equation for iron reacting with sulphur is

Fe	**+**	**S**	→	**FeS**
1 atom	reacts with	**1 atom**		
56 grams	reacts with	**32 grams**		(using relative atomic masses)

Now do this

1 You have 2 g of hydrogen.
  a You want the same number of atoms of carbon. How much do you weigh out?
  b You want twice as many atoms of oxygen. How much do you weigh out?

Formula masses

When we weigh out substances made of more than one atom, we have to add up the masses of all the atoms inside the formula. This is called the **formula mass**. It is the mass of one mole of the molecule.

A hydrogen molecule is H_2	The formula mass for H_2 is	$1 + 1$	=	2
An oxygen molecule is O_2	The formula mass for O_2 is	$16 + 16$	=	32
A methane molecule is CH_4	The formula mass for CH_4 is	$12 + 1 + 1 + 1 + 1$	=	16
Sodium chloride is NaCl	The formula mass for NaCl is	$23 + 35.5$	=	58.5

Calculating amounts used in chemical reactions

When chemicals react, their atoms join together in different ways. All the atoms at the start of the reaction are still there at the end. In a reaction the atoms never disappear, new atoms never appear. For example,

$$H_2 + Cl_2 \rightarrow 2HCl$$

This means that the mass of the chemicals is the same at the end of the reaction.

The mass of H_2 and Cl_2 at the start = H + H   + Cl   + Cl
     = 1 + 1   + 35.5 + 35.5 = 73
The mass of 2HCl at the end   = H + Cl   + H   + Cl
     = 1 + 35.5 + 1   + 35.5 = 73

The total mass of all the reactants will equal the total mass of all the products.

Moles and formula masses

You can work out how many moles there are of a chemical if you know its formula mass and how many grams of the chemical you have.

$$\text{Number of moles} = \frac{\text{mass}}{\text{formula mass}}$$

Calculating yields and formulae

Sometimes the amount of product is less than expected. The starting chemicals don't always completely react, and it is hard to get all the product out of the reaction mixture. Small amounts always 'get lost' somewhere.

Here are some reasons for 'missing' product:
- loss in filtration
- loss in evaporation – for something that can evaporate
- loss in heating – for something that can evaporate
- loss in transferring liquids.

Moles in solution

The molarity of a solution is the number of moles that are dissolved in one dm^3 of the solution.

A one **molar** solution contains one mole dissolved in one dm^3 of solution.

A three **molar** solution contains 3 moles per dm^3 of solution

Number of moles = molarity × volume (in dm^3)

Percentage yields

The **percentage yield** is the amount of product actually collected compared to the amount that was expected.

$$\% \text{ yield} = \frac{\text{actual mass of product}}{\text{expected mass of product}} = \times 100$$

If a reaction produced 46 g of product, but we expected to have 80 g, the % yield

$$= \frac{46 \times 100}{80}$$

$$= \frac{4600}{80}$$

$$= 57.5\%$$

Some relative atomic masses

hydrogen	H	= 1
lithium	Li	= 7
carbon	C	= 12
nitrogen	N	= 14
oxygen	O	= 16
sodium	Na	= 23
sulphur	S	= 32
chlorine	Cl	= 35.5
iron	Fe	= 56
copper	Cu	= 64

Now do this

2   A reaction produced 32 g of chemical. You expected it to produce 50 g of chemical. What is the percentage yield?

How to find a formula from reacting masses

To work out a formula you must know the mass of each element inside the substance. The sort of question you might have to answer is:
3.5 g of lithium reacts with 4 g of oxygen to make lithium oxide. What is the formula of lithium oxide?
(Relative atomic masses: Li = 7, O = 16)

These are the stages to go through.

Stage 1
Find out how many moles of each element you used.

3.5 g of lithium is made of $\frac{3.5}{7} = 0.5$ moles of lithium

4 g of oxygen is made of $\frac{4}{16} = 0.25$ moles of oxygen.

Now do this

3   8 g of copper combine with 1 g of oxygen. What is the formula of the copper oxide? (Relative atomic masses O = 16, Cu = 64)

4   4 g of copper combine with 1 g of oxygen. What is the formula of this copper oxide?

Stage 2
Find the ratio of the numbers of moles of the different elements – this is the formula.

0.5 moles of lithium atoms react with 0.25 moles of oxygen atoms.
2 mole of lithium atoms react with 1 mole of oxygen atoms.
The formula of lithium oxide is Li_2O.

Atoms, isotopes and electron shells

An atom is made of a tiny positive nucleus surrounded by shells of electrons.

The nucleus is made of protons and neutrons. Protons have a positive charge. Neutrons are neutral. They are both heavy particles.

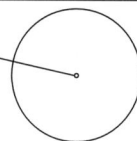

The electrons fit in shells around the nucleus. They have a negative charge and weigh almost nothing

Atoms are neutral. Their negative and positive charges cancel out. This means that the number of electrons must be the same as the number of protons.

Name	Charge	Mass	Where found
proton	+1	1	inside the nucleus
neutron	0	1	inside the nucleus
electron	−1	0	outside the nucleus, in shells

The number of protons in an atom is called the **atomic number** or the **proton number**. It tells you what element you have. If an atom has one proton, the element is hydrogen, two protons means helium and so on.

The mass of an atom is made up of all the protons and neutrons, because both are heavy particles. Add the two numbers together to make the **mass number**. The electrons don't weigh enough to matter.

We write all this information in a standard way.

The number of neutrons is the mass number minus the proton number.

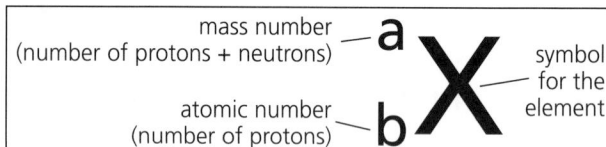

mass number
(number of protons + neutrons) — a X — symbol
for the
element
atomic number — b
(number of protons)

Isotopes

Many elements have more than one mass number. These different forms of the same element are called **isotopes**.

$^{35}_{17}Cl$ has 17 protons, so it is chlorine. Work out how many neutrons it must have (mass number – proton number). You should have the answer 18 neutrons.

$^{37}_{17}Cl$ has 17 protons, so it is chlorine. Work out how many neutrons it must have (mass number – proton number). You should have the answer 20 neutrons.

The only difference between them is the number of neutrons in the nucleus. This makes one isotope heavier than the other, but otherwise it doesn't have much effect.

Now do this

1   What is the difference between $^{16}_{8}O$ and $^{18}_{8}O$?

2   How many protons are in $^{56}_{26}Fe$?

3   How many neutrons are in $^{56}_{26}Fe$?

How are the electrons arranged in an atom?

In a neutral atom the number of electrons outside the nucleus is the same as the number of protons inside the nucleus. Electrons are negative, protons are positive, and so the two sets of charges cancel out and the atom is neutral. Remember that the number of protons is the atomic number.

Electrons fit into shells around the nucleus. Two electrons fit into the first shell, then up to eight electrons fit into the next shell. Eight electrons is a stable number for all shells after the innermost shell.

Sodium has 11 electrons, so its electron arrangement is 2,8,1. This means that there are two electrons in the first shell, eight in the next and one in the outer shell.

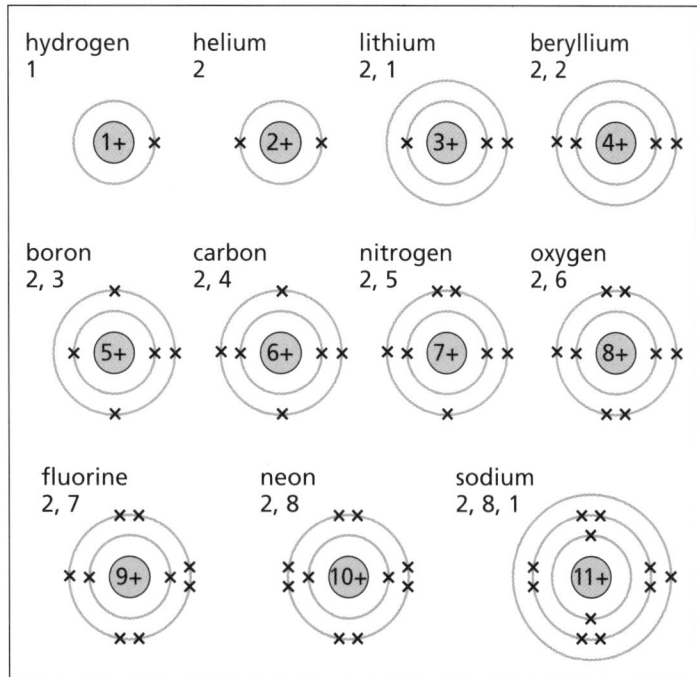

hydrogen 1	helium 2	lithium 2, 1	beryllium 2, 2
boron 2, 3	carbon 2, 4	nitrogen 2, 5	oxygen 2, 6
fluorine 2, 7	neon 2, 8	sodium 2, 8, 1	

Ions

If the outer shell of an element is only a few electrons away from the eight, the element will form an ion. Electrons are gained or lost to end up with the eight. If more than two electrons have to move, the element usually won't form an ion. It shares electrons instead.

Elements whose atoms gain electrons to form ions

If there are 7 electrons in the outer shell, then gain one electron → X^- ion.

If there are 6 electrons in the outer shell, then gain two electrons → X^{2-} ion.

Elements whose atoms give away electrons to form ions

If there is 1 electron in the outer shell, then give away one electron → X^+ ion.

If there are 2 electrons in the outer shell, then give away two electrons → X^{2+} ion.

Now do this

4 The atomic number of nitrogen is 7.
 a How many protons has it got?
 b How many electrons has it got?
 c How are the electrons arranged?

5 The atomic number of sodium is 11. What is its electron arrangement?

6 The atomic number of potassium is 19. What is its electron arrangement?

The Periodic Table

A Periodic Table is is a list of all the elements in order of their increasing proton numbers (atomic numbers). The order goes from left to right along each row, starting with the top row. A Periodic Table will be printed on the back of your examination paper.

Elements which are similar fit into vertical lines called **Groups**. The group numbers are written in Roman numerals, and are at the top of the table. They go from Group I to Group 0. Sometimes the last group on the right is called Group VIII. Hydrogen is the one element that is sometimes not put into a group.

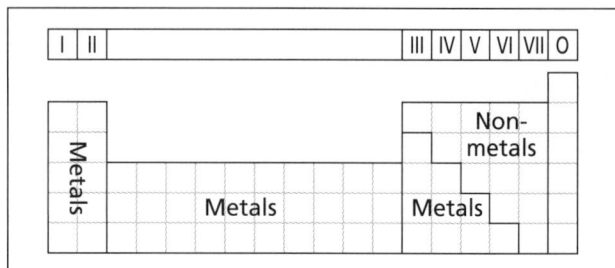

Do this. Find the proton number (atomic number) of sodium.

Metals and non-metals

There are two sorts of elements, metals and non-metals. The zig-zag line shows the boundary between them. Metals are on the left-hand side of the table, non-metals are on the right.

Metals will:
• react with oxygen to form oxides which are basic.

Most metals will also:
• react with water to form hydrogen and oxides or hydroxides
• react with acids to form hydrogen and a salt.
The most reactive metals are at the bottom left.

Non-metals often form acidic oxides. The most reactive non-metal is at the top of Group VII – it is fluorine.

Groups and electrons

The group number is the same as the number of electrons in the outer shell. These outer electrons are the most important electrons of an element, because that is where atoms touch, so the outer electrons dictate the chemical properties.

All the elements in a group have the same number of outer electrons. They are all similar, although there is a regular change in properties of the elements as you go down the group.

Eight electrons make a stable shell. Elements in groups which have only one or two electrons in the outer shell lose those electrons and form positive ions. Elements in groups which have six or seven electrons in the outer shell gain electrons and form negative ions.

Group number	I	II	III	IV	V	VI	VII	0
Outer electrons	1	2	3	4	5	6	7	8
Ion formed	M^+	M^{++}				X^{--}	X^-	

Now do this

1 Explain why elements in Group II form double positive ions.

2 Why don't Group 0 elements form ions?

Group I: The alkali metals

The Group I elements are called the **alkali metals**. You need to know about the first three: lithium, sodium and potassium.

Element	Symbol	Mass	Melting point (°C)
lithium	Li	7	180
sodium	Na	23	98
potassium	K	39	63
rubidium	Rb	85	39
caesium	Cs	133	29

As these elements are in Group I they all have only one electron in the outer shell, and they lose that electron to form single positive ions. They are all very reactive, and get *more* reactive going down the group. The melting points and boiling points get lower going down the group.

The alkali metals are all very similar. Like all metals they are shiny and conduct electricity. Unlike most metals they have such low density that they will float on water. They are soft, and get softer as you go down the group.

Alkali metals all tarnish rapidly because they react with the oxygen in the air, so they are stored under oil to stop them reacting.

Reactions with water

All alkali metals float on water and react strongly to make alkaline solutions. They force hydrogen gas out of the water and make the metal hydroxide.

lithium	+	water	→	lithium hydroxide	+	hydrogen
$2Li$	+	$2H_2O$	→	$2LiOH$	+	H_2

The reaction with water gets more violent as you go down the group.
- Lithium reacts but does not melt because it is the least reactive.
- Sodium melts and moves about the surface of the water as it reacts.
- Potassium melts, moves about the surface and bursts into flame.

Testing for alkali metals

The metals and their compounds give coloured flames.
You can use this to find out which metal is in a compound.
- Lithium burns with a red flame.
- Sodium burns with a yellow flame.
- Potassium burns with a lilac flame.

Alkali metal compounds

Alkali metal compounds melt at high temperatures. They dissolve in water and have colourless solutions.

Many of the compounds are very useful. Sodium chloride is salt, sodium hydrogen carbonate can neutralise acid in upset stomachs. Potassium nitrate is a fertiliser.

Use safety screens and goggles!

Sodium and potassium melt as soon as they are dropped in water. Lithium does not melt because it is the least reactive metal. Caesium is so reactive that it explodes when it touches water.

Now do this

3   Write a word equation for the reaction of sodium with water.

4   Write a balanced chemical equation for the reaction of sodium with water.

Group VII: The halogens

The Group VII elements are called the **halogens**. You need to know about
chlorine, bromine and iodine.

Element	Symbol	Relative atomic mass	Normal state	Colour
fluorine	F	19	gas	
chlorine	Cl	35.5	gas	green
bromine	Br	80	liquid	orange
iodine	I	127	solid	black

Halogens all have seven electrons in the outer shell, so they are very reactive
and they all gain one electron to form a single negative ion. They get *less*
reactive going down the group. Melting points and boiling points increase
going down the group.

The halogens are all very similar non-metals. They are poisonous (bromine
and chlorine should be handled only in a fume cupboard). They are acidic,
they react with metals and their compounds usually dissolve in water.

Reactions with metals

The halogens react with lots of different metals. In each
case they form a salt called a **halide**. Even less reactive
metals, such as iron, will react vigorously with a halogen.

iron + bromine → iron bromide

Reactions with hydrogen

The halogens will all react with hydrogen.
They form hydrogen chloride, HCl;
hydrogen bromide, HBr; and hydrogen
iodide, HI. These compounds are colourless
gases which dissolve in water to give strongly
acidic solutions. A solution of HCl in water
is called hydrochloric acid.

Now do this

1   Write a word equation for the reaction
between hydrogen and chlorine.
2   Sodium chloride has the formula NaCl.
Write a balanced equation for the reaction
between sodium and chlorine.

What are the halogens used for?

Chlorine is used
• as a bleach to get rid of stains
• for killing bacteria in drinking water and in
swimming pools
• for making plastics and insecticides
• to make hydrochloric acid. This has many uses
including etching metals and making plastics.

Iodine is an antiseptic.

Bromine and iodine are used to make silver
bromide and silver iodide. These chemicals turn
black in sunlight, so they are used in
photographic films.

How can you tell which halogens are in a compound?

Dissolve the compound in water, then add
silver nitrate solution.

Chlorine compounds give a white solid
(precipitate) $Ag^+(aq) + Cl^-(aq) \rightarrow AgCl(s)$

Bromine compounds give a cream solid
(precipitate) $Ag^+(aq) + Br^-(aq) \rightarrow AgBr(s)$

Iodine compounds give a yellow solid
(precipitate) $Ag^+(aq) + I^-(aq) \rightarrow AgI(s)$

Group 0: The noble gases

The noble gases are helium, neon, argon, krypton, xenon and radon. They are colourless gases and have almost no reactions. This is because they all have a stable outer shell (usually eight electrons, except helium, which has two), so they don't form any bonds. As their atomic numbers increase down the group their boiling points and densities increase.

Uses of the noble gases

Helium is used to fill balloons because it is light and it will not burn. Neon, argon and krypton are used in different sorts of lights, especially coloured 'neon' lights, and in lasers. They are also used when an inert atmosphere is needed – as a replacement for air if you have a chemical which would react with air.

The transition metals

The **transition metals** contain common metals, such as iron and copper, and also silver and gold. They are all what we normally think of as metals – they conduct electricity and heat, are shiny, hard, strong, dense and have high melting points.

Transition metals and their compounds can make good catalysts, for example iron is the catalyst in the Haber Process for making ammonia.

Compounds of the transition metals

Most of the transition metal compounds are coloured. The colour is due to the metal ion inside the compound. The colour tells you which transition element is present. The blue and green compounds of the copper ion are well known.

Heating the transition metal carbonates

If you heat transition metal carbonates they break apart into carbon dioxide and the metal oxide. The metal oxide is often a different colour from the carbonate. You can show that carbon dioxide is formed because it turns limewater milky.

copper	→	copper	+	carbon
carbonate		oxide		dioxide
green		black		

Remember that sodium carbonate does not break down when heated.

Testing with sodium hydroxide solution

Sodium hydroxide forms a green precipitate with Fe^{2+} ions.

$$Fe^{2+}(aq) + 2OH^-(aq) \rightarrow Fe(OH)_2(s)$$

Sodium hydroxide forms a red-brown precipitate with Fe^{3+} ions.

$$Fe^{3+}(aq) + 3OH^-(aq) \rightarrow Fe(OH)_3(s)$$

Sodium hydroxide forms a blue precipitate with Cu^{2+} ions.

$$Cu^{2+}(aq) + 2OH^-(aq) \rightarrow Cu(OH)_2(s)$$

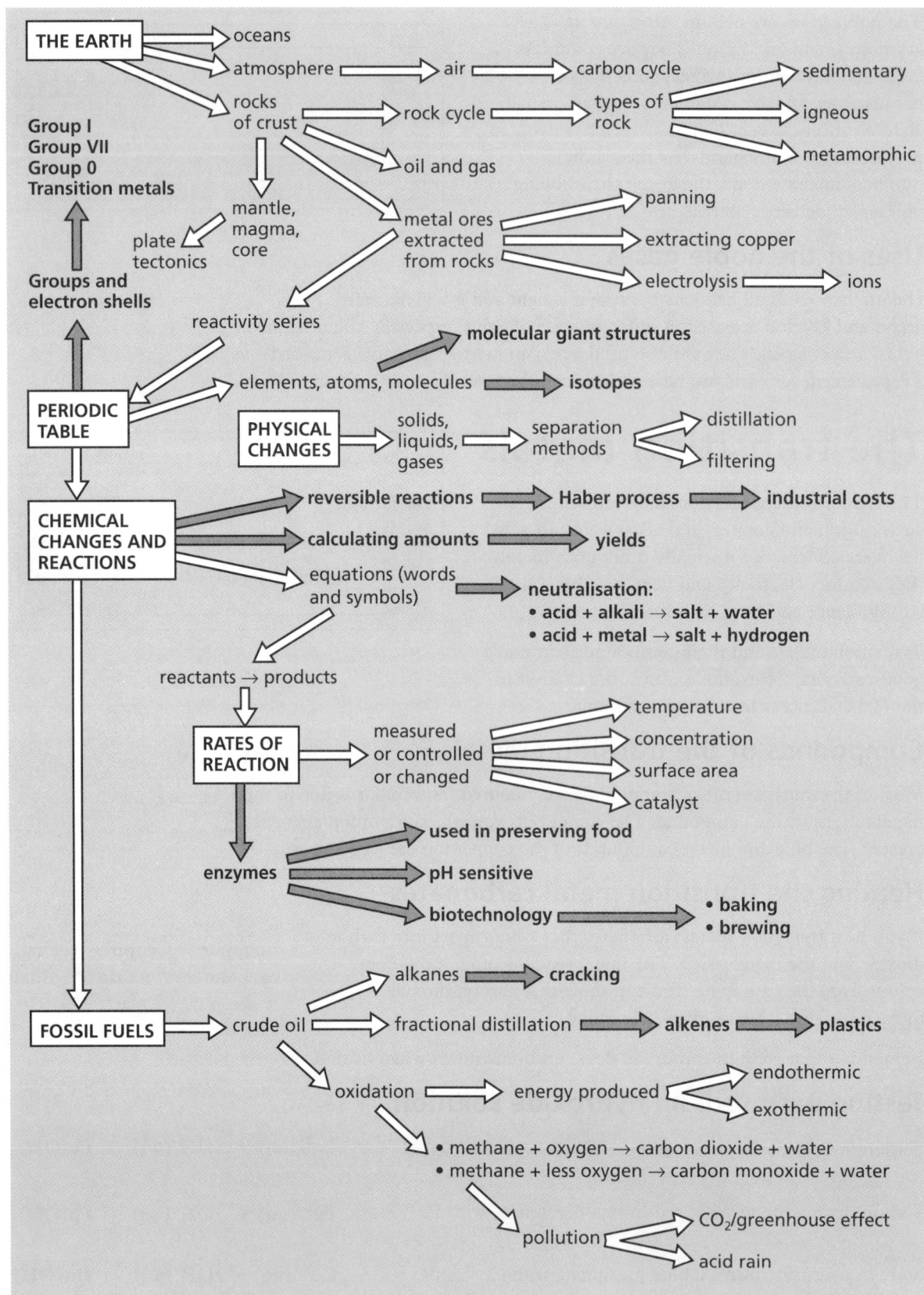

Concept map

THE EARTH → oceans

→ atmosphere ⟹ air ⟹ carbon cycle

⟹ sedimentary
→ igneous
⟹ metamorphic

rocks of crust → rock cycle ⟹ types of rock

Group I
Group VII
Group 0
Transition metals

→ oil and gas

mantle, magma, core

plate tectonics

Groups and electron shells

metal ores extracted from rocks → panning
⟹ extracting copper
⟹ electrolysis ⟹ ions

reactivity series

molecular giant structures

elements, atoms, molecules ⟹ **isotopes**

PERIODIC TABLE

PHYSICAL CHANGES → solids, liquids, gases ⟹ separation methods → distillation
→ filtering

CHEMICAL CHANGES AND REACTIONS → **reversible reactions** ⟹ **Haber process** ⟹ **industrial costs**

→ **calculating amounts** ⟹ **yields**

→ equations (words and symbols) ⟹ **neutralisation:**
• **acid + alkali → salt + water**
• **acid + metal → salt + hydrogen**

reactants → products

RATES OF REACTION → measured or controlled or changed → temperature
→ concentration
→ surface area
→ catalyst

enzymes → **used in preserving food**
→ **pH sensitive**
→ **biotechnology** ⟹ • **baking**
• **brewing**

alkanes ⟹ **cracking**

FOSSIL FUELS → crude oil ⟹ fractional distillation ⟹ **alkenes** ⟹ **plastics**

oxidation ⟹ energy produced → endothermic
→ exothermic

• methane + oxygen → carbon dioxide + water
• methane + less oxygen → carbon monoxide + water

pollution → CO_2/greenhouse effect
→ acid rain

Exam questions

1 The flow chart shows how ammonia is made.

a i Air is a raw material used to make ammonia. Write down the name of the other raw material. [1]

ii Write down two uses of ammonia. [2]

iii What are three of the costs in making ammonia? [3]

b A catalyst is used in this reaction.

i What is a catalyst? [2]

ii Which catalyst is used in this process? [1]

c The Haber Process is a reversible reaction. What is meant by the term 'reversible reaction'? [1]

d The graph shows what percentage of ammonia is produced by the Haber Process at different pressures.

i The plant is usually operated at about 250 atmospheres pressure. What percentage of ammonia should this produce? [1]

ii It is too expensive to build a factory which works at a higher pressure, even though a higher percentage of ammonia would be produced. Suggest one reason why it is more expensive to use a higher pressure. [1]

e The equation for the Haber Process is
$$N_2 + 3H_2 \rightleftharpoons 2NH_3$$
What happens to the position of the equilibrium as the pressure is increased? [1]

[13 marks]

2 When the nuclear power station at Chernobyl released radioactive dust into the air, some of the dust fell on the Lake District in Britain. Sheep ate the dust that settled on the grass and produced radioactive milk. Sheep normally use calcium from the grass to make milk, but this time they were using strontium-90 from the dust as well.

a i Find strontium in the Periodic Table and decide how many protons are in the nucleus of a strontium atom. [1]

ii Strontium-90 is an isotope of strontium. What is the difference between two isotopes of the same element? [1]

b i Use the Periodic Table to decide how many electrons are in the outer shell of a strontium atom. [1]

ii Explain why sheep are likely to take in strontium as well as calcium. [2]

c An element has an atomic number of 13 and an atomic mass of 27.

i How many neutrons are in its nucleus? [1]

ii Write down the number of electrons in each shell, starting with the innermost shell. [1]

[7 marks]

3 Ammonia solution is an alkali. You can make fertiliser by neutralising ammonia solution with an acid. A student investigated neutralisation reactions by adding acid from a burette to alkali in a flask. She measured the pH during the investigation.

a i Suggest the pH of the alkali in the flask at the start. [1]

ii Suggest the pH of the solution when she had added just enough acid to neutralise the alkali. [1]

iii Suggest the pH of the solution if she added one drop too much of the acid. [1]

b Complete the equation
acid + alkali → _____ + water [1]

c The fertiliser that she made was ammonium nitrate, $(NH_4)_2NO_3$.

i How many atoms of nitrogen are in the formula of ammonium nitrate? [1]

ii How many different elements are in ammonium nitrate? [1]

iii The relative atomic mass (A_r) of hydrogen (H) is 1. The relative atomic mass (A_r) of nitrogen (N) is 14. The relative atomic mass (A_r) of oxygen (O) is 16.
What is the relative formula mass of ammonium nitrate? [1]

d If fertilisers contaminate ponds or lakes, wildlife will be harmed.

i What do we call this effect? [1]

ii Briefly describe how the damage is done [3]

[11 marks]

4 Use this diagram of the Periodic Table to help you answer this question.

a i Where on the Periodic Table is the most reactive metal? [2]

ii Where on the Periodic Table is the most reactive non-metal? [2]

b Use ideas about electron shells to explain why the Noble Gases (Group 0) are not reactive. [1]

c Oxygen has eight electrons and is in Group VI.

i How many electrons are in the inner shell of an oxygen atom? [1]

ii How many electrons are in the outer shell of an oxygen atom [1]

d Magnesium has two electrons in its outer shell. What is the charge on a magnesium ion? [2]

[9 marks]

5 Ethane, C_2H_6, and ethene, C_2H_4, are hydrocarbons with slightly different formulae.

a How many atoms of carbon are in a molecule of ethane? [1]

b Hydrogen and carbon are both non-metals.

i What happens to the electrons on the two atoms when they form a bond? [1]

ii A carbon atom has a total of six electrons around its nucleus. How are they arranged in their shells? [2]

c Ethane is part of the alkane group.

i What group is ethene part of? [1]

ii What chemical test could you use to tell the difference between ethane and ethene? [1]

iii What would you see if you tried this test on ethene? [1]

iv State what you would see if you tried this test on ethane. [1]

d Ethene is used to make polythene, a polymer.

i Use the symbol –E– for ethene to draw part of a polythene molecule. [1]

ii Ethene does not form polythene without help. Give two things that you must do so that the ethene will react. [2]

e Use this table about different plastics to answer the questions below.

Plastic	Information
Acrylic	flexible, will take up dyes
Polycarbonate	rigid, tough and transparent
Polythene	flexible, easily formed into thin sheets, very cheap
PVC	can be rigid, tough, fairly cheap

Which plastic would be best for making:

i plastic drainpipes

ii different coloured clothes

iii plastic bags to put shopping in

iv safety spectacles? [4]

[15 marks]

6 We think that wine was first produced by accident when wild yeasts landed on some crushed grapes and made them ferment.

a i What are the three important conditions for fermentation to go well? [3]

ii What are the sugars in the grapes converted to during fermentation? [1]

b Yeast contains biological catalysts called enzymes.

i What does a catalyst do to a reaction? [1]

ii What can you say about a catalyst at the end of a reaction? [1]

c Yeast is also used in breadmaking. What does yeast produce to make the bread rise? [1]

d If bread is left in a cold place the yeast will only work very slowly. What will happen to the speed that the yeast works at as the temperature increases? Explain your answer. [4]

[11 marks]

7 Sodium and chlorine will react to form sodium chloride. Find sodium and chlorine in the Periodic Table.

a i How many electrons are in the outer shell of a sodium atom? [1]

ii How many electrons are in the outer shell of a chlorine atom? [1]

iii What sort of bond is formed when sodium reacts with chlorine? [1]

iv Explain what happens to the electrons as this bond is formed. [2]

b What sort of boiling point will sodium chloride have? [1]

c i Will solid sodium chloride be an electrical conductor or an insulator? [1]

ii Will molten sodium chloride be an electrical conductor or an insulator? [1]

[8 marks]

8 The energy of combustion of a fuel was found out by using it to heat 500 g of water in a beaker. The water temperature went from 20°C to 46°C.

a What do we call reactions that give out heat? [1]

b In what units do we measure heat? [1]

c Calculate the energy transferred by the fuel to the water. (It takes 4.18 J to heat 1 g of water by 1°C.) [2]

d Scientists are worried that burning fuels will add to the greenhouse effect. Explain how the greenhouse effect could raise the temperature of the Earth. [3]

[7 marks]

9 A student wanted to see how fast magnesium reacts with hydrochloric acid. She used the same amount of acid and the same mass of magnesium for each experiment.

a Use the idea of particles to explain why the reaction in beaker B was faster than A. [2]

solid magnesium and dilute acid at 20°C

powdered magnesium and dilute acid at 20°C

b Use the idea of particles to suggest and explain **two** reasons why the reaction in beaker C was faster than D. [4]

c Suggest **two** other ways of speeding reactions up. [2]

[8 marks]

Static electricity

Jo walks across the room. Her feet rub against the carpet, pulling tiny particles (**electrons**) off it. As the number of electrons on her builds up, Jo becomes **charged** with **static electricity**. She acquires a **negative charge** because she has gained some electrons. The carpet acquires a **positive charge** because it has lost electrons.

electrons transferred from carpet to Jo

carpet

$+ + + + + + +$

electrons move quickly from Jo to handle

When Jo reaches the door, she touches the metal handle. All the electrons which she pulled off the carpet flow rapidly through her into the metal handle. She **discharges** herself, but gets an electric shock at the same time.

Conductors and insulators

Materials which allow electrons to move through them are **conductors**. Things which electrons can't move through are **insulators**. Metals and water are conductors. Most other materials (such as glass, wood and plastic) are insulators.

Now do this

1 What can move through conductors but not through insulators?

2 Name two materials which are insulators.

3 Name two materials which are conductors.

4 Copy and complete the following sentences. A nylon comb is an _____. When it passes through hair, _____ are pulled off the hair and carried away by the _____. This leaves the comb _____.

Types of charge

There are two sorts of charge, called **positive** and **negative**. The sort of charge picked up by objects when they are rubbed against each other depends on the two materials involved.

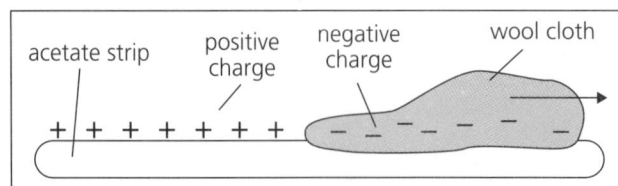

acetate strip

positive charge

negative charge

wool cloth

$+ | + + + + + + | - - - - - - -$

In this example, acetate becomes positive when rubbed with wool. This is because the electrons transferred from the acetate to the wool have a negative charge. The acetate becomes positive because it has lost some negative charge.

Polythene becomes negative when it is rubbed with wool. The wool becomes positive.

Now do this

5 Copy and complete the following sentences. Fur becomes positive when rubbed on glass. This is because electrons are transferred from the _____ to the _____ during the rubbing. Electrons have a _____ charge. Objects which have lost electrons have a _____ charge.

6 When glass is rubbed with silk, electrons are transferred from glass to silk. What are the charges of the glass and the silk after rubbing?

Attraction and repulsion

Objects with any charge attract objects with no charge.
Objects with the same charge always repel each other.
Objects with different charges always attract each other.

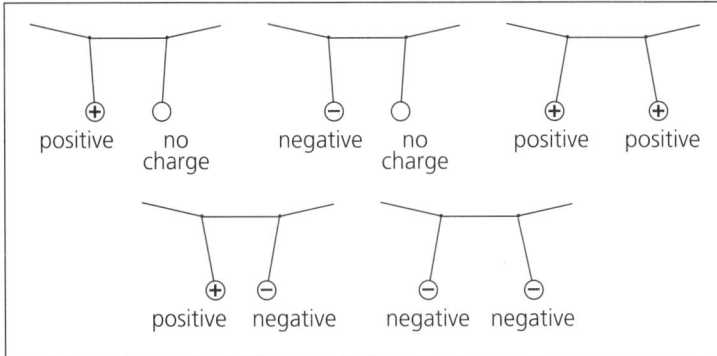

| positive | no charge | negative | no charge | positive | positive |

| positive | negative | negative | negative |

Now do this

7 The table shows the effect of bringing object L close to object R. Complete the table with the words attract and repel.

Charge on L	Charge on R	Effect
positive	negative	
positive	none	
negative	negative	

Using static electricity

Electrostatic forces are very useful.

Droplets of paint spray can be charged. They then repel each other, to give a fine mist which is strongly attracted to any uncharged metal objects nearby. The result is a very even coat of paint on the object, even round the back.

sprayer

pump and power supply

mist of charged paint

paint attracted to back of metal object

Photocopiers and laser printers use static electricity. Reflected light from a document is used to coat an insulating surface with a pattern of positive charge. This attracts tiny particles of negatively charged toner. The pattern of toner is then transferred to paper which has been strongly positively charged. The toner is fixed to the paper by heating to create a copy.

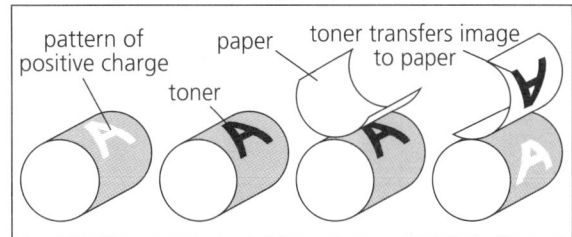

pattern of positive charge   paper   toner transfers image to paper
toner

Electrostatic discharge can be dangerous.

Airplanes in flight become charged as they move rapidly through the air. The charge must be removed safely when the aircraft lands. Otherwise, there may be a **spark** between the airplane and the metal nozzle of the refuelling pipe. The spark (which is a rapid flow of electrons through the air) could ignite the fuel.

Now do this

8 Name two devices which use static electricity.

9 Explain why static charge can be dangerous when flammable substances are present.

10 Suggest why you can get an electric shock when you touch the body of a car after a journey.

Electrical circuits

Here is the **circuit diagram** for a **lamp** connected to a **battery** by a pair of **wires**.

Chemical energy in a cell makes electrons in the metal parts of the circuit flow from the negative terminal ⊖ to the positive one ⊕. A flow of electrons or charge is called a **current**. There is only a current if there is a complete conducting circuit between the terminals of the cell. Several cells make a **battery**. The current is the rate of flow of charge.

$$\text{current} = \frac{\text{charge}}{\text{time}} \qquad I = \frac{Q}{t}$$

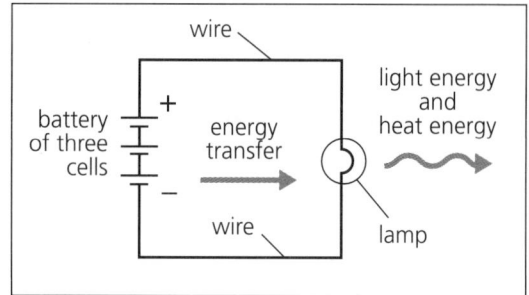

Symbol	Meaning	Units of measurement
I	current	ampere or A
Q	charge	coulomb or C
t	time	second or s

Worked example

Q A current of 250 mA flows in a lamp for 2 minutes. How much charge passes through the lamp?

A $I = 250$ mA $= 0.25$ A
       $Q = ?$
       $t = 2$ minutes $= 120$ s

$$I = \frac{Q}{t}$$

$Q = I\,t \qquad ? = 0.25 \times 120 = 30$ C

Now do this

1 Calculate the charge which flows through a 500 mA lamp in 30 s.

2 If 1200 C of charge passes through a motor in a minute, what is the current in it?

Component	Circuit symbol	Energy output
lamp		light and heat
resistor		heat
buzzer		sound
motor	M	kinetic
LED		light

Now do this

3 Name five different electrical components. Draw their circuit symbols and state what type of energy they produce.

4 Draw the circuit diagram for a motor run off a battery.

Voltage

All electrical components have a **voltage rating**. This should be the same as the voltage of the electricity supply. You can run more than one component from one supply by connecting them in **parallel** with each other. If you put components in **series** with each other, low voltage components can be run off a high voltage supply.

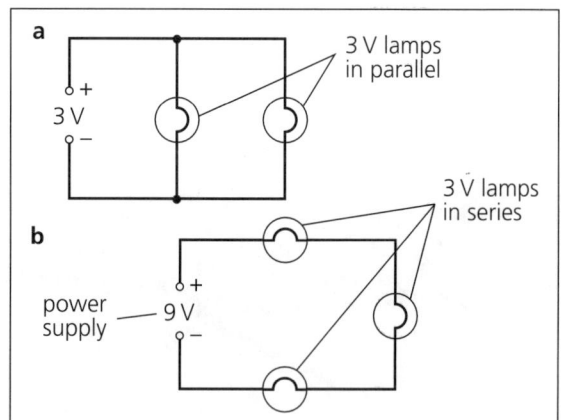

Current

The amount of current in a component is measured with an **ammeter**. The meter is connected in **series** with the component.

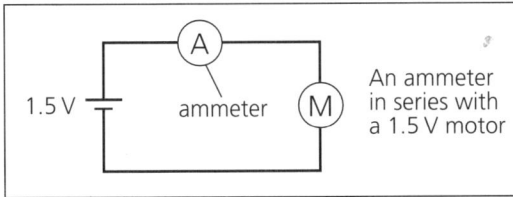

An ammeter in series with a 1.5 V motor

1.5 V — ammeter A M

Current is measured in **amps** (**A**). It has the same value all the way round a series circuit. When components are connected in parallel, the current drawn from the electricity supply is the sum of the currents in the components.

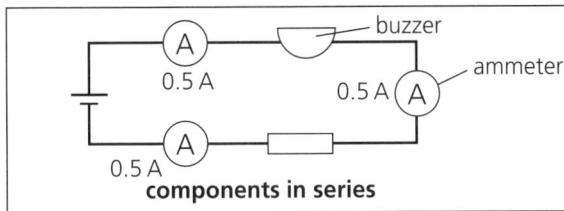

buzzer
A 0.5 A   0.5 A A ammeter
A 0.5 A
components in series

lamps rated at 6 V, 0.5 A
A 2 A   + 6 V –
components in parallel

Measuring voltage

The voltage drop across a component is measured by connecting a **voltmeter** in **parallel** with it. Voltage (or **potential difference**) is measured in **volts** (**V**). The voltage at a point in a circuit is the energy of each coulomb of charge at that point.

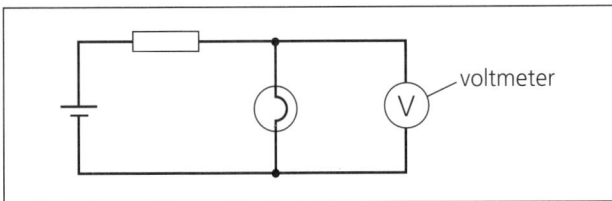

V voltmeter

Types of electricity

There are two **sources** of electrical energy: **direct current** (or **d.c.**) and **alternating current** (or **a.c.**). Batteries supply d.c., dynamos and generators supply a.c.

direct current   CRO   screen
current goes one way

alternating current   CRO   screen
current changes direction
G generator

Now do this

5 Draw a diagram to show how to measure the current in a lamp being run off a 6 V battery.

6 Fill in the readings of the ammeters in this circuit.

+ 3 V A – A
lamp rated at 3 V, 2 A

7 A single 60 W lamp draws a current of 0.25 A when connected to a 240 V supply. How much current will be drawn by 8 bulbs connected in parallel to 240 V?

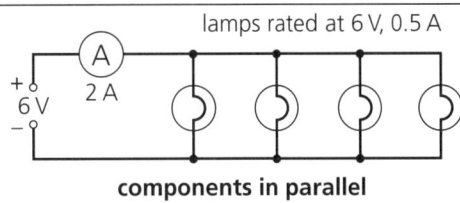

Now do this

8 A resistor and a motor are connected in series with a 12 V battery. Draw a circuit diagram to show how the voltage across the motor can be measured.

9 There is a voltage drop of 12 V across a lamp. How much energy is delivered to the lamp when 8 C of charge flow through it?

A **cathode ray oscilloscope** (or **CRO**) can be used to show the difference between a.c. and d.c. supplies.

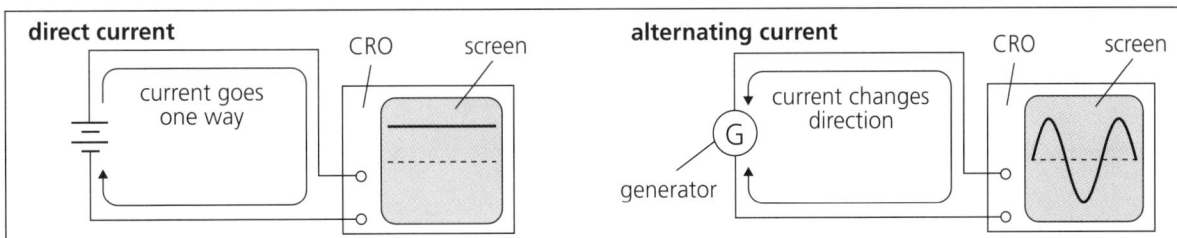

Power

The **power** of an electrical component is given with this formula:

power = current × voltage $P = IV$

Symbol	Meaning	Units of measurement
P	power	joules/s or watts (W)
V	voltage	volts or V
I	current	amperes or A

Worked example

Q There is a current of 2 A in an electric drill connected to 230 V. Calculate the power of the drill.

A $P = ?$ $V = 230\,V$ $I = 2\,A$

$P = I \times V$

$? = 2 \times 230 = 460\,W$

Now do this

1 Write down the symbols and units for power, voltage and current. State the formula relating them.

2 There is a current of 5 A in a lamp connected to a 12 V battery. Calculate the power of the lamp.

3 Draw a circuit diagram to show how an ammeter and a voltmeter should be connected to measure the power of a motor.

4 A 100 W lamp is connected to a 250 V supply. Calculate the current in the lamp.

Resistance

Resistors control the current in a circuit. A big **resistance** means a small current. Two bulbs in series have a larger resistance than just one on its own. A **rheostat** is a variable resistor which controls the current in a circuit by altering its resistance.

As the voltage across a resistor increases, so does the current.

Now do this

5 Which of these circuits has the highest resistance?

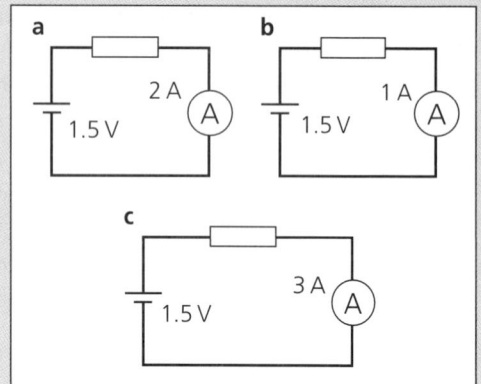

The **resistance** of an electrical component is calculated with this formula:

resistance = $\dfrac{\text{voltage}}{\text{current}}$ $R = \dfrac{V}{I}$

Symbol	Meaning	Units of measurement
R	resistance	ohms or Ω
V	voltage	volts or V
I	current	amperes or A

Worked example

Q There is a current of 0.2 A in a resistor connected to a 3.0 V battery. Calculate the resistance.

A $R = ?$

$V = 3.0\,V$ $R = \dfrac{V}{I}$ $? = \dfrac{3.0}{0.2} = 15\,\Omega$

$I = 0.2\,A$

Now do this

6   Write down the formula for electrical resistance. Explain the symbols and give their units.

7   A resistor has a current of 0.5 A when the voltage across it is 24 V. Calculate its resistance.

8   Show how a rheostat can be used to adjust the brightness of a lamp connected to a battery.

9   What is the current in a 3 Ω resistor when the voltage across it is 12 V?

10 What is the voltage across a 25 Ω resistor when there is a current of 4 A in it?

Switches

Switches are used to control the flow of electrical energy in a circuit. When the switch is **open** charge cannot flow through it. There can only be a current in a switch when it is **closed**.

Temperature and light-sensitive components

Things which contain a lot of free electrons have a low resistance. The number of free electrons in a metal is fixed, but can be changed in a **semiconductor**. The electrons in thermistors and LDRs can be freed by giving them extra energy. Increased light reduces the resistance of a light-dependent resistor (LDR). Similarly, increased temperature reduces the resistance of a thermistor.

Voltage–current curves

These graphs show how the current in a wire resistor and a lamp depend on the voltage across them. Neither of these components have a polarity, so the graphs look exactly the same if the voltage is reversed.

The resistance of a **diode** depends on the voltage across it. The current rises steeply when the **anode** voltage rises above the **cathode** voltage.

Now do this

11 Using the diagram, complete this table with the words **on** or **off**.

Switch L	Switch R	Lamp	Motor
open	open		
open	closed		
closed	open		
closed	closed		

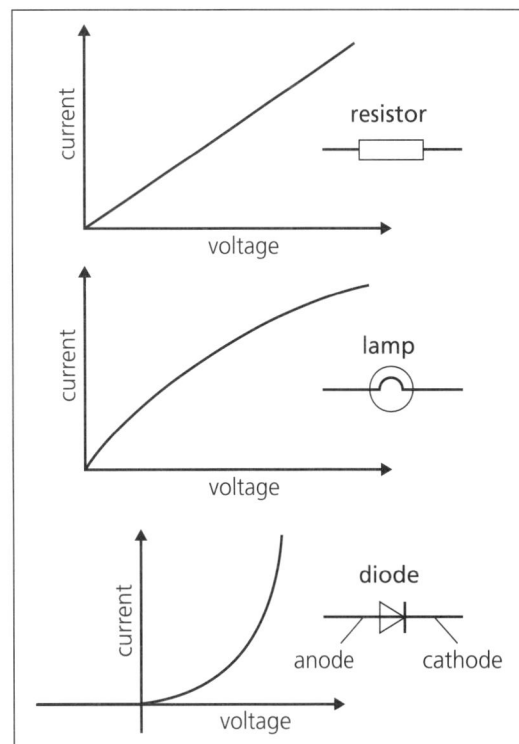

Work, energy and power

Jo lifts up a brick from the floor. She puts it on the table. This increases the **potential energy** (**PE**) of the brick. This extra energy comes from Jo.

| Chemical energy in Jo's muscles | = | Potential energy in the brick | + | Heat energy in Jo |

Jo does work

brick gains energy

Calculating work

The **work** done by Jo equals the PE gained by the brick.

work = force × distance $W = F \times s$

Symbol	Meaning	Units of measurement
W	work	joules or J
F	force	newtons or N
s	distance	metres or m

Worked example

Q   Sam moves a table across the floor, pushing with a force of 20 N. How much work does he do if the table moves 4 m?

A $W = ?$ $F = 20\,N$ $s = 4\,m$

$W = F \times s$ $? = 20 \times 4 = 80\,J$

PE and KE

Moving objects have **kinetic energy** (**KE**). The faster they go, the more KE they have. Like all forms of energy, both PE and KE are measured in joules.

Sam does work on Jo

Jo gains kinetic energy

Now do this

1   Write down the formula for work. Explain the symbols and their units.

2   A brick weighs 25 N. Calculate the work needed to raise a brick by 3 m. How much PE does the brick gain in the process?

3   If 1000 J of work is done lifting a block of weight 50 N, through what height is it raised?

4   50 000 J of work must be done to stop a car going at 10 m/s. If the car stops in a distance of 20 m, how big a force is required?

Now do this

5   Jo applies a force of 50 N to her bike. It moves forwards on level ground. How much KE has it gained after moving 10 m?

6   Which of these situations involve doing work:
   a lifting up a weight from the floor
   b stretching an elastic band
   c holding a weight still above your head
   d thinking out these answers?

Sam throws ball of clay into the air. As it rises, it **transforms** its KE into PE. The clay has maximum PE at the top of its flight. On the way down again, the PE is transformed back into KE. When the clay lands on the ground, all of the KE that Sam gave it becomes heat energy.

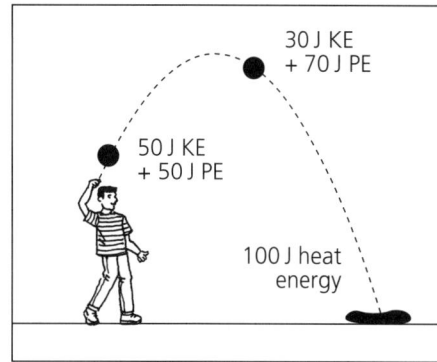

30 J KE + 70 J PE

50 J KE + 50 J PE

100 J heat energy

Now do this

7   Copy and complete the following sentences.
    Sally climbs up the ladder of a slide, transforming
    _____ energy into _____ energy. As she moves
    down the slide, she transforms _____ energy into
    _____ energy. As she slides to a halt at the end,
    all of the KE has become _____ energy.

Calculating KE and PE

KE and PE can be calculated with the help of these formulae.

$$KE = \frac{1}{2}mv^2 \qquad PE = mgh$$

Symbol	Meaning	Unit
KE	kinetic energy	J
PE	potential energy	J
m	mass	kg
v	speed	m/s
g	acceleration of free fall	m/s^2
h	height raised	m

Worked examples

Q   Calculate the KE of a 500 kg car at 15 m/s.

A   KE = ? m = 500 kg v = 15 m/s
        $KE = \frac{1}{2}mv^2$? = $0.5 \times 500 \times (15^2) = 56\,250$ J

Q   A ball has a mass of 0.5 kg. Calculate the increase in PE when it is thrown 20 m into the air. Assume that the acceleration of free fall is 10 m/s^2.

A   PE = ?   PE = mgh m = 0.5 kg g = 10 m/s^2 h = 20 m
        ? = $0.5 \times 10 \times 20 = 100$ J

Now do this

8   Calculate the KE of a 70 kg man running at 10 m/s.

9   Calculate the increase in PE of a 50 kg girl who climbs a vertical distance of 5 m up a ladder.

Machines (such as motors) are often labelled with their **power**. This tells you how much work they can do in a second. A motor with a high power can deliver energy more quickly than one with a low power. So cars with high-power engines can accelerate and climb up hills faster than cars with low-power engines.

$$\text{power} = \frac{\text{work}}{\text{time}} \qquad P = \frac{W}{t}$$

Symbol	Meaning	Units
P	power	watts or W
W	work	joules or J
t	time	seconds or s

Now do this

10   A crane does 1600 J of work in 8 s. Calculate its power.

Worked example

Q   Joe does 2000 J of work lifting bricks up a building. This takes him 50 s. Calculate his power.

A P = ?
        W = 2000 J $P = \frac{W}{t}$ $P = \frac{2000}{50} = 40$ W
        t = 50 s

Electromagnetism

Magnets

Pieces of steel can be made into **magnets** by passing direct current through a coil wrapped around them.

Magnets attract **iron** and **steel** which has not been magnetised. They ignore all other metals except **cobalt** and **nickel**.

Magnetic fields

Here is the **magnetic field** around a bar magnet. Each **field line** has an arrow on it. The field lines tell you which way the needle of a **compass** points.

The two ends of a magnet have different names. One is called the **north pole**. The other is called **south pole**. The field lines come out of the north pole of the magnet and return at the south pole of the magnet.

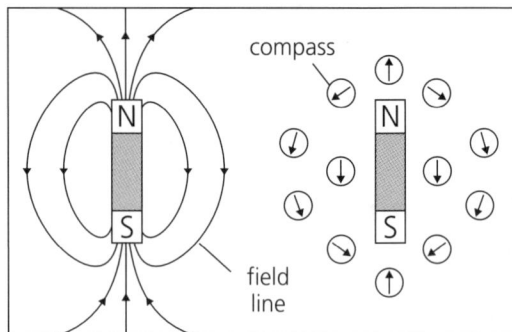

Now do this

1   Name the four materials which are attracted to magnets.

2   Name the pole at T on this magnet.

3   Which way will the compass needle point?

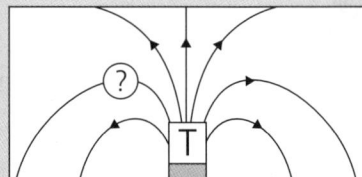

Either pole of a magnet will attract
unmagnetised iron.
Poles which are the same always
repel each other.
Poles which are different always
attract each other.

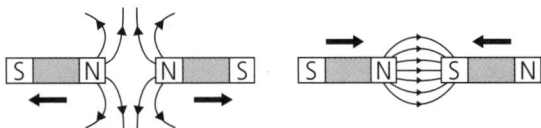

Now do this

4   Here are some pairs of objects. For each pair, state whether they repel, attract or ignore each other.

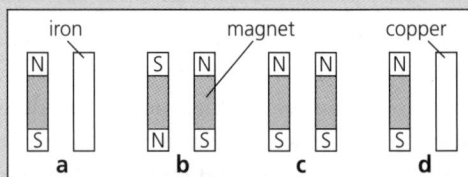

Forces on currents in magnetic fields

There is a **force** on a conductor which carries a current in a magnetic field. The force is at right angles to both the current and the field. The direction of the force can be reversed by reversing the direction of either the current or the field.

Now do this

5   The wire in diagram (a) is pushed to the left. Which way does the wire get pushed in diagrams (b) , (c) and (d)?

Electricity is **generated** whenever a wire is moved through a magnetic field. The voltage changes sign if the wire is moved the other way.

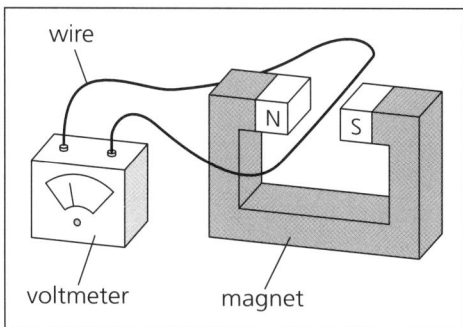

wire

N   S

voltmeter   magnet

The size of the voltage can be increased by speeding up the motion and increasing the strength of the field.

A voltage is **induced** across the ends of a coil of wire whenever the magnetic field inside it changes. The sign of the induced voltage changes when the change of magnetic field is reversed.

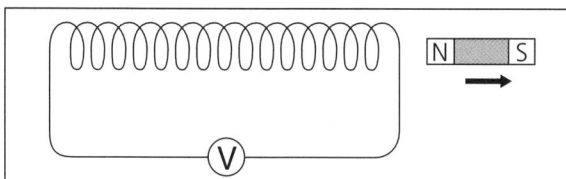

N   S

V

Electricity is generated on a large scale by spinning large coils of copper wire inside the fields of large magnets. The alternating current in the coil is brought out of the **generator** by **brushes** pressing on **slip rings**.

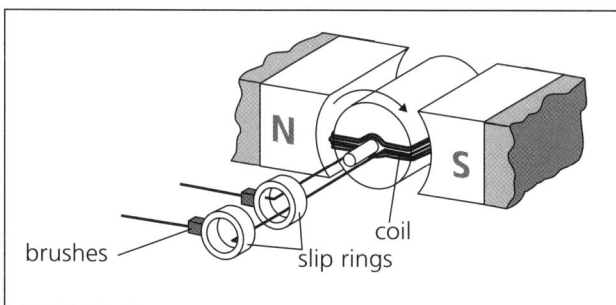

N   S

coil
brushes   slip rings

Now do this

6   The voltmeter reads +0.1V as the wire is pulled up through the poles of the magnet. What will it read when the wire is
   a pushed down
   b held still between the poles of the magnet?

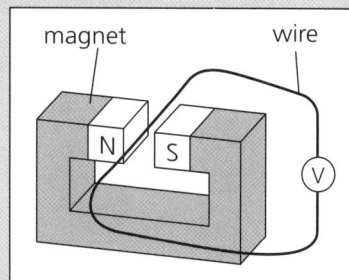

magnet   wire

N   S   V

7   State two things you could do to increase the reading of the voltmeter in question 6.

The size of the voltage can be increased by:
• speeding up the change of magnetic field
• increasing the number of coils of wire
• increasing the area of the coil
• winding the coil around soft iron.

Now do this

8   Copy and complete the following sentences. There is a positive voltage across a coil when a magnet is placed in it. The voltage is _____ when the magnet is left in the coil and becomes _____ as the magnet is removed from the coil.

9   State four ways of increasing the voltage induced in a coil when a magnet is brought close.

Now do this

10   A generator always contains lots of steel, soft iron and copper. Suggest what each material is used for in the generator.

11   Here is the voltage – time graph for a coil spinning in a magnetic field. How would the graph change if the coil spun round twice as fast?

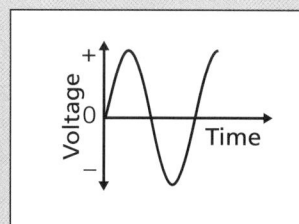

Voltage   +   0   –   Time

Generating electricity

Electricity is made on a large scale by boiling water to make high-pressure **steam**. The steam passes through a **turbine**, making it spin round. The turbine is connected to the shaft of a **generator**. Electromagnets are attached to the shaft. As it spins round, the magnetic field inside the coils of wire changes, generating electricity.

The water can be boiled by burning a fuel (such as coal, oil or gas) or by a nuclear reaction. Here is an energy flow diagram for a typical gas-fired electricity power station.

Efficiency

Each time the energy is **transformed**, some heat energy is lost. Overall, 1000 J of chemical energy in the gas becomes 400 J of electrical energy in the wires coming out of the generator. The remaining 600 J becomes heat energy at various places. The **efficiency** can be calculated with a formula.

$$\text{efficiency} = \frac{\text{useful output}}{\text{input}} \times 100$$

input = 1000 J
useful output = 400 J
efficiency = ?

$$\text{efficiency} = \frac{400}{1000} \times 100 = 40\%$$

The final value for the efficiency is quoted as a percentage. This is why it is sometimes called **percentage efficiency** (% efficiency).

Now do this

1 Describe how electricity is generated from oil.

2 Draw an energy flow diagram for a power station.

3 State the places where heat energy is lost in a power station.

4 Write down the formula for calculating efficiency.

5 200 J of chemical energy in coal becomes 50 J of electrical energy in a power station. Calculate the efficiency of the power station. What happens to the 150 J which doesn't become electricity?

Transporting electricity

Electricity is carried from power stations around the country by the **National Grid**. The electric current in this network of wires generates some heat energy. This is a waste of energy and it reduces the efficiency of the network. The efficiency is improved by keeping the wires in the grid at a very **high voltage**. This reduces the current in the wires, resulting in less wasteful heat energy.

power station generator · step-down transformer

G 115 V · grid wires · 115 000 V · 230 V · LOAD

step-up transformer

1000 kJ of electrical energy from generator → 50 kJ of heat energy in grid wires

→ 950 kJ of useful energy in load

Now do this

6 What is the National Grid? What does it do?

7 For every 1000 kJ of electricity fed into a grid, only 950 kJ can be extracted from it. What happens to the missing energy? Calculate the efficiency of the grid.

8 Explain why running the grid at a high voltage increases the efficiency of electricity transmission.

Transformers are used to raise and lower the voltage of the alternating current as it enters and leaves the grid.

A transformer is a loop of **soft iron**. Alternating current (a.c.) in the **primary coil** (made of **insulated copper**) continually changes the magnetism of the iron. This change of magnetism generates a voltage across the ends of the **secondary coil**.

Transformers have a very high efficiency. Very little electricity gets converted to heat energy on the way through them.

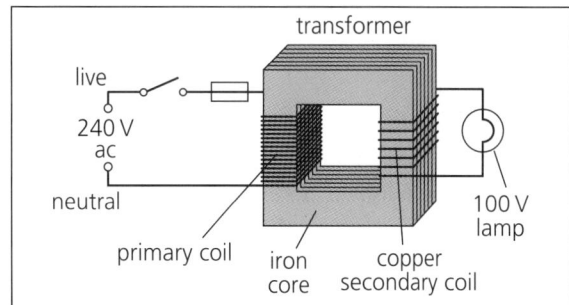

transformer

live · 240 V ac · neutral

primary coil · iron core · copper secondary coil

100 V lamp

$$\frac{\text{primary voltage}}{\text{secondary voltage}} = \frac{\text{primary turns}}{\text{secondary turns}}$$

$$\frac{V_p}{V_s} = \frac{n_p}{n_s}$$

Worked example

Q A transformer steps down 230 V to 12 V. If it has 60 turns of wire in its secondary coil, how many turns does it need in the primary coil?

A $\frac{V_p}{V_s} = \frac{n_p}{n_s}$ so $\frac{230}{12} = \frac{?}{60}$

therefore $? = 60 \times \frac{230}{12} = 1150$

Now do this

9 Draw a labelled diagram of a transformer.

10 Explain why there is always a transformer between a generator and the National Grid.

11 Do transformers operate from a.c. or d.c.?

12 1000 J of electricity enters the primary coil of a transformer. 20 J of heat energy appears in the transformer. Calculate the efficiency of the transformer.

13 The primary and secondary coils of a transformer have 920 and 48 turns of wire. If the primary coil is connected to a 230 V a.c. supply, what voltage appears at the secondary coil?

Gravity

Terminal speed

Jo drops a ball over the edge of a high cliff. As it falls, the ball picks up speed until it reaches its **terminal speed**. The ball stays at that speed until it hits the ground.

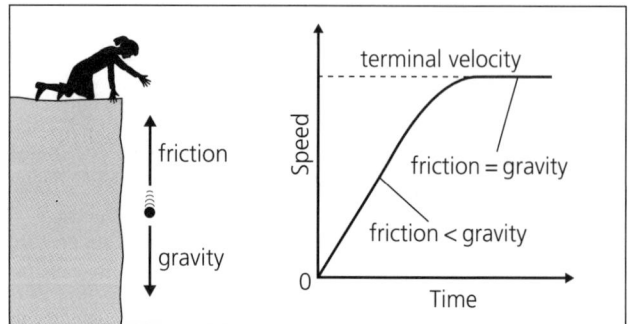

Gravity tugs the ball downwards, towards the centre of the Earth. So the ball speeds up. But as it speeds up, **friction** increases. At the terminal speed, the friction force has the same size as the gravity force.

The two forces become **balanced** – they have the same strength, but act in opposite directions.

Free fall

In the absence of friction, all objects in free fall near the surface of the Earth have the same acceleration. The value of this acceleration g is about 10 m/s^2. So the speed increases by 10 m/s for every second that an object falls, if the friction is negligible.

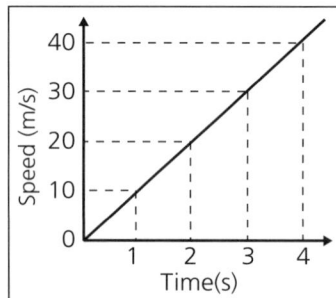

Gravity and weight

The force of gravity on an object is **weight**. It depends on the mass of the object and the acceleration of free fall, g.

weight	=	mass	×	g		
(in newtons)		(in kilograms)		(in metres per second squared or newtons/kilogram)		

The mass of an object does not depend on where it is. This is because mass is fixed by the number and type of atoms. However, the weight of an object changes as it moves from one place to another. This is because the value of g depends on the size and density of the planet. g is sometimes called the **gravitational field strength**.

Now do this

1 Name the two forces on a falling object. In which direction do they act?

2 Copy and complete the following sentences.
When an object is released _____ acts on it, so its _____ increases. The motion through the air produces the force _____ which acts _____. The friction _____ as the speed increases. At the terminal speed, the forces are _____ and the speed _____.

Now do this

3 A ball is dropped down a deep well. It is released from rest and hits the bottom after 3 s. If there is no friction with the air, calculate
a the speed of the ball after 3 s
b the average speed of the ball during its flight
c the depth of the well.

Worked example

Q An astronaut has a weight of 800 N on Earth, where g is 10 m/s^2. What is his weight on the Moon where $g = 1.6$ m/s^2?

A On the Earth: weight = mass × g
800 = mass × 10   so mass = 800/10 = 80 kg
On the Moon: weight = mass × g
weight = 80 × 1.6 = 128 N

Now do this

4 State the formula for calculating weight from mass. What are the units of weight and mass?

5 Explain why the weight of an object depends on its location but its mass does not.

6 Anita weighs 500 N on Earth. What are her mass and weight when she goes to Mars ($g = 4\,m/s^2$)?

Circular motion

The **velocity** of an object tells you two things about it:
- how fast it is moving, in m/s
- the direction in which it is moving.

The size of the velocity is given in m/s.

An arrow gives the direction of velocity.

These objects have the same speed, but different velocities.

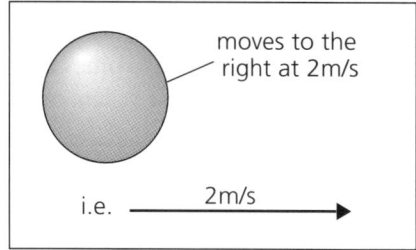

Now do this

7 What is the difference between speed and velocity?

Changing velocity

The velocity of an object does not change if the resultant force is zero. If all the forces balance out (or there are none in the first place), an object moves in a straight line with a constant speed.

If there is a non-zero resultant force, it will **accelerate** the object by changing its velocity.

$$\textbf{force} = \textbf{mass} \times \frac{\textbf{change of velocity}}{\textbf{time taken}}$$

Gravity pulls everything towards everything else.

Sometimes the velocity can be changed just by changing the direction of motion. If the force always acts towards the same point, the object may end up moving in a circle centred on that point. Although the speed of the object does not change, it keeps on changing its direction as it moves. So it is being accelerated by the **centripetal force**.

Gravity provides the centripetal force which keeps a planet in orbit around a star. The star pulls on the planet, continually accelerating it by changing its direction. The **orbit** of a planet can be circular or elliptical.

The planet pulls on the star with the same force as the star pulls on the planet. The acceleration of the star is very small because it has a very large mass.

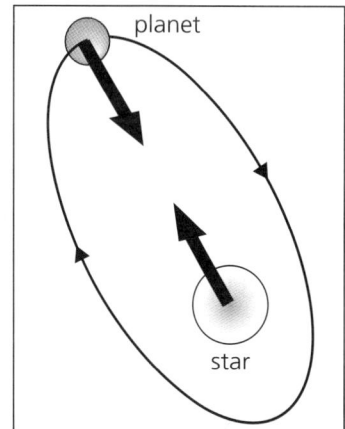

Now do this

8 An object moves in a circle at a constant speed. Which way must the force act on the object?

9 The force of gravity on Joe from the Earth is 750 N towards the centre of the Earth. What is the size and direction of the force of gravity on the Earth from Joe?

10 Name two things that a force can do to an object.

Space

The Earth we live on is a **planet**. It is a sphere of rock, surrounded by a very thin skin of gas and liquid (the atmosphere and oceans). Gravity pulls everything on the Earth towards its centre.

The **Sun** is much larger than the Earth. The Sun is our nearest **star**, a ball of hot gases (mostly hydrogen) which radiates a lot of light and heat energy. That energy comes from **fusion** reactions at the hot centre of the star. These reactions convert hydrogen into helium.

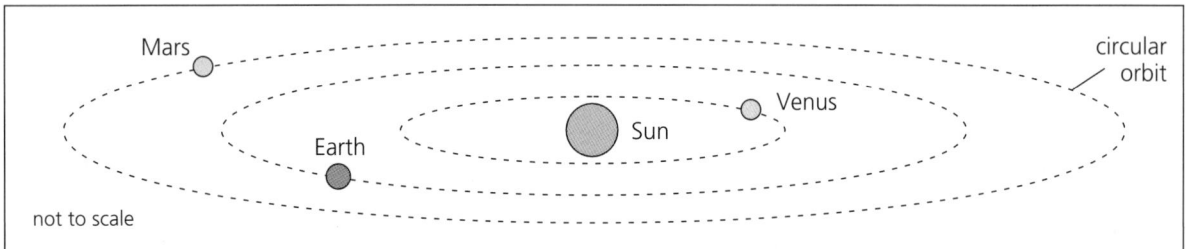

Earth

Mars   circular orbit   Venus   Sun   Earth

not to scale

The Earth is only one of several planets which orbit the Sun. Gravity tugs each planet towards the Sun. This force keeps each planet moving in either a **circle** or an **ellipse** around the Sun.

There is no friction in space, so orbits can keep going for billions of years.

Earth has just one **moon**. It goes once around the Earth in a month. A moon is a smaller lump of rock which orbits around a planet. Many planets have more than one moon.

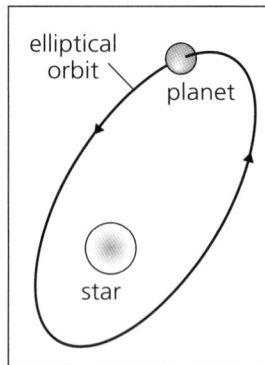

elliptical orbit
planet
star

Now do this

1   Describe a planet.

2   Describe a star.

3   Describe the motion of a planet around a star. Why does it move this way?

The Universe

The Sun, its planets and their moons make up a **solar system**. There are billions of solar systems clumped together in our local **galaxy**, the Milky Way. The **Universe** contains billions of different galaxies, separated by empty space.

Theories of the Universe
Until 450 years ago scientists thought (wrongly) that:

• the Earth was at the centre of the Universe
• the Sun took 24 hours to orbit once around the Earth, giving day and night
• the stars were all fixed on a sphere which rotated around the Earth.

Now do this

4   Here is a list of objects. Write it out in order of size. Start with the smallest.
     galaxy   moon   star   solar system
     Universe   planet

5   What is the difference between a planet and moon?

Moon orbiting Earth
outer sphere with stars and planets
fixed central Earth
Sun orbiting Earth

We now know that:

- the Earth orbits the Sun, taking one year to go round once
- day and night are caused by the Earth spinning, taking 24 hours to spin round once
- the stars are far away, at various distances, and only move very slowly.

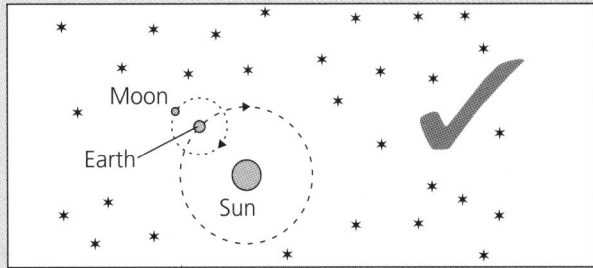

Now do this

6 Copy and complete the following sentences.
A year is the time for the _____ to orbit the _____. A day is the time for the _____ to spin once on its axis. A month is the time for the _____ to orbit the _____.

7 Explain why the stars appear to move across the sky at night.

The origin of the Universe

The Universe is about 15 billion years old. Scientists have evidence that it started with a Big Bang and has evolved into what we see around us today. Here are the main events in its life so far.

To start with, space is completely empty …
… then all the matter and energy suddenly appears at one point …
… the Universe expands rapidly, getting cooler as it does so …
… until, after 300 000 years, stable atoms of hydrogen and helium condense out …
… gravity makes these clouds of gas shrink, heating them up at the same time …
… until the temperature of the star reaches 15 million °C …
… and nuclear fusion begins to convert hydrogen into helium …
… and the heat generated stops the star collapsing further …
… after 10 billion years most of the hydrogen in the star's core is used up …
… so gravity collapses it a bit more, and helium atoms fuse to form heavier elements …
… when the core is mostly iron it becomes unstable and the star explodes as a supernova …
… the energy of the explosion creates a vast quantity of different atoms …
… which form a large cloud of dust and hydrogen …
… which gravity pulls in to form more stars …
… with planets orbiting around them.

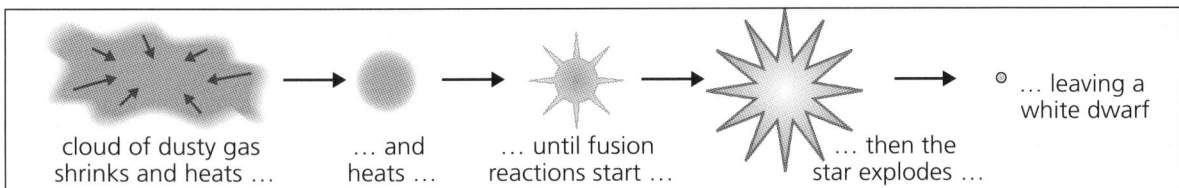

cloud of dusty gas shrinks and heats …   … and heats …   … until fusion reactions start …   … then the star explodes …   … leaving a white dwarf

Now do this

8 Write out a brief history of the Universe from the Big Bang to the present day.

Only very large stars explode. Smaller ones (like our Sun) will just run out of fuel and collapse into a cold lump.

Radioactivity

Some atoms have a nucleus which is unstable. It can break up, spitting out fragments which have a lot of energy. This process is called **radioactivity**.

All atoms contain a small **nucleus** at their centre. Most of the **mass** and all of the **positive charge** of an atom are in this nucleus.

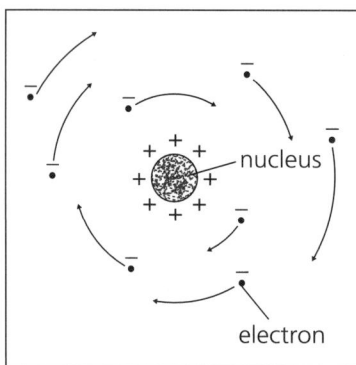

nucleus

electron

The rest of the mass and all of the **negative charge** are in the **electrons** which move around the rest of the atom.

Now do this

1 Describe the structure of an atom.

2 What is the charge of a nucleus?

3 What is the charge of an electron?

4 What is radioactivity?

Types of radiation

There are three different **nuclear radiations** from radioactive substances:

- **alpha (α) particle,** which is a heavy, positive helium nucleus
- **beta (β) particle**, which is a light, negative electron
- **gamma (γ) ray**, which is an electromagnetic wave with no charge.

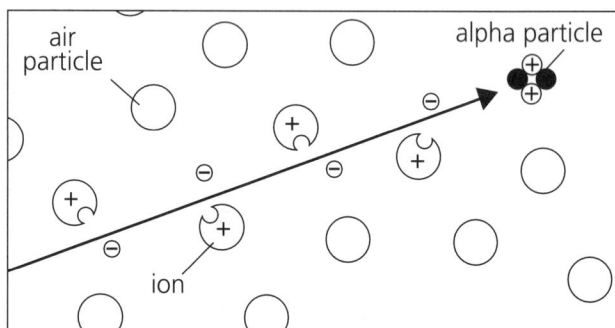

air particle

alpha particle

ion

All three radiations cause **ionisation** of the matter they pass through. They do this by knocking electrons out of the atoms which they pass through, leaving **ions**. The ions are positively charged.

Alpha particles are the least penetrating radiation. They can be stopped by a sheet of paper. Beta particles are stopped by a few millimetres of aluminium. Gamma rays can pass through several centimetres of lead, so they are the most penetrating.

paper   5 mm aluminium   ~5 cm lead

α   alpha

β   beta

γ   gamma

Dangers of radiation

Nuclear radiations are dangerous to living things. The ionisation that they cause can kill cells or change their genetic structure. Too much exposure to nuclear radiation can result in cancer.

Now do this

5 Name the three different nuclear radiations.

6 Which part of an atom does nuclear radiation come from?

7 State the charge of each of the nuclear radiations.

8 Name the radiation which **a** has the greatest mass **b** is a wave **c** is a nucleus **d** is an electron.

9 Here is a list of radiations. Write them down in order of ability to penetrate solids. Start with the least penetrating power.

  beta   gamma   alpha

Background radiation

We are exposed to radiation all the time. There are several causes of this background nuclear radiation:
- radioactive atoms, such as uranium, in rocks
- radioactive gases, such as radon, from the soil
- fallout from nuclear bomb tests and nuclear power stations
- cosmic rays from space.

Radioactive decay

The **activity** of a radioactive material goes down as time goes on. When the last unstable nucleus has split, the material is no longer radioactive. Some materials take a long time to decay, others are only radioactive for a short while.

Activity is measured in **becquerels** (**Bq**). It tells you the rate at which atoms are changing. So if the activity is 365 Bq, there are, on average 365 atoms decaying in one second.

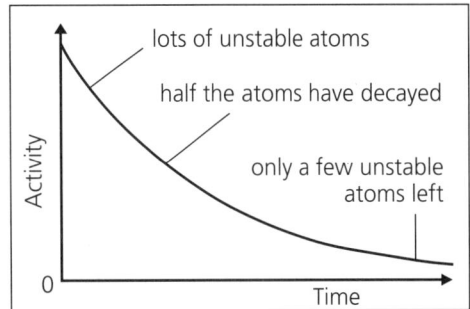

Now do this

10 Name the four sources of background radiation.

11 A radioactive source has an activity of 100 Bq. How many atoms in it decay in a minute?

12 How does the activity of a radioactive material change with time? Explain why.

The **half-life** of an element is the amount of time it takes for half of the atoms to decay. Each element has its own half-life.

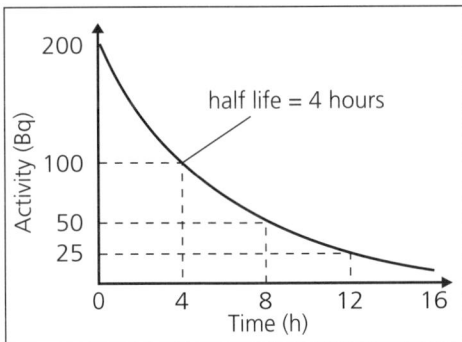

Worked example

Q A radioactive source has a half-life of 3 hours. If its activity is 400 Bq now, what will it be in 12 hours time?

A

Time (hours)	0	3	6	9	12
Activity (Bq)	400	200	100	50	25

so the final activity will be 25 Bq

Uses of radioactivity

Here are some uses of nuclear radiation and radioactive substances.
- Uranium can be used to boil water in a nuclear power station.
- Gamma rays can be used to sterilise surgical instruments.
- Alpha particle sources are used in smoke alarms.
- Beta particle sources can be used to measure the thickness of sheets of material.
- Gamma rays can be used to kill cancer tumours.
- Radioactive materials make good tracers in plants and people.
- The age of rocks can be measured with radioactivity.

Now do this

13 State one use for
  a alpha particles
  b beta particles
  c gamma rays
  d uranium.

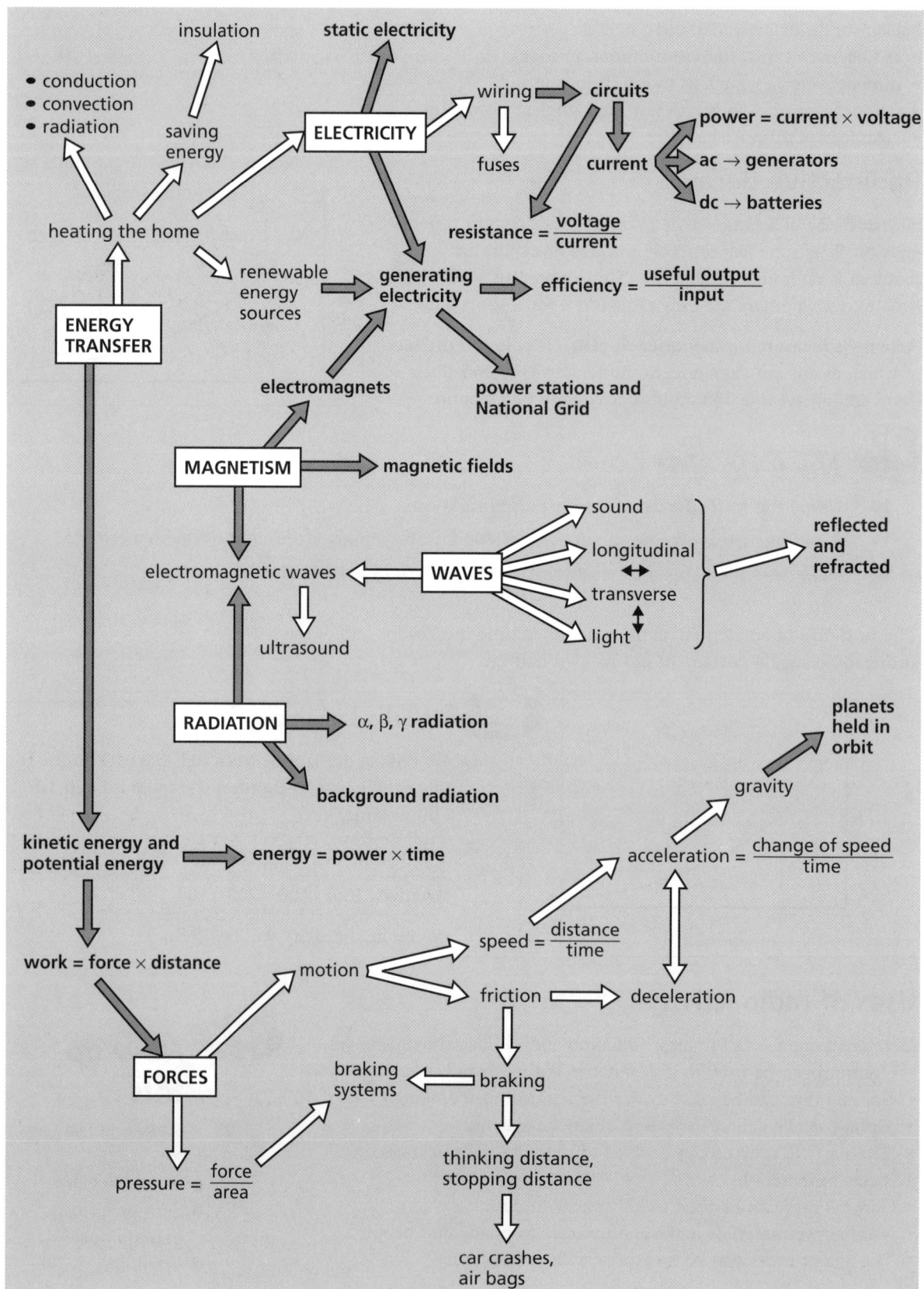

Concept map

insulation

static electricity

- conduction
- convection
- radiation

saving energy

heating the home

wiring → **circuits**

ELECTRICITY

fuses

current

power = current × voltage

ac → generators

dc → batteries

$$resistance = \frac{voltage}{current}$$

renewable energy sources

generating electricity

$$efficiency = \frac{useful\ output}{input}$$

ENERGY TRANSFER

electromagnets

power stations and National Grid

MAGNETISM → **magnetic fields**

electromagnetic waves ← **WAVES**

sound

longitudinal ↔

transverse

light ↕

reflected and refracted

ultrasound

RADIATION → α, β, γ **radiation**

background radiation

planets held in orbit

gravity

kinetic energy and potential energy → **energy = power × time**

$$acceleration = \frac{change\ of\ speed}{time}$$

work = force × distance

motion

$$speed = \frac{distance}{time}$$

friction → deceleration

FORCES

braking systems ← braking

thinking distance, stopping distance

$$pressure = \frac{force}{area}$$

car crashes, air bags

Exam questions

1 The diagram below shows an electrical circuit with a lamp and a motor.

The switch is open. The lamp glows dimly. The motor rotates slowly.

a Explain what happens to the lamp and the motor when the switch is pressed. Use your idea of electric current. [3]

b Look at the table.

component	power	voltage
lamp	6 W	12 V
motor	24 W	12 V

i The lamp and motor run off the same 12 V battery. Draw a diagram to show how. [1]

ii Which will have the greatest current? Explain your answer. [2]

iii Calculate the current drawn from the battery. [3]

[9 marks]

2 Mel measures the power of a motor connected to a cell.

a She uses a voltmeter and an ammeter. Draw a circuit to show this. [2]

b The voltmeter reads 1.2 V. The ammeter reads 0.6 A.

i Calculate the power of the motor. [3]

ii Calculate the resistance of the motor. [3]

c Mel puts a rheostat in series with the motor. This allows her to change its speed. Use your idea of resistance to explain this. [3]

[11 marks]

3 Sam combs his hair. His hair becomes positively charged.

a Use your idea of electrons to explain why his hair becomes charged. [3]

b Sam's hair stands on end after it is combed. Explain why. [2]

c Sam uses a plastic comb. Julie uses a metal comb. Her hair does not get charged. Why? [2]

[7 marks]

4 a Jane is driving a car. She puts on the brakes.

i Complete the sentence.
The brakes transfer the _____ energy of the car into _____ energy. [2]

The brakes exert a force of 500 N on the car. It stops in a distance of 20 m.

ii Calculate the work done on the car by the brakes. [3]

iii The car can stop in less than 20 m when it goes uphill. Use your idea of energy to explain why. [3]

b Jane pushes hard on the accelerator for 10 s. The engine transfers 50 000 J of kinetic energy to the car.

i Calculate the power of the engine. [3]

ii 200 000 J of chemical energy was transferred into the engine during the 10 s. Calculate the efficiency of the engine. [3]

[14 marks]

5 The diagram below shows an electromagnet.

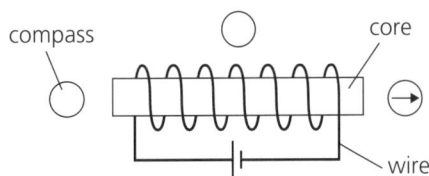

a What is the best material to use for the core? [1]

b Write down **two** things you could do to increase the strength of the electromagnet. [2]

c There are three compasses near the electromagnet. The needle has been drawn for one compass.

   i Draw in the other two needles. [2]

  ii What could you do to make the needles face in the opposite direction. [1]

[6 marks]

6 A power station burns coal to make electricity.

a Complete the sentences, choosing from:
generator   turbine   furnace transformer   boiler
The coal is burnt in the _____. The heat energy turns water into steam in the _____. The steam passes through the _____ to make kinetic energy. This is transferred to electrical energy by the _____. The voltage of the electricity is raised by a _____. [5]

b The station uses 250 MJ of chemical energy in the coal to make 75 MJ of electrical energy. Calculate the efficiency of the power station. [2]

c Useless heat energy appears at various places in the power station.

   i Describe three of the places. [3]

  ii Explain why the heat energy is useless [1]

[11 marks]

7 Earth and Venus are planets in the Solar System. Look at the diagram. It is not drawn to scale. There is a star at the centre.

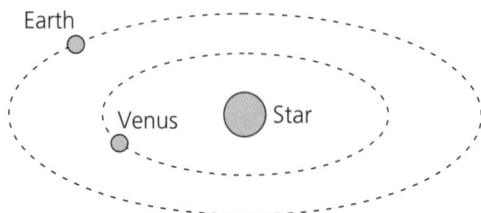

a What is the difference between a planet and a star? [1]

b Stars are kept hot by fusion. Describe the fusion reaction. [3]

c Stars start off as a large cloud of dust and gas. Explain how this can become a star. [4]

d Suggest what will happen to a star when its fusion reactions stop. Give an explanation. [2]

[10 marks]

8 There are satellites in orbit around the Earth.

a Name the force which keeps a satellite in orbit around the Earth. [1]

b Explain why there are satellites around the Earth. [2]

c The MEG satellite takes 90 minutes to orbit the Earth. It is 200 km above the Earth. The OCR satellite is 3000 km above the Earth.

   i What is its orbit time? Choose from:
less than 90 minutes   exactly 90 minutes more than 90 minutes [1]

  ii Explain your answer. [2]

[6 marks]

9 Radioactivity is dangerous.

a Why is radioactivity dangerous? [2]

b Explain why a piece of radioactive material becomes less dangerous as time goes on. [3]

c A radioactive source has an activity of 500 Bq now. Its half-life is 10 days. Calculate the activity of the source in 30 days time. [3]

[8 marks]

10 An LED is connected in series with a 3 V battery and a resistor.

a Draw the circuit diagram [1]

b Complete the sentences.
Choose from:
heat   light   sound   chemical   electrical

_____ energy in the battery becomes _____ energy in the wires. The LED transforms _____ energy into _____ energy [4]

c The voltage across the LED is 2 V when the current in it is 0.05 A.

   i Explain why the voltage across the resistor is 1 V. [1]

  ii Calculate the resistance of the resistor. [3]

[9 marks]

11 Complete the sentences.
Radioactivity is cause by the breakup of the
_____ of an atom. Two of the
radiations from radioactive materials are
particles. These radiations are called
_____ and _____ . The
radiation which is a wave is called
_____ . **[4 marks]**

12 a Here are the names of some waves:
infra-red, microwaves, radio,
ultrasound, X-rays.

 i Which wave is longitudinal? [1]

 ii Which wave has the longest wavelength? [1]

 iii Which wave can cause cancer? [1]

 iv Which wave can detect airplanes? [1]

 v Two of the waves can be used to find
broken bones. Which two? [2]

 b Infra-red can pass down optical fibres.

 i Describe what happens to a ray of infra-red
as it passes from air into glass. [2]

 ii Describe what happens to a ray of infra-red
when it hits the side of the fibre. [2]

 [10 marks]

13 Avril is going to install central heating in
her home. She can choose gas or electricity.

 a Write down one advantage and one
disadvantage of using electrical
central heating. [2]

 b It costs Avril £2000 to keep the inside of
her house at 25°C all winter.

 i State one thing that Avril could do to
reduce her heating bill. [1]

 ii Explain why it would reduce the heating
bill. [2]

 c Avril loses a lot of heat energy through the
roof of her house. Complete the sentences.
Choose from:
conduction, radiation, diffusion, convection.
Heat energy passes through the tiles of the
roof by _____ . Heat energy is
transferred from the surface of the roof by
_____ and _____ . [3]

 [8 marks]

14 Ann charges up a strip of plastic.

 a i Describe what Ann could do to charge the
plastic. [1]

 ii Use the idea of electrons to explain the
charging of the plastic. [2]

 b Ann knows that polythene rubbed with wool
becomes negatively charged. Describe an
experiment that Ann could do to find the
type of charge on her piece of plastic. [3]

 [6 marks]

15 A transformer has 1150 turns in its primary
coil and 30 turns in its secondary coil. Both
coils are wound on a metal core.

 a Suggest the best material for the core.
Explain why it is the best. [2]

 b If the primary coil is connected to a 230 V
supply, calculate the voltage across the
secondary coil. [2]

 c Use the idea of changing magnetic fields to
explain how a transformer works. [3]

 [7 marks]

16 Julie throws a ball high into the air. The ball
has a mass of 0.3 kg. The ball leaves Julie's
hand with 60 J of kinetic energy and 30 J of
potential energy.

 a Show that the ball leaves Julie's hand with a
speed of 20 m/s. [2]

 b At the top of its flight, the ball has 80 J of
potential energy.

 i How much kinetic energy does it have? [1]

 ii How high above the ground does the
ball rise? [3]

 c If the ball stays on the ground when it hits
it, what happens to its energy? [1]

 [7 marks]

Pages 2 and 3

2 Maggots, grass, oak tree.

3 **a** chloroplasts **b** cell membrane **c** cell wall.

4 To allow more room to take up oxygen.

Pages 4 and 5

1 Digestion is the breakdown of large food molecules into small soluble ones.

2 Bile is produced in the liver. It is released into the intestine to emulsify fats.

3 Enzymes speed up the breakdown of food.

4 Stomach acid provides the right conditions for stomach enzymes to work: kills microbes on food.

5 Stomach, pancreas.

6 If it is too cold enzymes do not move around very quickly and therefore they do not work very efficiently; too hot, and they are destroyed (denatured).

7 The small intestine is long, with lots of thin-walled villi to increase the surface area for absorption.

8 Peristalsis is the muscular contractions which squeeze food through the digestive system. It is so important because it ensures that food does not normally get stuck in the digestive system.

Pages 6 and 7

1 Any three from: water, digested food (e.g. glucose), hormones, waste products, urea, carbon dioxide.

2 They contain the oxygen carrier haemoglobin; they have no nucleus, therefore more room for haemoglobin, and they have a large surface area to take up more oxygen.

3 Oxygen enters in the lungs and leaves at respiring cells; carbon dioxide enters at respiring cells and leaves at the lungs; food enters at the small intestine and leaves at respiring cells.

4 It allows oxygen to be given up easily when the oxyhaemoglobin arrives at respiring cells.

5 Any two from: arteries have a narrow lumen; thick, elastic, muscular walls; contain blood at high pressure; do not contain valves. Veins have a wide lumen; thin, muscular walls; walls lack elastic fibres; blood at low pressure; contain valves.

6 It allows oxygenated blood to be sent from the heart at a higher pressure, giving a greater rate of flow to the tissues.

7 Right ventricle, left ventricle.

8 To prevent blood flowing backwards when the heart contracts.

9 There are valves in veins, to prevent the backflow of blood.

Pages 8 and 9

1 We need oxygen to release energy from food in respiration.

2 In the alveoli there is a higher concentration of oxygen than in the blood. Therefore oxygen moves down the diffusion gradient into the blood.

3 Three from: large surface area; thin walls; moist surface to aid diffusion; good transport system to carry the gases away.

4 Inhalation – diaphragm contracts and flattens, rib cage lifts, moving out and up; this increases the volume of the chest cavity and sucks air in. Exhalation – the diaphragm domes upwards, the ribs are lowered, the volume of the chest cavity decreases; therefore air is forced out.

5 The bronchi and larger bronchioles have cartilage to support them so that they do not collapse when the air pressure changes during exhalation.

6 Some of the chemicals in cigarette smoke are corrosive and attack the delicate lining of the alveoli, others stop the cilia beating; this causes mucus and trapped bacteria and dirt to accumulate in the lungs and set up infections.

Pages 10 and 11

1 Pressure receptors in the skin; chemical receptors in the nose; light receptors in the eye; pressure receptors in the ear, and the semi-circular canals.

2 Retina contains the light-sensitive cells to respond to the different patterns of light; iris controls the amount of light entering the eye; optic nerve carries messages to the brain; lens bends the light so that it can come to a focus on the retina.

3 Circular muscles in the iris contract and the radial muscles relax to make the pupil small.

4 Motor neurones are very long, enabling them to cover long distances in the body; often insulated to speed up transmission of the message; end at effectors such as muscles or glands.

5 Synapse is the tiny gap between two different neurones. Synapses ensure that messages can only pass in one direction along a neurone.

6 Stimulus, pain of dog bite – pain receptor in skin – sensory neurone – central nervous system – motor neurone – arm muscle – hand moves away from the dog.

Pages 12 and 13

1 Three from: start their menstrual cycle (have periods); develop breasts; grow pubic and underarm hair; grow taller.

2 Hormones are released into the blood and travel to their target sites in the blood as it travels around the body, whereas nervous messages travel in a direct route.

3 A pregnant woman maintains a high level of progesterone to keep the uterus lining in place for the baby to develop in, therefore the uterus lining cannot come away as menstruation.

4 It prevents the ovaries releasing eggs.

5 Oestrogen helps to repair and build up the lining of the uterus.

Pages 14 and 15

1 Two from: regulate plant shoot and root growth; control ripening of fruits; control flowering.

2 Auxins dissolve in water to move around the plant.

3 Light and gravity. Light is needed so that the plants can photosynthesise and produce the materials needed for them to grow; gravity ensures that whichever way a seed is planted, the roots will always grow down into the soil to obtain water and minerals.

4 Two from: rooting compound to ensure cuttings start to produce roots and shoots; selective weedkiller because it can accelerate the growth of certain plants to such an extent that they become too weak and die; enables farmers to pick fruit before fully ripe and then to complete ripening when required.

5 A selective weedkiller is one which kills only certain types of plants, and leaves others unharmed.

6 The shoot is positively phototropic and grows up towards the light; the root grows down towards gravity.

Page 16

1 The habitat – non-living part; the populations – the living part.

2 a Insects and other very small creatures.

b Plants.

c Small nocturnal animals.

Pages 18 and 19

1 a Producer – heather; primary consumer – rabbit, grouse, bees, deer; predator – fox, eagle.

b Any two starting with heather,
e.g. heather → grouse → fox.

c Should show a normal pyramid shape.

2 Light energy.

3 A food chain shows only one feeding relationship, whereas a food web is more realistic and shows many more feeding relationships.

4 In a pyramid of numbers, one oak tree is represented as the same as one grass plant, or one mouse. If you use the mass of each, you take account of their relative sizes.

5 Energy is lost at each trophic level, therefore there is insufficient energy to sustain more than four or five trophic levels.

Pages 20 and 21

1 Fungi and bacteria.

2 Decomposers recycle nutrients which would otherwise be locked away inside dead things.

3 Deforestation involves removal of trees, which would otherwise be removing carbon dioxide from the atmosphere for photosynthesis; burning these trees, or increased burning of fossil fuels, is increasing carbon dioxide in the atmosphere; increase in population leading to increased demand for cars, higher standard of living etc. leading to more fossil fuels being burnt and more carbon dioxide in the atmosphere.

4 Photosynthesis.

5 Nitrogen-fixing bacteria change nitrogen into nitrates; denitrifying bacteria convert nitrates into nitrogen; nitrifying bacteria convert ammonia into nitrates.

6 Beans have root nodules with nitrogen-fixing bacteria in. They therefore put a lot of nitrates back into the soil when ploughed in.

Page 23

1 Use – fertilisers to increase growth; pesticides to reduce crop damage and loss; herbicides to reduce losses caused by competition; intensive practices; biological control.

2 Pesticide increases yield, but may get into the food chain and kill other organisms which would naturally eat some of the pest species, leading to more pesticide required in subsequent years. It is also costly.

3 Nitrate rich materials drain through the soil and into waterways. Here they encourage growth of surface algae cutting off light to the plants below. These plants die and decompose, leading to the death of all the other living things in the waterway.

4 For example – more household waste, overcome by increasing public awareness and recycling facilities. Increased car use adding to the greenhouse gases, overcome by increased public awareness and improved public transport systems.

Pages 28 and 29

1 Hydrogen sulphide, sugar, nitric acid.

2 Salt and sand, salty water.

3 Evaporate; filter; filter, evaporate; dissolve, filter, evaporate.

Pages 30 and 31

1 Particles can move through the container. Particles are randomly arranged.

2 Particles are held in position and can't move closer.

3 Gets warm, difficult to change back again.

4 Condensed, dissolve, solvent, solution.

Pages 32 and 33

1

Formula	No. of atoms in formula	No. of different elements
HCl	2	2
H_2O	3	2
CH_4	5	2
$AlCl_3$	4	2
H_2SO_4	7	3
$C_6H_{12}O_6$	24	3

2 H_2S

3 NH_3

4 $MgCl_2$, Fe_2O_3

5 Reactant side: 1 atom of Mg, 2 atoms of O.
Product side: 2 atoms of Mg, 2 atoms of O.
Equation doesn't balance.

Reactant side: 1 atom of C, 4 atoms of H and 4 atoms of O.
Product side: 1 atom of C, 2 atoms of O and 4 atoms of H, 2 atoms of O.
Equation balances.

6   2, 2, 3, 4, 3

Page 35

1   Increase temperature, increase concentration of acid, increase surface area of the carbonate (use smaller pieces).

2   Increase temperature and concentration.

3   A. The slope is the steepest.

4   C

Page 37

1   Broken: $4 \times$ C—H, $1 \times$ Cl—Cl.
    Made: $3 \times$ C—H, $1 \times$ C—Cl, $1 \times$ H—Cl.

2   $400 \times 4.5 \times 4.2 = 7560$ J

3   Carbon dioxide, greenhouse, ultraviolet, infra-red, sulphur dioxide.

Pages 38 and 39

1   Respiration, combustion.

2   Photosynthesis.

3   80%, 20%, 0.04%, oxygen, carbon dioxide, respiration, combustion.

Pages 40 and 41

1–3 See page 40.

4   **a** Underneath, into the mantle   **b** they melt.

5   They get older.

Pages 42 and 43

1   Large, igneous, metamorphic.

2   Weathering, sedimentary, metamorphic, upthrust.

Pages 44 and 45

1   300°C, 100°C, 200°C.

2   Because it has a lower boiling point.

3   Because it has more carbon atoms.

4   Propane + oxygen $\rightarrow$ carbon dioxide + water

5   $C_3H_8 + 5O_2 \rightarrow 3CO_2 + 4H_2O$

6   $C_5H_{12} + 8O_2 \rightarrow 5CO_2 + 6H_2O$

Pages 46 and 47

1   Zinc + copper oxide $\rightarrow$ zinc oxide + copper

2   Copper oxide, silver oxide, the metal and water will be formed.

3   CABD

4   Reduced – iron oxide, oxidised – aluminium

5   Reduction

6   Carbon + copper oxide $\rightarrow$ carbon dioxide + copper

7   Conducts electricity.

8   The mixture glows.

9   **a** Zinc   **b** zinc is more reactive than iron.

Pages 48 and 49

1   Positive.

2   Negative.

3   Mg^{++}

4   The ions can't move through the solid.

5   Negative electrode (cathode).

6   **a** Positive **b** negative.

7   Negative electrode (cathode).

8   Negative electrode (cathode).

Pages 52 and 53

1   2000 Hz   2   4 m

3   Vibrations, compressions, rarefactions, frequency, hertz or Hz, wavelength, metres, longitudinal, energy flow.

4   3, 4 m, 25 cm

5   The energy flows from left to right but the wiggles are up and down.

6   $v = fL$ 7   24 m/s   8   50 m, 600 000 Hz

Pages 54 and 55

1   60°, 60°; 40°, 40°

2   50 cm behind the mirror.

3   See page 54.

4   60°, 30°.

5   Opposite to the way it entered the prism.

Pages 56 and 57

1   47 Hz, 900 Hz, 12 000 Hz, 24 kHz, 50 000 Hz, The last two.

2   37.5 m

3   Looking inside people.

4   p-waves are longitudinal, s-waves are transverse.

5   See the top of page 57.

Pages 58 and 59

1   –20°C. Conduction, convection and radiation.

2   Kinetic, vibrate, energy, conduction.

3   Lose energy. Air at the top cools, shrinks and falls. It is replaced by a flow of hot air from the base of the fridge.

4   Bad, bad, good, good.

5   Gets smaller.

6   Only particles with more than average energy can escape. Leaves particles with less than average energy behind in the liquid.

7   Wall cavities, double glazing and roof insulation reduce conduction. White walls and special window glass reduce radiation. Sheltered location and small surface area reduces convection.

Pages 60 and 61

1   Chemical energy in gas $\rightarrow$ heat energy in the air duct $\rightarrow$ heat energy in the room.

2   Cheap to install, no waste gases.

3   Electricity is expensive.

4   Coal, oil, natural gas. Less pollution, can be made from renewable sources.

5   Wood (from plants).

6   Look at the bottom of page 60!

7   5 years.

8   Insulator, air, conductor, metal.

Pages 62 and 63

1 7p   **2** 60p   **3** 0.1p

4 Live (brown), neutral (blue), earth (green and yellow).

5 Thin wires get hot, thick wires stay cool.

6 Live and neutral transfer electrical energy. Earth protects against electric shock.

7 Cuts off current before the wires get too hot.

8 Melts if the live wire touches the outer casing of an appliance.

9 In the live wire.

10 Double insulated.

11 Outer metal casing. To prevent electric shocks.

Pages 64 and 65

1 v (m/s), s (m), t (s)   **2** $v = s/t$ **3** 20 m/s

4 300 m/s   **5** 1.67 m/s   **6** 30.6 m/s

7 3000 m   **8** 5 s

9 1 = c, 2 = d, 3 = b

10 1 = c, 2 = a, 3 = b

11 **a** 25 m   **b** 100 m   **c** 50 m

12 **a** 2 m/s   **b** 0 m/s   **c** 2 m/s

Pages 66 and 67

1 Acceleration = change of speed/time taken, m/s^2

2 10 m/s^2 **3** 6 s   **4** 10 m/s

5 Air resistance, contact between tyres and road, moving parts in the wheels.

6 Steady speed, getting faster, slowing down.

7 6000 N   **8** 65 000 N   **9** 2 m/s^2

10 Distance moved before the brakes start to slow the car down. Lack of concentration, tiredness, intoxication.

11 Distance moved while the brakes are on. Incorrect adjustment, rain, bald tyres, badly inflated tyres.

12 21 m   **13** **a** 5 s   **b** 75 m

14 10.5 m, 2.5 s, 18.8 m

Pages 68 and 69

1 Force, length, smaller, elastic, inelastic, force.

2 10 cm, 60 N

3 Crumple zones absorb kinetic energy. Seat belts slow people down securely. Air bags provide a soft cushion.

4 Pressure (Pa) = force (N) /area (m^2)

5 1000 Pa, 10 000 Pa, 16 000 Pa.

6 $A = F/P$ **7** 0.025 m^2

Pages 74 and 75

1 Green plants use light energy to change carbon dioxide and water into sugars (food).

    carbon dioxide + water → glucose + oxygen

            chlorophyll and light energy

2 Carbon dioxide comes from the atmosphere; water from the soil via the root hairs.

3 Three from: broad; thin; lots of chlorophyll; good transport system; stomata.

4 Oxygen and water vapour.

5 No, because they need light to photosynthesise.

6 Plants appear green because they reflect green light. Light that they reflect cannot be used for photosynthesis, therefore green light is not very good for photosynthesis and plants do not grow well.

Pages 76 and 77

1 Three from: changed into sucrose for transport; changed into cellulose; changed into proteins; respired to release energy; changed into starch for storage.

2 It allows some materials to pass through it, but not others.

3 There is more water inside the chips than there is in the concentrated sugar solution around them, therefore water will move from a high concentration to a low concentration, leaving the cells and making them smaller; in the dilute sugar solution, the osmotic gradient is the other way round, with water moving into the cells and causing the chip to become longer.

4 The xylem, to transport absorbed water and minerals; the phloem to transport dissolved sucrose.

5 Magnesium is used to make chlorophyll, which makes plants look green. Chlorophyll is essential for photosynthesis, which makes the materials necessary for the plant to grow.

6 One crop will rapidly use up certain minerals in the soil, and if the crop is harvested rather than ploughed back into the soil, the minerals are removed as well. Farmers have to use fertilisers to replenish the lost minerals.

7 To absorb water and dissolved minerals.

Pages 78 and 79

1 A vascular bundle is a group of tissues concerned with transport, therefore it contains xylem and phloem.

2 Prevents the plant losing too much water by evaporation.

3 Transpiration is the evaporation of water from the leaves of a plant and its replacement by water from the xylem.

4 Three from: provides water for photosynthesis; cools the plant down; helps to move minerals up the plant; provides support because the cells are stiff when full of water.

5 **a** Carbon dioxide diffuses in through open stomata.

   b Oxygen diffuses out through the stomata from a high concentration to a relatively lower concentration in the atmosphere.

Pages 80 and 81

1 Respiration is the release of energy from glucose (food).

2 **a** glucose + oxygen → carbon dioxide + water + energy

b glucose → lactic acid + some energy

3 Two from: aerobic produces more energy; aerobic produces carbon dioxide; anaerobic produces lactic acid; only aerobic uses oxygen.

4 Respiration occurs in all the cells in the body.

5 Two from: breathing rate increases; heart beat increases; aerobic respiration increases.

6 Breathing rate, more oxygen; heart beat, faster delivery of oxygen and glucose to cells; more respiration, more energy to work the muscles.

7 During vigorous exercise the muscles have to respire anaerobically. This forms lactic acid. To get rid of lactic acid, oxygen is needed, therefore at the end of the exercise you have built up a lot of lactic acid which must be broken down. The oxygen needed to break it down is referred to as the oxygen debt.

Pages 82 and 83

1 Homeostasis means maintaining conditions in your body at a steady state (optimum level).

2 Pancreas, liver.

3 Water, urea, and salt as urine.

4 Carbon dioxide dissolves in the blood to form carbonic acid. A change in the blood pH will affect enzyme activity around the body.

5 On a hot sunny day you lose water through sweating, therefore there is less water in the body to be lost in the urine, so you produce more concentrated urine.

6 Brain.

7 Sweat uses some of our body heat to evaporate it from the skin, therefore some of the body heat is used up.

Pages 84 and 85

1 Tears contain antiseptic which destroys microbes.

2 Blood blocks the hole (platelets) and white blood cells launch a counter attack.

3 An antibody is a chemical produced to attack something our body recognises as foreign (antigen).

4 White blood cells leave the blood to reach any invading microbes so that they can launch an attack.

5 A drug is a substance that changes the way your body works.

6 Chemicals in cigarette smoke stop the cilia beating, therefore mucus and microbes lodge in the lungs rather than constantly being removed. In the lungs microbes can cause infections.

7 Depressant – slows down brain activity, e.g. alcohol.
Stimulant – speeds up brain activity, e.g. caffeine.

Page 87

1 Growth needs the production of identical cells, all carrying all the chromosomes. Only mitosis does this.

2

Mitosis	**Meiosis**
Occurs in growth and asexual reproduction.	Occurs in gamete formation.
Produces two identical cells.	Produces four non-identical cells.
Same number of chromosomes as parent cell.	Half the number of chromosomes as parent cell.

3 Down's syndrome.

4 Two or more genetically identical individuals.

5 Mitosis.

Page 89

1 50% blue, 50% brown; Bb × bb = Bb, Bb (both brown), bb, bb (both blue).

2 50% rollers, 50% non-rollers. Ratio 1 : 1.

3

Gametes	X	X^c	
X^c	XX^c	X^cX^c	— colour-blind girl
Y	XY	X^cY	

or

Gametes	X^c	X^c	
X^c	X^cX^c	X^cX^c	— all girls colour blind
Y	X^cY	X^cY	

4 Weight and body shape.

Page 91

1 Some body parts not fossilised; not many organisms die in the right conditions to form fossils; may not have found all the fossils formed.

2 Individuals best adapted to their environment survive and breed therefore are more likely to increase in number.

3 The soot-covered bark camouflaged the black version of the moth. Therefore they were less likely to be seen and eaten, and so survived and increased in number. Black moths were fitter because they were better adapted to their environment than the pale moths.

4 Species poorly adapted to their environments are likely to become extinct. If the environment changes and a species cannot adapt to the new conditions, it will become extinct.

Page 92

1 **a** speed.

b Selective breeding – pick two speedy parents, breed them and pick the fastest foal, repeat.

2 Animals reproduce by sexual reproduction, whereas plants can also reproduce asexually to produce genetically identical offspring.

3

Selective breeding	Genetic engineering
Advantages • Gradually produce living things with more and more desirable characteristics.	*Advantages* • Outcome is known. • Once set up it is quicker than selective breeding. • Can transfer genes from one species to another. • Can make large amounts of useful products, e.g. insulin.
Disadvantages • Time consuming. • Outcome not predictable.	*Disadvantages* • Expensive to set up. • Worries about transferred gene escaping into other species. • Worries about effects of eating genetically altered individuals. • Ethical worries, including how it might be applied to human beings.

Pages 96 and 97

1 Water, H_2O

Methane, CH_4

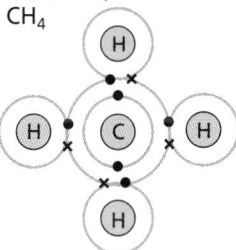

Carbon dioxide, CO_2

Nitrogen, N_2

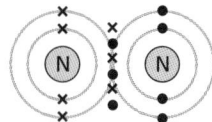

2 Molecular structure.
3 Giant structure.
4 Covalent bonds.
5 Weak forces.

Pages 98 and 99

1 1   **2** 6   **3**

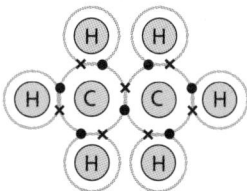

4 It has many weak forces.

5

6

Page 101

1 **a** It increases
   b It slows down and stops.
2 It is damaged (denatured).
3 **a** Alcohol, carbon dioxide   **b** Alcohol   **c** C.
4 Food flavouring.

Page 103

1 Falls.   **2** Baking soda.   **3** Iron sulphate.
4 **a** Magnesium chloride and hydrogen.
   b $Mg + 2HCl \rightarrow MgCl_2 + H_2$

Pages 104 and 105

1 A reaction that will go in either direction.
2 Nitrogen and hydrogen.
3 The cost of energy.
4 One of: make it quickly; recycle any unused gases.
5 **a** Make it quickly (use a catalyst), recycle any unused gases
   b Using a high temperature, high pressure.

Pages 106 and 107

1 $24\,g, 64\,g$ **2** 64%   **3** Cu_2O **4** CuO

Pages 108 and 109

1 Oxygen-18 has two more neutrons than oxygen-16.
2 26   **3** 30
4 a 7   **b** 7   **c** 2 in the first shell, 5 in the next.
5 $2:8:1$ **6** $2:8:8:1$

Pages 110 and 111

1 They have two outer electrons, which they lose to leave a stable shell.
2 Group 0 elements have a stable outer electron shell.
3 Sodium + water $\rightarrow$ sodium hydroxide + hydrogen
4 $2Na + 2H_2O \rightarrow 2NaOH + H_2$

Page 112

1 Hydrogen + chlorine $\rightarrow$ hydrogen chloride
2 $2Na + Cl_2 \rightarrow 2NaCl$

Pages 118 and 119

1 Electrons.
2 Glass and wool.
3 Iron and copper.
4 Insulator, electrons, comb, charged.
5 Fur, glass, negative, positive.
6 Glass is positive, silk is negative.
7 Attract, attract, repel.
8 Photocopier, paint sprayer.
9 Sparks can cause explosions.
10 The car is charged as it moves through the air, and the charge flows through you to earth.

Pages 120 and 121

1 $15\,C$ **2** $20\,A$

3 See the table on page 120.

4

5

6 They all read 2 A

7 2 A

8

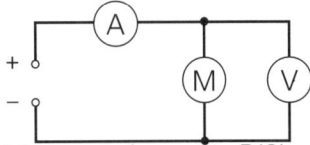

9 96 J

Pages 122 and 123

1 $P(W) = I(A) \times V(V)$ **2** 60 W

3

4 0.4 A   **5** b   **6** $R(\Omega) = V(V)/I(A)$

7 48 Ω

8

9 4 A   **10** 100 V

11 off + off, off + on, on + off, on + on

Pages 124 and 125

1 $W(J) = F(N) \times s(m)$ **2** 75 J, 75 J.

3 20 m   **4** 2500 N

5 500 J   **6** a, b

7 Chemical, potential, potential, kinetic, heat.

8 3500 J   **9** 2500 J

10 200 W

Pages 126 and 127

1 Iron, steel, cobalt, nickel. **2** North.   **3** Left.

4 Attract, attract, repel, ignore.

5 Right, right, left.

6 **a** –0.1 V   **b** 0.0 V.

7 Move faster, stronger magnet.

8 Zero, negative.

9 Iron core, faster motion, stronger magnet, more coils of wire.

10 Steel magnet, copper coil wound on soft iron.

11 Twice as many cycles, double the amplitude.

Pages 128 and 129

1 Burning oil heats water to make steam. Steam rotates turbine. Turbine turns generator.

2 Chemical energy in the fuel → heat energy in the steam → kinetic energy in the turbine → electrical energy in the generator.

3 Heat energy is lost up the chimney from the combustion of gases, from pipes carrying steam and friction in the turbine and generator.

4 Efficiency = $\dfrac{\text{output}}{\text{input}} \times 100$

5 25%, heat energy.

6 High-voltage wires which transport electricity over long distances.

7 Heat energy, 95%.

8 Reduces current in wires.

9 See page 129.   **10** To raise and lower the voltage.

11 a.c.   **12** 98%   **13** 12 V.

Pages 130 and 131

1 Gravity downwards, friction upwards.

2 Gravity, speed, friction, upwards, increases, balanced, stays the same.

3 **a** 30 m/s   **b** 15 m/s   **c** 45 m

4 Weight (N) = mass (kg) × gravity (N/kg or m/s²)

5 Mass is fixed by number of atoms, g is fixed by planet.

6 50 kg, 200 N

7 Velocity is both speed and direction.

8 Towards the centre of the circle.

9 750 N from centre of Earth towards Joe.

10 Change its speed and its direction of motion.

Pages 132 and 133

1 A sphere of rock or gas which orbits a star.

2 A ball of gases kept hot by fusion reactions.

3 The planet goes in a circle or ellipse around the star. Gravity pulls on it.

4 Moon, planet, star, solar system, galaxy, universe.

5 A moon is lighter than the planet which it orbits around.

6 Earth, Sun, Earth, Moon, Earth.

7 The Earth is spinning round.

8 See page 133!

Pages 134 and 135

1 A small central nucleus with electrons moving around it.

2 Positive.   **3** Negative.

4 The breakup of a nucleus.

5 Alpha, beta and gamma.   **6** Nucleus.

7 Alpha is positive, beta is negative and gamma has no charge.

8 **a** Alpha   **b** Gamma   **c** Alpha   **d** Beta.

9 Alpha, beta, gamma.

10 Uranium in rocks, radon in the air, nuclear fallout from bomb tests, cosmic rays from space.

11 6000

12 Goes down, as the number of unstable atoms decreases.

13 **a** Smoke alarms

b Thickness measurement

c Sterilising instruments, killing cancers

d Generating electricity.

AT2 – Year 10

Question			Answer	Marks	Total
1	**a**		Break it down into small; soluble bits. **b** Lipids or fats.	1 1	
	c		Emulsifies fats; providing a larger surface area for enzymes to work on.	2	
	d		Any two of: large surface area; very long or lots of villi; permeable surface; good blood supply.	2	**6 marks**
2	**a**		Any three of: permeable; moist; large surface area; good blood supply.	3	
	b		Support the bronchioles/bronchi; to prevent collapsing when pressure changes during inhalation and exhalation.	2	**5 marks**
3	**a**	**i**	Haemoglobin **ii** Oxygen + haemoglobin → oxyhaemoglobin	1 1	
		iii	Actively respiring; cells /body tissues.	2	
	b		Artery; small lumen with thick, elastic walls. To allow materials to be exchanged. Vein; valves.	5	**9 marks**
4	**a**		Hormones.	1	
	b		Any four from: increases heart rate; increases breathing rate; therefore more blood with oxygen and glucose delivered to the muscles; converts glycogen to glucose to increase glucose availability; diverts blood to muscles and brain away from gut and other less important areas.	4	**5 marks**
5	**a**		Phototropism.	1	
	b		Enables them to take up light; needed for photosynthesis.	2	
	c		Produced at the tip and diffuses back down the shoot; on light side auxin is destroyed; on shaded side auxin causes the cells to elongate; this side therefore grows whereas the side in the light stops growing.	3	**6 marks**
6	**a**		Receptor; sensory neurone; motor neurone; effector.	3	
	b		Two of: blinking; sneezing; swallowing; suckling.	2	
	c		Two of: long; insulating sheath; branched endings.	2	**7 marks**
7			Any four of: nitrates encourage growth of surface algae; these cut off light to plants below; plants cannot photosynthesise so die; decomposers rot the dead plants; they use up oxygen in the water; all other living things suffocate; waterway becomes largely uninhabited.	4	**4 marks**
8	**a**		Nucleus; contains genetic information to control activities of the cell.	2	
	b		To leave more room to transport oxygen.	1	
	c	**i**	To release energy by respiration **ii** To release the energy for it to swim.	1 1	
	d		Oxygen. **e** Water (can accept a named mineral)	1 1	
	f		A and D. Both have cell walls/both have a large vacuole.	3	**10 marks**
9	**a**		Speed up; they break down food (or break down large insoluble food molecules) into small soluble ones.	2	
	b		The enzyme has broken down the starch into glucose; which has passed through the semi-permeable membrane.	2	
	c		Blood.	1	
	d		Starch is too big a substance to pass through the membrane.	1	
	e		Nothing; boiling has destroyed the enzyme; therefore no glucose can be produced.	3	**9 marks**

Question	Answer	Marks	Total
10 a	Correctly labelled parts – check back to diagram in the text.	3	
b	Cornea starts to bend the light. Retina contains the light-sensitive cells. Lens completes bending of light to focus image on the retina.	3	
c	In dim light the circular muscles are relaxed; the radial muscles are contracted; making the pupil large; to allow in lots of light; reverse for bright light.	4	
d	Reflex action.	1	
e	Prevents excess light getting into the retina and damaging it.	1	**12 marks**
11 a	Lining of the uterus comes away/menstruation	1	
b	Causes the lining of the uterus to thicken c 14	1 1	
d	Level will stay high; because the yellow body stays active	2	
e	Other things may cause the body temperature to increase, for example a fever or 'flu'	1	**6 marks**
12 a	Randomly; place the quadrat on the ground and count; the number and types of plant species.	3	
b	Collect insects; sweeping net a set number of times through undergrowth; use pooter to collect insects for counting and identification.	3	
c	Collects nocturnal animals; add a bait; count and identify regularly.	3	**9 marks**
13 a	Must start with water lily, duckweed, pondweed or reeds; next level must contain insects, tadpoles or small fish. Arrows must point in the right direction.	3	
b	Energy flow.	1	
c	At each level there is energy loss; as respiration; death and decay; therefore less energy available to support next level.	2	
d	Pondweed, small fish, larger fish, heron, fox or larger fish, human.	3	**9 marks**
14 a	To make into proteins/nucleic acids.	1	
b	Nitrogen is unreactive; most living things need soluble nitrates.	2	
c	Conversion of nitrogen to nitrates.	1	
d	Add a fertiliser; plant a crop with root nodules.	2	**6 marks**

AT3 – Year 10

Question	Answer	Marks	Total
1 a	calcium + oxygen → calcium oxide *One mark for the reactants, one mark for the product.*	2	
c	$2Ca + O_2 \rightarrow 2CaO$ *One mark for the reactants, one mark for the product.*	2	**4 marks**
2 a	Any two of: larger hydrocarbons; have more intermolecular forces; which makes the molecules harder to separate.	2	
b i	Oxidation. ii Carbon dioxide and water.	1 2	
iii	$CH_4 + 2O_2 \rightarrow CO_2 + 2H_2O$ *One mark for correct formulae, one mark for correct balancing.*	2	
iv	Carbon monoxide and water.	2	
v	$CH_4 + 1.5O_2 \rightarrow CO + 2H_2O$ or $2CH_4 + 3O_2 \rightarrow 2CO + 4H_2O$ *One mark for correct formulae, one mark for correct balancing.*	2	**11 marks**

Question		Answer	Marks	Total
3	**a**	Igneous. **b** Interlocking crystals.	1 2	
	c	Rock A. It has small crystals.	1	
	d	The plate split, and the two halves moved apart.	2	**6 marks**
4	**a**	Ions. **b** To lower the melting point.	1 1	
	c	Ions can travel through the liquid but not the solid.	1	
	d	**i** Anode. **ii** Cathode.	1 1	
	iii	They go to the cathode and turn into atoms (they are neutralised).	2	**7 Marks**

AT4 – Year 10

Question		Answer	Marks	Total
1	**a**	**i** Transverse. Energy flow at right angles to displacement.	2	
		ii A **iii** 3 Hz **iv** 1.5 m/s	1 2 2	
	b	Jill's voice vibrates her cup. This sends a longitudinal wave along the string. This vibrates Tom's cup, creating a sound wave.	3	**10 marks**
2	**a**		1	
	b	All the reflected rays appear to come from a single point behind the mirror.	2	
	c	**i** A **ii** Rays from the lamp which reflect from the mirror emerge in the same direction, making a beam of light.	1 2	**6 marks**
3	**a**	Heat energy increases vibration of particles in the wall. Particles in solids touch each other, so the energy of vibration is passed from one particle to another.	2	
	b	**i** Fibre wool **ii** It contains air, which is a poor conductor.	1 2	
	c	**i** Block up gaps in windows and doors. **ii** 8 months	1 2	
	d	Double glaze windows to reduce heat conducting through. Reduce the temperature of the house to reduce heat flow to the cold outside.	4	**12 marks**
4	**a**	**i** 1.2 kWh **ii** 9.6p **b** Live, neutral, earth.	1 1 3	**5 marks**
5	**a**	**i** 3 m/s^2 **ii** 60 kg **b** 300 m	2 2 2	
	c	Friction is the only horizontal force, acting against her velocity. So she has a negative acceleration.	3	
	d	The helmet spreads the force of impact over a large area, reducing the pressure on her skull.	3	**12 marks**
6	**a**	Rise to room temperature.	1	
	b	Heat energy makes particles in solids vibrate. Particles are connected to each other. So the vibration is passed from particle to particle through the solid.	3	
	c	Heat radiation is reflected from a shiny material, so the rate at which heat energy enters the ice cream is reduced.	2	
	d	Wrap the ice cream in a material which contains trapped air. Air is a poor conductor of heat.	2	
	e	Cold air falls, so that all of the freezer gets cold.	1	**9 marks**

Question			Answer	Marks	Total
7	a	i	The time it takes for the driver to apply the brakes ii 0.67 s	1 2	
		iii	Tiredness, inebriation.	2	
	b	i	$-5.4\,\text{m/s}^2$ ii 933 kg	3 3	**11 marks**

AT2 – Year 11

Question			Answer	Marks	Total
1	a		Nucleus. **b** 46, or 23 pairs.	1 1	
	c		Any four of: caused by exposure to radiation; mutagens; ultraviolet light; results in changed genetic code which may cause cancers; birth defects or developmental defects.	4	
	d		Mutations; not inherited the same combination of genes from the mother and father.	2	**8 marks**
2	a		B, A, D, C E **b** 8	4 1	
	c		Two of: asexual reproduction; growth; repair.	2	
	d		Any two of: cells formed only contain half the number of chromosomes; the cells formed are not identical genetically; 4 daughter cells are formed rather than 2.	2	**9 marks**
3	a		Any four of: selecting plant for required characteristics; chopping it into a large number of pieces of tissue; keeping aseptic technique; transferring pieces of tissue to suitable culture medium; growing them under suitable conditions.	4	
	b		**Advantages** – genetic outcome guaranteed; lots produced relatively cheaply. **Disadvantages** – genetically identical therefore no variation to help overcome adverse environmental conditions; all susceptible to the same microbes and diseases.	4	**8 marks**
4	a		Smooth regular-shaped petals.	1	
	b		Will only show in the phenotype if homozygous.	1	
	c		Use any letter – e.g. R for regular, r for jagged **d**	4 4	

$RR \times rr$

Gametes	R	R
r	Rr	Rr
r	Rr	Rr

Gametes	R	r
R	RR	rR
r	Rr	rr

all will be regular, because R is dominant.   three will be regular but one will be jagged.

Question			Answer	Marks	Total
	e		Jagged are recessive homozygous; therefore if she breeds jagged with jagged, all the offspring should be jagged.	3	**13 marks**
5			Any five of: grey squirrels have out-competed red ones; because they are better suited to the environment; they can live in a variety of habitats, not just pine woods; they can eat a wider range of foods; they are bigger and can therefore beat red ones if they do end up in the same habitat; they have a greater reproductive potential than red ones; therefore there will be more of them each year; this is an example of survival of the fittest.	5	**5 marks**

Question			Answer	Marks	Total
6	a		Any three of: transparent epidermis; long thin palisade cells tightly packed; lots of chloroplasts; air spaces in the mesophyll; stomata to allow the gases in and out; internal surface area to volume ratio very large.	3	
	b		Carbon dioxide concentration.	1	**4 marks**
7	a		All the cells of the body.	1	
	b		$C_6H_{12}O_6 + 6O_2 \rightarrow 6CO_2 + 6H_2O$ (+ energy)	3	
	c		The water on Max's skin is using his body heat; to evaporate it.	2	**6 marks**
8	a		Stimulants increase the transmission of messages across synapses in the brain.	1	
	b	i	Addiction is when the drug produces a dependence within the drug taker, so that they then have to keep taking the drug; withdrawal symptoms are unpleasant effects which the person experiences if they stop or are prevented from taking the drug.	2	
		ii	When the body gets used to a level of the drug and requires more and more to be able to experience the same effect; this leads to the user having to obtain greater amounts of the drug with associated cost implications.	2	**5 marks**
9	a		+ 1; –2; –4; –5.	4	
	b c		If graph plotted correctly, the point at which the length remains unchanged is the answer to **c**, which is 1.1 mol/dm^3 sugar solution (+ or – 0.1).	5	
	d		Water moves out of the cells; due to osmosis; down the concentration gradient; therefore all the cells are a little smaller and the cylinder seems to shrink.	4	**13 marks**
10	a		Homeostasis.	1	
	b		Water; salt; pH; temperature; glucose; carbon dioxide; urea.	3	
	c		Blood is filtered; useful molecules, such as glucose, are reabsorbed; urea and leftover water remain in the kidney tubule to form urine.	4	
	d		On a hot day you would sweat; therefore less water needs to be lost from the body in urine; small volume of concentrated urine; reverse argument for cold day.	3	**11 marks**

AT3 – Year 11

Question			Answer	Marks	Total
1	a	i	Crude oil.　　**ii**　To make nitric acid *or* fertiliser *or* explosives.	1　2	
		iii	Wages, raw materials, energy, building the factory, etc.	3	
	b	i	A substance which speeds up a reaction and can be recovered.	2	
		ii	Iron.　　**c**　The reaction will go in either (and both) direction.	1　1	
	d	i	43%　**ii**　Cost of compressors *or* need for thicker walled reaction vessel.	1　1	
	e		Moves to the right.	1	**13 marks**
2	a	i	38　　**ii**　The number of neutrons.　　**b i** Two	1　1　1	
		ii	Strontium and calcium are in the same group/have the same number of outer electrons, so will have very similar properties.	2	
	c	i	14　　**ii**　2, 8, 3	1　1	**7 marks**

Question			Answer	Marks	Total
3	**a**	**i**	Between 9 and 14. **ii** 7 **iii** Between 6 and 4.	1 1 1	
	b		Salt **c i** Two **ii** Three **iii** 80	1 1 1 1	
	d	**i**	Eutrophication	1	
		ii	Any three from: algae grow on the surface; this cuts the light to the lower plants; plants die and rot; using up oxygen from the water; killing animals such as fish.	3	**11 marks**
4	**a**	**i**	Bottom of Group I. **ii** Top of Group VII.	2 2	
	b		They have a stable outer shell *or* they have eight electrons in the outer shell.	1	
	c	**i**	2 **ii** 6 **d** Double positive.	1 1 2	**9 marks**
5	**a**		Two. **b i** They are shared.	1 1	
		ii	Two electrons in the first shell, four in the second.	2	
	c	**i**	Alkene group. **ii** Bromine water. **iii** Goes colourless.	1 1 1	
		iv	Stays orange/brown.	1	
	d	**i**	–E–E–E–E–E–E–E–E–E–E– **ii** Use high pressure and a catalyst.	1 2	
	e	**i**	PVC. **ii** Acrylic. **iii** Polythene. **iv** Polycarbonate.	1 1 1 1	**15 marks**
6	**a**	**i**	Sugar, moisture, warmth. **ii** Alcohol (ethanol).	3 1	
	b	**i**	Speeds up the reaction. **ii** It can be recovered.	1 1	
	c		Carbon dioxide gas.	1	
	d		Speeds up, to reach its maximum rate at 37°C, then slows down as the yeast is killed and stops.	4	**11 marks**
7	**a**	**i**	One. **ii** Seven. **iii** Ionic.	1 1 1	
		iv	The outer electron is given from the sodium to the chlorine so that each ends up with eight outer electrons.	2	
	b		High. **c i** Insulator. **ii** Conductor.	1 1 1	**8 marks**
8	**a**		Exothermic **b** Joules or kilojoules	1 1	
	c		$500 \times 4.18 \times 26 = 54340\,J$ *or* 54.340 kJ	2	
	d		Any three from: ultraviolet (short wavelength radiation) comes in from the Sun; the Earth gives out infra-red (long wavelength) radiation; greenhouse gases trap this long wavelength radiation preventing heat loss.	3	**7 marks**
9	**a**		Collisions: greater surface area/more places for collision.	2	
	b		Particles move faster, collide more often. Particles have more energy so can break bonds more easily.	4	
	c		Increase the concentration, use a catalyst.	2	**8 marks**

AT4 – Year 11

Question		Answer	Marks	Total
1	**a**	The motor stops because all the current takes the low resistance path through the switch. The lamp glows brightly because there is more current in the circuit, since the resistance of the motor has been removed.	3	

Question			Answer	Marks	Total
b	**i**		**ii** $P = IV$, so motor has 2 A, lamp has only 0.5 A	1 2	
			iii 2.5 A	3	**9 marks**
2	**a**		**b i** 0.72 W **ii** 2 Ω	2 3 3	
	c		As the resistance of the rheostat increases the current decreases, lowering the power of the motor, so reducing its speed.	3	**11 marks**
3	**a**		The comb pulls electrons off his hair. Electrons are negative, leaving the hair positive.	3	
	b		Like charges repel. Each hair is repelled by all the other hairs, forcing it upright.	2	
	c		Plastic is an insulator, so carries the electrons away from the hair. Electrons removed from hair by a metal comb can flow through it back to the hair.	2	**7 marks**
4	**a**	**i**	Kinetic, heat. **ii** 10 000 J	2 3	
		iii	Some of the KE can become PE as the car moves up, so the brakes need to do less work.	3	
	b	**i**	5000 W **ii** 25%	3 3	**14 marks**
5	**a**		Soft iron. **b** increase current, wrap more coils of wire.	1 2	
	c	**i**	**ii** Reverse the direction of the current in the wire.	2 1	
					6 marks
6	**a**		Furnace, boiler, turbine, generator, transformer. **b** 30%	5 2	
	c	**i**	Waste gas from the furnace, from the cooling tower where the steam condenses, heat radiated from the hot boiler.	3	
		ii	Because it is too spread out to be converted into electricity.	1	**11 marks**
7	**a**		Stars generate heat energy within them.	1	
	b		Hydrogen atoms collide and join to form helium atoms.	3	
	c		Gravity pulls the particles towards each other, giving them kinetic energy. So the cloud collapses and heats up. Eventually, the pressure and temperature are high enough for fusion to start.	4	
	d		The heat of the star will radiate into space, so it will cool down.	2	**10 marks**
8	**a**		Gravity	1	
	b		To allow communication between different parts of the Earth, to monitor the climate and weather.	2	
	c	**i**	More than 90 minutes	1	
		ii	Gravity gets weaker as you go away from the Earth, and the satellite has a much larger distance to cover in one orbit.	2	**6 marks**
9	**a**		The emissions can break up molecules in living cells, killing them or damaging their DNA.	2	
	b		Each nucleus can only decay once. As time goes on, there are fewer and fewer nuclei left to decay.	3	
	c		63 Bq	3	**8 marks**

Question		Answer	Marks	Total
10 a			1	
b		Chemical, electrical, electrical, light	4	
c	**i**	3V from battery is shared between LED and resistor. **ii** 20 Ω	1 3	**9 marks**
11		Nucleus, alpha, beta, gamma.	4	**4 marks**
12 a	**i**	Ultrasound **ii** Radio **iii** X-rays **iv** Microwaves	1 1 1 1	
	v	X-rays, ultrasound.	2	
b	**i**	It changes direction, with the angle of refraction smaller than the angle of incidence.	2	
	ii	It reflects with the angle of incidence equal to the angle of reflection.	2	**10 marks**
13 a		Cheap to install, but expensive to run.	2	
b	**i**	Install double glazing.	1	
	ii	Reduce conduction of heat through the windows by having a layer of trapped air in the window.	2	
c		Conduction, radiation, convection	3	**8 marks**
14 a	**i**	Rub it with a cloth.	1	
	ii	Electrons are negative. So if the rubbing removes or adds electrons to the plastic, it ends up charged.	2	
b		Suspend the charged plastic from a thread. Bring it close to the charged polythene. If it attracts, the plastic is positive. If the plastic repels, it is negative.	3	**6 marks**
15 a		Iron, because it is easily magnetised. **b** 6V	2 2	
c		Alternating current in the primary creates a changing magnetic field in the secondary, which induces an alternating voltage in the secondary coil.	3	**7 marks**
16 a		Use KE = 1/2 mv^2	2	
b	**i**	10 J **ii** 27 m. **c** Heat energy	1 3 1	**7 marks**

Index